AF676271

ALCOHOLISM

ALCOHOLISM

ITS NATURAL HISTORY, CHEMISTRY AND GENERAL METABOLISM

WILLIAM J. HAUGEN LIGHT, Ph.D.

Institute for the Study of Drugs,
Alcohol, and Addictive Behaviors
Metropolitan State College

and

Graduate School of Public Affairs
University of Colorado at Denver
Research Associate
California Academy of Sciences

CHARLES C THOMAS • PUBLISHER
Springfield • Illinois • U.S.A.

Published and Distributed Throughout the World by

CHARLES C THOMAS • PUBLISHER
2600 South First Street
Springfield, Illinois 62717

This book is protected by copyright. No part of it may be reproduced in any manner without written permission from the publisher.

© *1985 by* CHARLES C THOMAS • PUBLISHER

ISBN 0-398-05147-X

Library of Congress Catalog Card Number: 85-8054

With THOMAS BOOKS *careful attention is given to all details of manufacturing and design. It is the Publisher's desire to present books that are satisfactory as to their physical qualities and artistic possibilities and appropriate for their particular use.* THOMAS BOOKS *will be true to those laws of quality that assure a good name and good will.*

Printed in the United States of America
Q-R-3

Library of Congress Cataloging in Publication Data

Light, William J. Haugen.
Alcoholism: its natural history, chemistry, and general metabolism.

Includes bibliographies and index.
1. Alcoholism. I. Title. [DNLM: 1. Alcoholism. WM 274 L723a]
RC565.L54 1985 616.86'1 85-8054
ISBN 0-398-05147-X

To Ruth, Deborah and Carolyn, for making the Universe appear less lonely, and for creating a space in which I am content.

The five volumes in this series are:

1. *Alcoholism: Its Natural History, Chemistry and General Metabolism*
2. *The Neurobiology of Alcohol Abuse*
3. *The Psychodynamics of Alcoholism: A Current Synthesis*
4. *Alcoholism and Women, Genetics, Fetal Development, and Polydrug Abuse*
5. *Alcoholism, Co-Dependency, Recovery and the Role of the Clinician*

PREFACE

THIS SERIES of volumes is written as an introduction to the complex and often bewildering illness of alcoholism. It is directed primarily to health care professionals, particularly medical students, practicing physicians, psychiatric and psychological clinicians and trainees, nurses, alcoholism counselors, and other practitioners who regularly confront alcoholism as either the primary illness or as a major complicating factor in their patients or clients. One may legitimately ask, why another series on alcoholism? They seem to be coming off the presses at a brisk rate already from nearly every quarter — as though another new fad has burst upon us and one is not really "with it" unless one is either a recovered alcoholic intent upon telling his or her own story, or else is involved in treating them in some way. One can scarcely keep up with the literature in one's own specialty, let alone the proliferation of books and articles about alcoholism. Why burden us with yet more?

My response is that the works currently available overwhelmingly treat the subject from the fairly narrow perspective in which the authors or editors are themselves research experts, or out of the need to advance a favorite model or theory about the cause(s), course, and preferred treatment of the problem. Or if they are more general and ecclectic in scope, the discussion is far too superficial to be of any real value for professional workers who wish to know the current state of our knowledge of "ethanology." The last ten years or so have seen an enormous growth in our understanding about alcohol and alcoholism research. At some point in the very recent past we acquired a critical mass of accurate, scientific information about the pharmacological mechanisms by which alcohol (and many other addictive agents, as well) affects membrane systems and leads to pharmacological tolerance and physical dependence. These data, coupled with an increasingly sophisticated understanding of the psychodynamic and biochemical factors contributing to psychiatric illness in general and our ability to effectively intervene in such disorders to an unprecedented degree, have permitted an understanding of alcoholic disorders at a most fundamental level — a level that rivals our comprehension of our world and our universe in the other cognate sciences.

This information, unfortunately, is widely scattered in numerous professional journals and symposium volumes in the fields of medicine, toxicology and pharmacology, physiology, psychiatry and psychology. It is also heavily burdened with highly technical jargon and it assumes a command of the relevant background literature that is rarely possessed by anyone not actively working in the research frontiers of the respective discipline. These comments also apply to recent state-of-the-art reviews on the subject (for example, Lieber 1982).

It was my intention to bring together the substance of this vast literature, organize it into what I hope is a holistic and coherent picture, and translate it into comprehensible English that can be readily understood by any reasonably intelligent and educated person. I am convinced that this can be accomplished without sacrificing any of the scientific accuracy or subtle nuances of understanding to be obtained from close attention to the fine details and interrelationships of the various systems involved.

Thus, an adequate comprehension of the many factors contributing to alcoholic liver disease requires a detailed knowledge of liver structure and function. It is especially important to know how the structural units of the liver typically described in medical texts correlate with the physiologically more useful "functional" hepatic units, the liver acini, and how the latters' concentric zones of increasing anoxia toward the perivenular areas lead to specific regional hepatic lesions, necrosis, and ultimately, fibrosis. One must also be aware of the biochemical details of the mixed-function monooxygenases (which are only now beginning to be adequately taught in medical schools), basic pharmacokinetics and enzymatic processes, general lipid metabolism, the involvement of the pituitary-adrenal axis and catecholamine release upon peripheral free fatty acid mobilization, and the bewildering array of metabolic consequences of altered redox states resulting from alcohol oxidation.

This series is meant to be a current synthesis of information from many different fields and an examination of the disease of alcoholism as I have come to know it over nearly seventeen years of professional study. It is based, among other things, upon my experience in working with alcoholics and their families as supervising counselor for the National Council on Alcoholism in the San Francisco Bay area. It incorporates a background and education spanning many years as a professional scientist and educator and which includes formal training in toxicology at the University of Wisconsin at Madison. It grew out of a series of lectures that I developed for a wide range of audiences, ranging from youngsters on probation for alcohol and drug-related offenses, through volunteer workers and counselor-trainees in alcohol intervention, to formal classes of nursing and medical students at the University of San Francisco and the University of California School of Medicine at San Francisco, and finally, both undergraduate and graduate level courses in pharmacology of addictions at Metropolitan State College and the University of Colorado, both schools in Denver.

Although I have assumed no particular background or professional training on the part of the readers, it is expected that they have at least some basic concept of the nature of chemical bonds and understand the simple structural formulas presented herein. Those with absolutely no comprehension of these concepts are referred to the chapter(s) on the chemistry of life in any good introductory biology test. Some readers will perhaps have psychological foundations, some medical, some may be members of the clergy, some paraprofessional counselors of various persuasions with or without formal scientific training, and some may be interested laypersons who are themselves recovering or recovered alcoholics or the close friends and significant others of alcoholics. Because of the disparate backgrounds of the readership to which this series of books is directed, I have introduced each topic with a basic examination of the terminology and processes under discussion. The reader is led step-by-step through ever more advanced and sophisticated concepts up to and including the latest information, ideas, and thinking entertained by current researchers in the field.

Therefore, a family practice or general physician may be initially annoyed at elementary discussions of such things as oxidation-reduction reactions. These are included, however, so that someone from another discipline, let us say clinical psychology, will be able to follow subsequent treatments of the metabolic significance of altered redox states consequent to the oxidation of large amounts of alcohol and the ultimate effects of these processes upon human cognition and behavior.

The medically or biologically sophisticated reader will soon enough encounter very detailed presentations of biochemical phenomena that are currently at the forefronts of scientific investigation — subjects that will most certainly not have been studied if he or she has been in practice for even a very few years (like less than four or five). Indeed, many of these subjects have yet to be incorporated into standard medical texts or curricula. At the same time, our clinical psychologist will have been educated up to the medical or research level, at least insofar as is immediately relevant to a full understanding of the topic under consideration. Elsewhere the situation will be reversed, so that it is now the psychiatrically erudite reader who must tolerate the initial, elementary presentation of such things as depressive-spectrum disorder, sociopathy and its relationship to primary and secondary alcoholism, and the rudimentary concepts of decompensation and regression, narcissistic trauma and entitlement loss. But here, too, the discussion will soon lead into such topics as the interrelationship between narcissism and paranoid ideation in alcoholics, dyadic versus triadic conflicts, and the relative degrees of bonding and socialization in the development of the psychoses, neuroses and personality disorders. The latest concepts involving imbalances of central neurotransmitter substances as major factors in psychiatric disturbances, including alcoholism, are explored in depth and fully integrated with more traditional psychodynamic models. I believe this series represents the only work to date that truly accomplishes this goal in a fundamental coherent way.

I am introducing a number of ideas of my own about alcoholism which are presented for the first time in this series of volumes. I do have personal biases about this disorder, as does anyone who has thought about it seriously for more than ten minutes. Some of these ideas conflict with certain theories of some other authors. This is most evident in the portions dealing with the etiological factors underlying alcoholism, a subject which has spawned much often acrimonious debate. However, my suggestions are quite in line with the medical and psychiatric consensus about alcoholic disorders, and they are thoughts to which I have given careful considerations and brought wide-ranging knowledge and experience. I cannot prove some of these ideas, but I think they are as valid as anyone's. They are based upon personal insight and understanding, both intuitive and scientifically objective, of the various dynamics involved. They are certainly no more flimsily grounded than is most of the clinical and psychiatric literature, which is similarly anecdotal. The major portion of this work is, of course, firmly based upon solidly demonstrated, scientific data — particularly those sections dealing with the pharmacological and biological aspects of alcoholism.

Although much of the material contained in these volumes is difficult and complex, it is presented in what I hope is an easy, communicative, and readable style. I have provided a great many graphic illustrations to aid the users of these books, and innumerable footnotes supply additional information to enhance a point or to correlate the discussion with other related phenomena. I have not encumbered the text with extensive citations from the professional literature. This information is in the public domain and is well documented by the references which I do include. This series is also not intended to be an exhaustive, encyclopaedic catalog of facts and statistics about alcoholism. Rather, it attempts to provide a comprehensive and holistic synthesis of the many interrelated psychodynamic and biological processes which contribute to the etiology and manifestations of alcoholic disorders. The information contained herein is the product of a huge army of investigators and clinicians in many fields whose work spans many decades. I have served primarily as an interpreter.

I have covered little of the ground previously discussed for general audiences by other authors, although some review of such information is appropriate and is included. An example is a detailed presentation of the course of primary alcoholism as originally described by the late Dr. E. M. Jellinek. But even here, the discussion has been modernized and tempered with a much wider clinical experience than was available in Jellinek's time. And a few qualifying remarks of my own are included. I will not go very deeply into the various debates on treatment modalities, although I will present a broad approach based upon the overwhelming medical and psychiatric consensus in the final volume of this series. And I do not propose to engage in the endless debate about whether alcoholics can safely return to drinking on a social basis. I will categorically state my firm conviction that they cannot, and that any attempt to suggest that they can is medically and psychiatrically irresponsible. As to the sections dealing with the pharmacology, toxicology and metabolism of alcohol, and the genetics, biology, natural history and medical aspects of alcoholism, my discussions are confined to hard, scientifically-verifiable facts and interpretations, and any inferences I may draw are based upon these hard data and are also supported in the professional literature.

I had originally intended to write a book for the recovering alcoholic and his or her family, inasmuch as many of them, regardless of the particular treatment modality in which they may be participating, are largely ignorant about the disease, its causes, course, and medical and psychological consequences (as are the great majority of health care professionals). Although many alcoholics make full recoveries and are able to lead rich and satisfying lives, many others are plagued by recurrent or chronic depressions of profound proportions and are afflicted by a variety of physical and emotional problems that require professional intervention – a form of assistance they all too rarely get.

But as the manuscript progressed it became apparent that I was getting far too deeply into the scientific details and complexities of the alcoholic disorders to keep the attention of most laypersons for long. This was obviously the case despite my efforts to make it palatable to a wide range of readers and clearly understandable to any fairly intelligent and literate person willing to put in the necessary effort. About this time my wife, who is a practicing physician, suggested that I was actually writing for a professional audience and that I should continue in that genre. She observed that a much less detailed synopsis of this work would be more appropriate for the average reader.

What I have done in this series is to provide a thorough and detailed introduction into each discipline so that nonspecialists will understand the many intricacies of normal function of each system under consideration. Thus, the volume dealing with the effects of alcohol and alcoholism upon the human nervous system begins with a review of basic neurobiology. One has to know how neurons function and transmit information before one can appreciate how alcohol affects those processes. Similarly, one cannot really appreciate the ways in which alcohol ravages embryonic development or understand fetal alcohol syndrome without some basic knowledge of normal human fetal development. So each topic is presented as a detailed minicourse for those who know little or nothing about it. This is true of the psychodynamics volumes as well as the biologically- and medically-oriented ones. Following the introductory sections, the effects of alcohol and alcohol abuse upon the respective systems are presented in great detail. A summary is provide at the end of each section for those without the heart or inclination to wade through all the heavy scientific material.

This series of volumes presents, I believe, as complete and integrated picture of alcoholism as it is currently possible to create. And I think the model described in this series is a powerful and useful one. Alcoholism, perhaps more than most psychiatric disorders, can be understood at several fundamental levels. This series of books is my contribution to that end.

This work took four years to complete, and the final manuscript was more than one thousand pages and a quarter of a million words in length. There are approximately 90 full page illustrations. Because of the enormous cost of producing a single or even two-volume book from this manuscript, costs which would have priced this work far beyond the reach of most of us (including myself), the publisher and I agreed to present this as a series of five volumes, each about 200 to 250 pages long. To fully grasp the entire picture requires all five of these volumes. Nevertheless, each one is self-contained and presents a complete picture of alcoholism and the respective topics contained therein.

I, at least, have grown enormously both professionally and personally by writing this series. It has enabled me to provide my students at the Institute for the Study of Drugs, Alcohol and Addictive Behaviors at Metropolitan State College and the University of Colorado at Denver with extraordinarily valuable information and insight to take with them into the world of addiction prevention, intervention, treatment, and education.

ACKNOWLEDGMENTS

I OWE an enormous debt to many individuals, organizations, and institutions who made this series possible. Among these are: Mrs. Florette White Pomeroy, retired executive director of the National Council on Alcoholism - Bay Area, who gave me free rein during my tenure there and staunchly supported my sometimes unusual methods of intervention; Dr. Mary Fortin, formerly of the School of Nursing at the University of San Francisco; Dr. Mark I. Levy, a loyal companion in a common cause who walked an enormous distance with me along the incredible path of discovery and enlightenment; Dr. Antonio J. Ferreira, who freely shared many of his keen insights with me deriving from his private psychiatric practice focusing on alcoholics and their families; Mr. Mitch Capor of the Alameda County Probation Department, California, who provided an ongoing opportunity to gain valuable insight into the special problems of teenage substance abuse; my wife, Dr. Ruth Lewert Light, who has been a constant source of strength and inspiration throughout both our lives together and the writing of this manuscript; and my students in introductory and advanced courses in pharmacology and psychodynamics of addictions at the Institute for the Study of Drugs, Alcohol, and Addictive Behaviors at both Metropolitan State College and the University of Colorado at Denver, who force me to continually consolidate, sharpen, and refine my thoughts about the subject and who always remind me of my vast ignorance.

Words cannot express my deep gratitude to the many thousands of men and women in Alcoholics Anonymous and its sister fellowship, Al-Anon. Perhaps this series of volumes may be regarded as a small repayment for all the pain and joy that they have shared with me and for the many lifetime friendships that have sprung up between us. This work is for them, the recovered and recovering alcoholics and co-alcoholics, who have shown the way to so many thousands of suffering victims of this most horrible of afflictions.

Finally, I wish to thank Drs. John J. Magnuson and Ronald D. Hinsdill of the University of Wisconsin at Madison, who provided more than they know, who good naturedly tolerated my eccentricities, and who generously allowed me to wear both my hats simultaneously. The writing of this manuscript was supported in part by the Department of Health and Human Services Public Health Service National Research Award 5 T32 ES07015 to the University of Wisconsin from the National Institute of Environmental Health Services.

CONTENTS

LIST OF FIGURES

ALCOHOLISM

Section 1
INTRODUCTION

THE ALCOHOLISMS: A NATURAL HISTORY

ALCOHOLISM, like most disorders with strong behavioral components, continues to elude a precise medical, social, or even legal definition. This is due in large measure to the fact that its (or more accurately *their*) causes have not yet been clearly determined in spite of general agreement within the medical profession that its etiology is multifactorial and involves both biological and psychosocial factors. Part of the reason also lies in the fact that alcoholism is not one, but several diseases, each with multiple causes, although they have many features in common and the outlook is generally similar in most of them. The following definition was proposed jointly by the National Council on Alcoholism and the American Medical Society on Alcoholism in 1976:

> "Alcoholism is a chronic, progressive and potentially fatal disease. It is characterized by tolerance, physical dependence and/or pathological organ changes, all of which are the direct/indirect consequence of the alcohol ingested."

Like many chronic diseases, alcoholism persists essentially throughout the life of the individual afflicted. It cannot be "cured" in the sense that true alcoholics, with very few exceptions, are unable to engage in or resume normal, so-called "social" drinking without the near certainty of eventual, severe relapse once the alcoholism has been established. It is typical of chronic diseases that they can only be remitted or arrested, but never cured, by complete avoidance of the precipitating agent(s) (in this case, alcohol) and careful management of the associated psychological and physiological cofactors. Like a number of other chronic disorders, alcoholism is progressive and the symptoms and consequences become cumulatively worse over time as the active phase of the disease state continues, or as subsequent relapses are suffered during periods of remission. Alcoholism represents a true addiction, as reflected in increasing tolerance to the effects of the drug (ethanol), requiring ever larger doses to achieve the same desired state of inebriation, and in the manifestation of physical dependence by obvious signs and symptoms of withdrawal upon reduction or cessation of the drug, at least late in the course of the disease.

The foregoing definition, however, is very vague and general — almost philosophical, in fact. It does not permit a diagnosis or evaluation of the existence of alcoholism in a given individual and is thus of limited value. A more operational and diagnostic definition is one also proposed by the same two professional groups which is herein paraphrased as: whenever an individual suffers deleterious consequences to any aspect of his social, marital or family, occupational, economic or legal life, or endures any serious medical complications as a result of his drinking of beverage alcohol, *and that person continues to drink in the face of these consequences,* then that individual is an alcoholic. This approach is far more useful, since it allows experienced and insightful professional workers in alcoholism or medicine to make fairly reliable diagnoses, even in early stages of the disease. It is the major idea behind the famous *Twenty Questions* of Alcoholics Anonymous and of similar questionnaires put out by the National Council on Alcoholism and similar agencies, in which positive answers to several key questions indicate a strong inference of alcoholism.

In 1972, the Criteria Committee of the National Council on Alcoholism, composed of several senior medical authorities on the subject, published a series of diagnostic criteria for use by physicians to ensure a more objective, scientific, and reliable assessment of the presence of alcoholism in patients seen in treatment, especially in emergency rooms where alcoholics commonly appear for a variety of alcohol-related disorders and traumas. Among these criteria are several listed at the diagnostic level of 1; that is, the existence of any single criterion with that diagnostic level means that alcoholism is considered to be "definite . . . [present and] obligatory. A person who fits this criterion *must* be diagnosed as being alcoholic [italics mine]" (Criteria Committee, National Council on Alcoholism 1972). Included among these primary diagnostic criteria are the following indicators of physiological dependency (addiction):

(1) the presence of gross tremors resulting from drinking which are not the result of other complicating conditions such as hypoglycemia;
(2) hallucinosis due to drinking, as distinguished from hallucinations resulting from functional psychoses (e.g. schizophrenia);
(3) withdrawal seizures other than those due to epilepsy and other neurological disorders not resulting from alcoholism;
(4) having a blood alcohol content exceeding 150 mg-percent [= 150 mg of alcohol per 100 ml of blood] or 0.15% without obvious signs of intoxication (this is a characteristic feature of many alcohol-tolerant alcoholics who can "drink anyone under the table");
(5) having a blood alcohol level *at any time* of more than 300 mg-percent [300 mg/100ml] or 0.30%.
(6) consuming a fifth of a gallon of hard liquor daily or the beer or wine equivalent for more than one day by a 180-pound person.

As we shall see, alcoholism has multiple causes and involves both a genetic and constitutional predisposition to the disease, as well as a host of environmental factors. It is not a matter of nature *versus* nurture (a pitfall that traps many academic and intellectuals who find ambiguity hard to live with), but one of both nature *and* nurture.

Recovered alcoholics frequently speak of having an "allergy" to alcohol. That idea is presented in the "Big Book" of Alcoholics Anonymous and stems from the concept of allergies in vogue during the 1930s when it was written. The allergy theory was espoused by Dr. William Silkworth, a psychiatrist who was treating Bill W., one of the cofounders of AA. It may be a useful idea for the recovering victim of alcoholism (and for his family) who needs some sort of model for what ails him or her, but it is biologically and medically inaccurate. An allergy is now understood to be a hypersensitive response of the body's *immune system* to foreign substances or particles that do not stimulate such reactions in normal people. This involves very special proteins in the blood that do not interact with alcohol in any way, not even in alcoholics.[1] Common allergic reactions include so-called "hay fever," generally involving the nasal and sinus areas and manifested by sneezing and postnasal drip; asthma, involving labored breathing and wheezing due to spasmodic contractions of the bronchii of the lungs; food allergies involving the digestive tract; and a variety of skin rashes and other actions. The foreign substance stimulating the allergic response is called an *antigen* or *allergen*. It is recognized by the body as an alien substance, and in normal individuals these allergens are captured and combined with a special class of circulating proteins in the blood called *immunoglobulins* or *antibodies,* which are produced by specialized blood cells known as *B-lymphocytes*. These allergen-immunoglobulin complexes cause certain cells in the adjacent tissues known as *mast cells* to release *histamines* in susceptible individuals. These histamines cause local inflammation and capillary dilation, resulting in a drop in blood pressure and in fluid release. They can also produce contractions of the smooth muscle tissues of the bronchii in the lungs and induce secretions of digestive enzymes in the stomach. In some cases of extremely allergic reactions to such things as insect stings or certain drugs like penicillin or novocaine (the latter are very rare), the response may end in profound *anaphylactic shock* — an extremely dangerous and life-threatening situation. In summary, alcoholism is most definitely a disease of the body, at least in part, but it is not an allergy. This may seem like nit-picking (and it is), but referring to alcoholism as an allergy often creates unnecessary barriers to communication with medical professionals about a disorder that is already overburdened with such obstacles.

Some psychologists and sociologists argue that labelling alcoholism as a disease risks providing problem drinkers with a convenient rationale for avoiding the acceptance of personal responsibility for their lives. They assert that the

[1]Substances with a low molecular weight such as ethyl alcohol (ethanol) do not normally elicit antibody production and cannot form antigen-immunoglobulin complexes.

alcoholic will tend to use this idea as a justification for continued drinking. I do not believe that the evidence supports this contention. Anyone who has any experience with alcoholics knows that they are the ultimate masters of rationalization and denial — they need no assistance in inventing all manner of extravagant and ingenious excuses for their drinking behavior. If they are still looking for excuses, they will find them regardless of what anybody does or says, or *doesn't* do or say. If, on the other hand, they have had a bellyful of the consequences of their alcoholism and are "sick and tired of being sick and tired" (to borrow a phrase commonly heard in AA circles), then a realistic explanation to them of what alcoholism is and what one's options are certainly can do no harm. Quite the contrary, the concept that alcoholism is a known medical illness with a more or less standard course and prognosis, and that it afflicts millions of decent and otherwise responsible people is usually of major therapeutic value for the victims of this disorder. Most alcoholics are ridden with guilt and full of remorse over what they perceive as their own moral degeneracy. Alcoholic persons typically have extremely high, perfectionistic standards for themselves, although they are often tolerant of "human" frailties and weakness in others. It is themselves on whom they are the hardest. The demoralization suffered by such a rigid perfectionist in the face of repeated behavior that is universally condemned as outrageous, disgraceful, and disgusting can scarcely be imagined by anyone who has not experienced it. A common reaction expressed by many alcoholics when they first come to understand that they have a known and treatable disease is one of enormous *relief.* At least they are not insane or moral pariahs, which is what they feared most.

The disease concept of alcoholism is not only medically accurate, it is essential if one is to treat it in a responsible way. A diabetic person can take personal responsibility for managing his disease by appropriate dietary measures and, where necessary, insulin therapy only if he is very clear about what is wrong with him and exactly what is needed to counteract the problem. He must also have full knowledge of what the consequences will be should he become sloppy about his treatment program. The knowledge that one suffers from a disease state over which he has no control in no way absolves him of the responsibility of avoiding those situations (in the case of alcoholism, the first drink) which will almost certainly precipitate a relapse.

Arguments advanced against the disease model for alcoholism by many social scientists represent nothing more than pure sophistry. They reflect the intellectual's own need to regard man as a *tabula rasa* as proposed by John Locke in the Eighteenth Century — a "blank slate" which can be completely molded by man's willpower and intellect. This is a humanistic view, but it is not an accurate one. It ignores completely an overwhelming body of biological and medical information that we do, indeed, carry an enormous genetic load of predispositions and restricted options from birth. I am also convinced that many of these anti-disease-concept professionals still believe on some basic level, either consciously of unconsciously and in spite of their loud protestations to the contrary, that alcoholics *are,* in fact, moral lepers. I suspect that their real opposition comes out of a fear that the disease model may allow alcoholics to escape punishment for their "sins" by being relieved of the burden of guilt. It is interesting that the more the burden of evidence shifts in favor of a genetic predisposition to alcoholism, the more vociferous and uncompromising the anti-disease-concept humanists become in their resistance. I submit once again that alcoholism, like most other complex and poorly understood disorders, is not a simple matter of nature *or* nurture, but is rather one of *both.*

The late Dr. E. M. Jellinek was one of the first to purpose a disease model for alcoholism. He recognized several different major patterns of alcoholic drinking, which he described as follows:

(1) *alpha alcoholism* — psychological dependence upon alcohol; prodromal alcoholism.

(2) *beta alcoholism* — long-term, daily heavy drinking with ensuing medical complications, often serious, but without the overt behavioral and socioeconomic deterioration commonly seen in other forms of alcoholism; said to be common in France and Italy.

(3) *delta alcoholism* — chronic alcoholism, so-called maintance drinking; high daily level of consumption involving tolerance (may be evidenced by reverse tolerance in late stages) and physical addiction, and inability to abstain.

(4) *gamma alcoholism* (including *epsilon alcoholism*) — binge-drinking; dipsomania; the so-called *periodic* alcoholic, in which bouts of uncontrolled drinking are followed by short to protracted periods of "controlled" drinking or complete abstinence. Physical addiction is present and is manifested by severe withdrawal following binges, often including hallucinations, seizures and/or frank *delerium tremens.*

The foregoing classification was an early attempt to approach the subject from a scientific perspective, but it is no longer in general use and is of doubtful validity. The patterns suggested by Jellinek do not appear to describe real, discrete entities, and they are often observed to blend into one another. As an example, periodic binge-drinkers (gamma-type) commonly lapse into chronic, daily, maintenance (delta-type) drinkers, and vice versa. And beta-type alcoholics commonly show signs of obvious physical addiction, withdrawal, and inability to abstain.

Another way of looking at the problem is perhaps more realistic. Alcoholic drinking can be classified as *primary alcoholism* when that is the major disorder present and when most of the more serious psychiatric disturbances result from, rather than precede, the drinking. This by no means implies that there are no premorbid personality disturbances or neurotic factors, but only that the general psychosocial adjustment was reasonably intact prior to the onset of pathological drinking. About 60-70 percent of alcoholics appear to be of this type (Schuckit 1979a, 1979b). The general picture in primary alcoholism is a dismal one, usually with an insidious onset, followed by a gradual and progressive deterioration in social, economic, psychological and physical well-being, accompanied by ever more serious drinking, inability to abstain, and physical addiction. Unless there is a successful intervention in the course of this disease, the eventual outcome is far too often death from a variety of alcohol-related causes. There appears to be a strong genetic basis for the development of primary alcoholism.

Secondary alcoholism is commonly encountered in persons with a previously existing psychosis, especially schizophrenia or manic-depressive disease, or in persons with a *sociopathic [psychopathic or antisocial] personality disorder.* With psychotic alcoholics, an effective intervention in the psychotic symptomatology is usually necessary in order to bring them back to reality sufficiently for them to have some chance of attaining and maintaining sobriety. This generally requires the use of antipsychotic medications, such as the phenothiazines (for example, Thorazine®, Stellazine®, Mellaril®) or butyrophenones (haloperidol) for schizophrenics and lithium salts for manic patients. The important point is that for such people, the major problem is a severe, functional psychosis, and alcoholism cannot possibly be successfully treated unless the psychiatric disturbance is also being effectively handled. Some manic-depressives presenting only the manic phase appear to be able to drink "normally" during periods when their psychosis is in remission, but this does not seem to be true for alcoholics with both manic and depressive episodes, nor for those with unipolar depression.

Sociopathic alcoholics are generally included under the category of secondary alcoholism, even though they often closely resemble primary or "garden variety" alcoholics in their drinking patterns and behavior. Their psychiatric maladjustment is well established by early childhood and long predates their pathological drinking. There are also major differences between sociopaths and garden variety alcoholics in their psychological states and drinking patterns, and sociopaths are far more likely to be involved in overt criminal behavior. These differences are treated in a subsequent volume. Pre-alcoholic sociopathy is seen in about 20 percent of male and 5 percent of female (where it is often termed *hysterical personality* or *Briquet's syndrome*)[2] alcoholics; pre-alcoholic depressive illness is seen in 20-25 percent of female and 5 percent of male alcoholics (Schuckit et al. 1969; Schuckit 1973). Less than 5 percent of alcoholics exhibit schizophrenia (Schuckit 1979) or other major psychiatric disorders.

[2]There is considerable confusion regarding these diagnostic entities. Some authorities regard hysterical or histrionic personality and sociopathy in females as the same disorder, but there is much disagreement about this.

Certain individuals, especially sociopaths and some women, are subject to dramatic and severe alcoholism almost from their first encounter with the drug. Similarly, some persons (again, frequently women) who have refrained from using alcohol until later in adulthood may exhibit a sudden onset of florid alcoholism despite an apparently good premoid psychosocial adjustment. Many of the former group would appear to represent alcoholism secondary to a preexisting major psychiatric disorder although the issue is far from clear. Those whose onset of alcoholism coincides with the giving up of a teetotaling lifestyle in later years may simply reflect a progressive primary alcoholism whose symptoms only become manifest upon exposure to the drug.

Primary alcoholism has a very strong genetic component, whereas secondary alcoholism appears to be due largely to a serious underlying psychiatric disorder (which disorder may itself be at least in part genetically based). Some cases of so-called secondary alcoholism appear to be just that. However, I strongly suspect that others, particularly severe and progressive cases, may in fact represent a case of primary alcoholism superimposed upon a *coexisting affective* disorder or sociopathic personality structure. In other words, these individuals are likely to be suffering simultaneously from two disease states: alcoholism and an additional major psychiatric disorder, usually either major depression or sociopathy depending upon the sex involved. These clinical entities are by no means mutually incompatible, and multiple psychiatric diagnoses are not rare in clinical practice. The distinction between primary and secondary alcoholism is a useful one, nevertheless. As is true for most psychiatric categories, however, the boundaries between them are often blurred and individual patients may progress from one diagnostic category to another (see also the comments on depression below).

There are also well documented cases of *transient situational pathological drinking* which may spontaneously remit with the passage of time or with resolution of the life circumstances surrounding the alcohol abuse. Such cases do not appear to represent any of the true alcoholisms, all of which follow a more or less progressive course, are chronic in nature, and which, except for *extremely rare* cases, require a complete and permanent cessation of drinking and usually entail a rather thorough restructuring of the personality as well in order to effect a recovery. Moreover, in those very few cases where apparent "alcoholics" have been able to resume normal drinking, the diagnosis is open to challenge — in a sense, one of the main diagnostic features of this disease lies in its chronicity and the inability to resume controlled drinking for any prolonged period. Sociopathic personalities are sometimes observed to "burn out" at about age thirty-five to forty, and this may coincide with a spontaneous remission of active alcoholism. Such cases of remission almost surely represent secondary alcoholism. However, many remitted sociopaths show a continuing, progressive alcoholism (Goodwin & Guze 1979), and this very likely represents a coexisting primary alcoholism. The relationship between primary and secondary alcoholism remains complex and clouded.

Some individuals exhibit *pathological intoxication* after ingesting small to moderate amounts of alcohol during which they become abusive and assaultive, often with little or no provocation. This reflects a severe underlying personality disorder or a neurological problem such as epilepsy, and these people usually have no recall of the event after sobering up. Many garden variety alcoholics only manifest such behavior after considerable progression of the disease has occurred, probably as a result or personality deterioration due to long-term alcohol abuse. Finally, *acute alcoholism* refers to the medical syndrome of severe intoxication, usually involving a number of serious medical complications and often presenting as an emergency situation with life-threatening potential. This term refers to a specific intoxication episode and is not synonymous with the disease of alcoholism, although nonalcoholics would scarcely be normally found in such straits.

Jellinek (1960) and the World Health Organization Alcoholism Subcommittee (1952) cautioned that the disease concept of alcoholism does not properly apply to all types of pathological drinking. This is an important point to keep in mind. These investigators distinguished between *alcohol addiction* and *habitual symptomatic excessive drinking*. The disease concept is considered to apply only to the former category, approximately equivalent to primary alcoholism, in which *loss of control* over drinking develops after several years of exposure to alcohol. Although excessive drinking in both groups reflects an underlying psychopathology, the habitual excessive drinkers do not exhibit such loss of control; they are not thus true alcohol addicts and the disease concept does not properly apply to them.

It was also Jellinek and the WHO subcommittee that made famous the progressive model of primary, addictive alcoholism and divided the typical course of this disease into several major categories (see Fig. 1).

(1) In the *pre-alcoholic symptomatic phase,* the alcoholic-to-be usually begins his or her drinking career the way most other people do, although they frequently start somewhat earlier in life, sometimes even prior to the teens. They drink because their friends and peers do, and because alcohol is very effective in promoting "conviviality" (to quote Father Joseph C. Martin in his famous movie, *Chalk Talk*) and a sense of social well-being and ease at social gatherings. Moreover, persons headed for alcoholism generally experience something extra from alcohol, even in the earliest stages. Whereas most people experience a mild blunting of anxiety and tension, the developing alcoholic, to his delight, discovers almost from his first encounter with alcohol that he has suddenly been totally and completely relieved of a very heavy burden of insecurity, anxiety, and social uneasiness *that he never even knew he had until that moment when it dissipated.* For the early alcoholic, tension, anxiety, and dysphoria are totally eliminated and he feels a

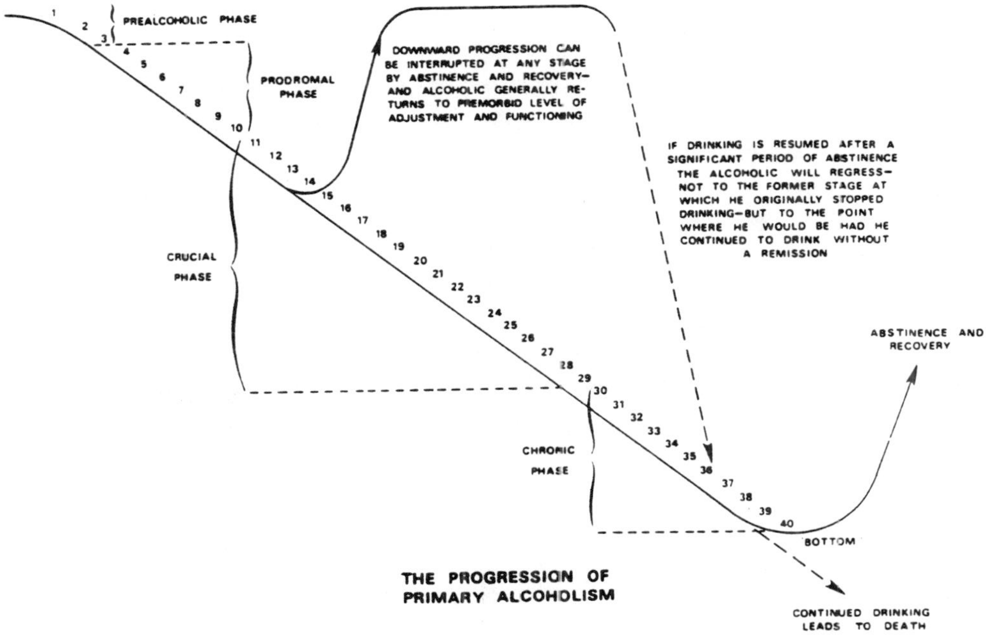

Figure 1. The numbers refer to the signs and symptoms typically occurring in the course of primary alcoholic progression. Not all of these necessarily occur in all individuals nor in exactly the order presented above. Italicized signs and symptoms are important indicators initiating the onset of major phases. (1) occasional relief drinking (2) constant relief drinking (3) increase in tolerance (4) *onset of palimpsests (blackouts)* (5) surreptitious drinking (6) preoccupation with alcohol (7) increasing dependence on alcohol (8) feelings of guilt about drinking (9) avoids subject of alcohol in conversation (10) blackouts increase (11) *loss of control* (12) rationalization and alibis for behavior (13) onset of social, marital, occupational, financial and/or legal consequences (14) pathological intoxication – gradiose and aggressive behavior (15) persistent remorse (16) vain efforts to control drinking (17) tries geographical escapes and periods of total abstinence (18) life now completely focused on alcohol (19) avoids family and friends (20) may quit job without good reason (21) unreasonable resentments develop (22) marked self-pity (23) protects and hoards alcohol supply (24) decreased libido and impotence (25) paranoid jealousy (26) begins to neglect personal hygiene and nutrition (27) first hospitalizations for alcoholism (28) tremors and early morning (matutinal) drinking (29) sudden decrease in tolerance to alcohol (30) *onset of regular matutinal drinking* (31) onset of lengthy intoxications (binges) (32) physical deterioration now apparent (33) moral and mental deterioration – impaired thinking (34) onset of alcoholic psychoses (35) seeks far inferior drinking companions (36) undefinable fears, constant tremors and psychomotor inhibition (cannot initiate action without alcohol) (37) obsessive drinking (38) vague religious desires (39) all alibis now exhausted (40) alcoholic now openly admits defeat.

Adapted and modified from H. M Glatt (1957), *British Journal of Addiction* 54, and Jellinek (1962).

soaring freedom and relief that cannot be readily comprehended by nonalcoholic "Earth people." He has found his magic medication (although he may not yet be fully aware of it) and he is like a person reborn – as indeed he is. From the very first, the developing alcoholic has a very special relationship to ethyl alcohol and he knows it deep in his being. He reacts to it quite differently, both psychologically and physiologically, than do his nonalcoholic peers. For one thing, hang overs are usually nonexistent or much less severe for the alcoholic-to-be, at least in the early stages. The alcoholic soon develops a *conditioned response* to *self-medicate* with alcohol and it becomes an effective, and ever increasingly, his sole device for coping with life's stresses. Nonalcoholics simply do not obtain the kind of relief that alcoholics do, nor do their tensions and fears appear to be as pronounced in the first place in the absence of other psychological disturbance.

The prealcoholic phase may persist from several months in cases of extremely short progression to (more usually) several years, during which time the drinker passes gradually from occasional relief drinking to alleviate anxiety to chronic, daily drinking. He gravitates more and more toward drinking-related functions and situations. Indeed, drinking may often be the only attraction, and he may find himself drawn to alcohol-related events in which he would otherwise have no interest. He begins to focus on drinking and alcohol more than ever and perhaps finds that he requires a few drinks before going to a social function where there will be additional drinking. Similarly, he may have to keep a supply at home in order to have the increasingly necessary nightcap or two before retiring to help him get to sleep. He may notice that he now needs more alcohol to achieve the former desired effect; he is now developing tolerance to the drug.[3] Many developing alcoholics are proud of this ability to drink everyone else under the table. He drinks more and more, and anticipates ever more eagerly that point in the day which he can "relax" from life's tribulations over his favorite alcoholic beverage.

He now drinks significantly more than his nonalcoholic friends do, but his drinking is not yet conspicuous to others. He is far from being out of control and he does not need to drink constantly, but he cannot imagine life without alcohol. It gives him the necessary courage to function in life, especially in social situations and with members of the opposite sex (at least in the case of heterosexual alcoholics). His associates and companions are likely to be for the most part people with the same orientation to alcohol as his own.

(2) The *prodromal phase* is generally ushered in by the appearance of alcoholic *blackouts* which superficially resemble the amnesic or fugue-like states seen in some cases of hysterical neurosis (now referred to under the rubric of dissociative disorders). These blackouts are not to be confused with *passing out,* which represents a true state of coma. An individual experiencing a memory

[3]See also discussion about metabolic and pharmacodynamic tolerance in Section 2. Although an enhanced ability to metabolize alcohol is induced by long-term exposure to large amounts of the drug, this cannot completely account for the high degree of tolerance seen in many alcoholics. Most of this accommodation appears to occur in the central nervous system and involves increasing neural membrane resistance to the fluidizing effects of alcohol.

blackout will have no recall for part or all of the events surrounding a drinking episode, but he will have ample evidence that he was active and functioning during the period in questions. Blackouts may be precipitated by as few as one or two drinks, and they do not appear to be related to the degree of intoxication.

Blackouts are terrifying experiences, as anyone who has ever had one can attest. If he can muster the courage to ask them about it, his friends may report that his behavior appeared to be perfectly normal during the period for which he has no recall. On the other hand, he may well have manifested pathological intoxication and engaged in behavior that caused him social embarrassment (when he learns of it) or resulted in his arrest. He is very frightened, and with good reason. He may have gotten married, enlisted in the military, committed a crime, or find himself in a distant city with no idea of how he got there. But the point is, *he doesn't know what happened!* One alcoholic surgeon of my acquaintance performed several successful operations in blackout states with no recall of having ever been in the operating room.

These alcoholic blackouts are often referred to in the professional literature as *palimpsests,* from the Greek, meaning parchments upon which several items have been superinscribed, with the earlier writings partially or wholly erased. Nonalcoholic individuals can also experience blackouts, but they are much rarer than in alcoholics. The occurrence of more than two alcohol-induced blackout events is strongly suggestive of alcoholism.

By now the alcoholic is beginning to experience some of the consequences of his alcoholic drinking. Feelings of self-doubt and guilt become more prevalent. He may not show up for work on an occasional Monday morning (or a Wednesday or Thursday) or he may become late more often. He may find it necessary to refortify himself with alcohol during increasingly long lunch breaks. If married, he begins to experience marital discord centered around his drinking and its consequences. He is now dependent upon alcohol and probably drinks a good deal on most days. Denial becomes increasingly important, and he may rationalize his drinking in a variety of ways: *I can't be an alcoholic* (this, even when no one has made such a suggestion). *After all, I can go 5 days in a row without a single drink — why, I did that just last month on a camping trip. Besides, I never drink before 5:00 in the afternoon. I can take it or leave it — I just choose to take it, that's all. I'll definitely know when to quit before it gets to me!*

And yet, increasingly, his denials break down as he enters the stage of needing a "hair of the dog that bit him" in the morning, his work begins to suffer, or he accumulates DWIs (driving while intoxicated arrests). He begins to drink surreptitiously and more and more avoids the subject of alcohol and alcoholism in his conversation. He may become exceedingly uncomfortable when the subject arises. His blackouts increase in number and in seriousness. His marriage may fail or be threatened with failure, and he may make repeated pledges and efforts to go on the wagon. Inevitably, he only suffers repeated relapses and further demoralization.

(3) Somewhere along the line he has passed into the *crucial phase* of alcoholism, which is characterized by *loss of control.* A single drink may produce an uncontrolled binge of alcoholic drinking that may persist until the alcoholic is forced to stop from sheer exhaustion and physical collapse. He can now no longer predict what will happen once he takes the initial drink, and his alcoholic condition has become obvious and apparent to everyone, even to the alcoholic himself. Former rationalizations that sporadic drunken episodes with pathological behavior were caused by one or another combination of adverse life circumstances can no longer be sustained, not even by the alcoholic himself. He drinks when he is sad and when he is happy (by now an increasingly rare mood for him) — the plain truth is that he drinks simply because he drinks! The typical alcoholic finds the concept of social drinking as alien and incomprehensible as normal drinkers view the pathological and obsessional drinking of the alcoholic. To an alcoholic, it is just not conceivable that one could have "just one drink." It's hardly worth the effort!

His family, if he still has one, is almost certainly sucked up into the psychological and social tornado of an alcoholic lifestyle. They are probably in collusion with his efforts to generate alibis and deceive his superiors on the job. They may fall into the trap of trying to resist his alcoholism by hiding his supply (which he is now hoarding and trying to protect), or taking money out of his pockets and wallets to prevent his being able to buy more. Such efforts are foredoomed to failure, however, and they only aid and abet the alcoholic's machinations to avoid taking personal responsibility for his predicaments. Furthermore, no matter how destitute, alcoholics never fail to obtain an adequate supply of alcohol in one form or another.

The alcoholic now associates with companions much lower on the socioeconomic scale and begins to engage in increasingly obnoxious and perhaps even overtly aggressive behavior. He becomes more isolated as family and friends desert him and his only associates are likely to be a few drinking buddies as bad off as himself. He has probably begun to quit jobs either without reasonable grounds, or before he anticipates being fired. He attempts one or more *geographic cures,* hoping to leave his problems behind him in physical space. He may try to change his drinking patterns in a vain effort to recapture control of his drinking, all to no avail. He longs desperately for the days long since past when alcohol was still his friend which allowed him to feel good about himself and at peace with the world. But those days are forever gone, and deep down he knows it.

His sexual life is long since quite thoroughly disrupted, and he has probably been impotent for several years, at least off and on, due to a combination of psychological and physiological factors resulting from alcohol abuse. He is racked by unreasonable fears and resentments, and may exhibit *alcoholic paranoia* or insane jealousy towards his wife (or girlfriend) because of his own projections resulting from his sexual inadequacy.[4] A normally heterosexual man may experience *homosexual panic* as latent homosexual impulses become conscious, particularly if he should find himself in an alcoholic homosexual situation which, to his horror, he finds pleasurable. Such feelings of sexual ambivalence exist in all men and women, but they are generally well suppressed by the intact repressive mechanisms of a healthy personality. But it must be stressed that alcoholics are no more latently homosexual than the rest of the population, despite certain theories suggesting that latent homosexuality underlies the development of alcoholism in males.[5] Alcoholics generally seem to suffer some deficit in their psychological defense system and their ability to repress unwanted subconscious material. This filtering deficit may account for some of the heightened tension and anxiety levels they experience early in life, and alcohol appears to help blot out these sources of tension at least at first. Long-term alcohol abuse quite thoroughly disrupts these already weak defense mechanisms, and as negative and undesired subconscious impulses surge into conscious awareness on an ever increasing basis, the sufferer feels overwhelmed by guilt and remorse over his feelings, thoughts and behavior. These catastrophic feelings of self-loathing may drive him to commit or attempt suicide.

(4) The final, or *chronic phase* of alcoholism is characterized by prolonged intoxications or benders, often lasting for days. Obvious signs of physical addiction follow such episodes, including very severe tremors, and in a small percentage of alcoholics (about 10%), even *alcoholic hallucinosis* with auditory and tactile hallucinations. The auditory hallucinations frequently involve accusing voices, sometimes with a homosexual content or directing threats against the hallucinator. Visual hallucinations are less common, and when present are often accompanied by great fear. They often take the form of small, brightly colored and fast-moving animals. There may be delusions and the victim may be disoriented in space and time. There may be great panic associated with this syndrome, especially with hallucinatory homosexual accusations, and suicide is a serious threat. Alcoholic hallucinosis superficially resembles paranoid schizophrenia, but the latter disorder persists in the absence of drinking within the previous ten days or so. Schizophrenia is further characterized by thought disorder, depersonalization, inappropriate and/or flattened affect or emotional response, and autistic features.[6] For obscure reasons, alcoholic hallucinosis is more common among American black males than among other segments of the population (Goodwin 1976). *Grand mal* seizures can occur upon cessation or

---

[4] Either he cannot acknowledge his own impotence and must therefore blame his wife's projected indifference (which he thinks can only result because she is seeing someone else), or he becomes convinced that she must be having an outside affair, since he is (or believes he is) unable to perform adequately or satisfy her needs.

[5] This subject is treated in detail in the volume dealing with psychodynamic aspects of alcoholism.

[6] These terms are explained in the volume on psychodynamics.

reduction of alcohol intake, usually between 24 hours and seven days afterwards. A lowered seizure threshold due to magnesium deficiency resulting from metabolic acidosis (see below in Section 2) may be partly responsible. About 10 percent of alcoholics experience one or more episodes of *delerium tremens,* which is marked by profuse sweating, a coated tongue and foul breath, a weak and rapid pulse, seizures, elevated temperature and frank delerium, often with *confabulations* or fabricated tales which may be quite absurd. Delerium tremens is a life-threatening medical emergency.

Moral and ethical decompensation and intellectual deterioration may also occur at this stage. He now exhibits *reverse tolerance* to the effects of alcohol, and a very small amount of alcohol can produce severe intoxication; this is due at least in part to impaired liver function. His former ability to outdrink his companions has long since vanished. Further socioeconomic decline usually follows, perhaps even as far down as skid row, and the chronic alcoholic exhibits a gross neglect of his physical health and malnutrition, poor hygiene, and a variety of serious medical prolems. Death frequently occurs before the sufferer reaches skid row status due to a number of different medical complications, including cirrhosis of the liver (about 10% of alcoholics), cardiac arrest, hypoglycemic shock, and similar causes. Alcoholics are subject to all types of fatal and near-fatal trauma, including shooting, stabbing, beating, burns, and car accidents. Only about 3 to 5 percent of all alcoholic persons ever reach skid row; the rest either die beforehand or remain at a higher social level.

A few alcoholics (less than 5%, Schuckit 1979) may develop *Wernicke-Korsakoff syndrome,* due in part to an acute and severe vitamin B_1 deficiency (see also below, Section 2) and partly to the direct toxic action of alcohol on the brain. This syndrome is characterized by a clouded consciousness with confusion, paralyzed eye muscles, disorientation in space and time, both *anterograde amnesia* (the loss of memory for immediately preceeding events) and *retrograde amnesia* (memory loss for past events), and the resulting *confabulations* or falsification of memory with fantastic and bizarre ficticious narratives to cover up the memory blanks, as well as various neurological symptoms and signs. The outlook for such individuals is poor, although some do recover marginally in a few weeks with adequate vitamin B_1 (thiamine) therapy in a hospital setting. Wernicke-Korsakoff patients are typically aggressive and violent sociopaths with a history of barroom brawling prior to the onset of this syndrome. With the occurrence of Korsakoff-stage problems, the personality becomes apathetic and passive and almost all interest in alcohol disappears (Butters & Cermak 1980). The final progressive stage of alcoholism is so-called *wet brain syndrome,* characterized by constant muttering, fixed or frozen facial features *(fixed facies),* purposeless picking movements of the hands, and coma. The prognosis is very grave and death is, mercifully, usually not long in coming.

The foregoing characterization is an encapsulated account of a typical, unchecked course of primary or garden variety alcoholism. Although it by no means always results in Wernicke-Korsakoff or wet brain syndromes, such outcomes are common enough. The story has many variations, the course may be rapid or slow and the milestones may not follow exactly the foregoing sequence. There are also major differences in the etiology and alcoholic patterns and between men and women (see Volume 4 of this series). But the theme remains essentially the same: a progressively deteriorating entrapment and compulsion to drink coupled with true psychological and physical addiction, and leading to a total disruption of every aspect and parameter of the victim's life and the lives of family members, as well. The drinking pattern in later years may be a periodic one, but is more commonly manifested as daily, maintenance drinking. The course may run itself out to the bitter end, or the sufferer may get off the downward plummeting elevator at any floor and begin the recovery process. Some alcoholics, especially many younger ones, are recognizing their disease as early as the prodromal stage, probably due to increased public awareness and alcoholism educational programs, and they are entering Alcoholics Anonymous and other treatment programs much sooner in the course of the disease than has been typically true in the past. Regardless of the particular scenario or "bottoming-out" point, every alcoholic knows well the feeling of total dispair as very few other people ever experience it. This is true whether he went all the way to skid row or reached his nadir as a "high-bottom drunk" still living in his own house and sleeping between clean sheets at night.

It is not just family and friends of the alcoholic who cannot understand this strange compulsion to self-destruct; the victim of this horrible affliction is himself equally at a loss to explain his behavior. He is like a complete madman, and yet beneath his insane behavior he is really quite sane and rational. His constant attempts to rationalize his chaotic life only reflect his own inability to comprehend his inexplicable situation. He more than likely started out in life with an excess of superior qualities: intelligence, charm, creativeness, industriousness, and a strong sense of morality, fair-play, justice, and compassion. He is often the person considered "most likely to succeed" by his associates. What, then, goes wrong? I believe that alcoholics are people who generally possess more than their share of plusses, but that as part of the genetic package with which they were endowed, they also contain the seeds of their own destruction once they encounter ethyl alcohol. In other words, the very combination of traits that makes many of them more "fit" at the same time predisposes them ultimately to be less able to function in life than their nonalcoholic counterparts. This idea is discussed in greater depth in Volumes 3 (psychodynamics) and 4 (genetics) of this series. At this juncture I want to go into the concept of alcoholism in more detail.

A MULTIFACTORIAL DISEASE

Many recovered alcoholics often refer to alcoholism as a "disease of the body, the mind, and the spirit." That is an accurate, if somewhat simplified statement. As we shall see, it has multiple causes involving strong genetic and constitutional predispositions overlain with complex socioeconomic, cultural, and psychological factors. There have been a number of studies aimed at elucidating the role of genetic factors in the etiology of alcoholism relative to personality and environmental components. But almost no professional attention has been paid to the last aspect of alcoholism – the spiritual one – except perhaps by a few theologians and lay treatment groups like Alcoholics Anonymous. Of course, spiritual matters have traditionally been considered to be not really proper subjects for scientific investigation. All such experiences are quite internal, subjective, and highly personal and they offer little by way of external, objective evidence that can be approached by the methods known to science. Nonetheless, I believe that spiritual impoverishment and isolation is probably the most important factor of all, and that alcoholics tend to be people with unusually profound spiritual needs, whose expression is blocked by a variety of attitudes, intellectual convictions, and rebellion against previous religious training. Indeed, one investigator has suggested that a field of "research theology" should be developed to "explore . . . the so-called spiritual factors in etiologies of problem drinking" (Hoff 1969: 88).

On scientific and biological grounds I am convinced that mankind has an innate, deep-seated need for religious and spiritual fulfillment. Indeed, man could very appropriately be defined as the *religious animal.* I intend no theological inferences of any kind, either pro or con, by this suggestion, but I do believe it reflects anthropological reality. As *Homo sapiens,* each one of us has spiritual needs that must be satisfied one way or another. Many people hold one or more of a variety of theological and/or mystical concepts and engage in more or less organized rituals and practices. Some are more casual about it, but they also hold at least some vague religious or spiritual ideas from which they derive some sense of support. Some turn to magical thinking, sorcery, astrology, and belief in such things as Tarot Cards and *I Ching* (especially in this day of iconoclasm and easy acceptance of almost anything that looks like it is alien to established ideas and principles). Others pursue one or more of a great many meditation techniques, including Transcendental Meditation, Yoga, or Zen, or they find spiritual fulfillment by getting close to Nature or in music and the arts. And of course, many intellectually persuaded persons seek their religion in academic endeavors and humanistic philosophy (both rather rigid belief systems), quasi-extremist politics, or in outright atheism. Man either embraces spirituality or he resists it, but he is not indifferent to it. These needs are stronger in some than in others, but few of us are immune to a profound sense of awe when we truly consider the immensity of the Cosmos and our relationship to it.

Students of Zen Buddhism undergo long years of rigorous training by confronting a series of *koans* – unsolvable, paradoxical statements or questions designed to break down the rational mind and open the Inner Being to a direct experience of Self (or of God, in the western Judaeo-Christian tradition). *What is the sound of one hand clapping?* is one famous *koan,* and, *Show me your face before your parents were born!* is another. In the Rinzai sect, nearly 600 such *koans* must be directly experienced and transcended by the student before he can be considered enlightened enough to become a qualified *roshi* or Zen master. By focusing one's total concentration on such a *koan* for a long enough period of time (usually months or even years), one's mental processes ultimately break down and fail. And at the instant of total intellectual collapse and emotional despair one is open to the full mystical or religious experience (*satori* or *kensho* in Japanese). This experience is a nonrational one which cannot be obtained by mere belief or conviction on the part of the mind. Neurophysiological investigations into Zen have shown that a Zen disciple's success in "solving" his *koan* are correlated with his brainwave pattern at the time (Restak 1984). Experienced Zen meditators can almost immediately enter deep, stage 4 meditation in which normal alpha brainwave activity is changed to slower theta waves. Zen masters apparently never accept a student's answer to his *koan* unless the student is emitting theta waves at the time.

I believe alcoholism represents an inescapable, living *koan* to its victims. Superficially, it consists of the fact that alcoholics cannot drink and they cannot *not* drink. Like the Zen monk, student alcoholics can transcend this absolute impasse only by experiencing a profound emotional, intellectual, and spiritual crisis. Only after hitting such a "bottom" can they surrender to their situation and (to quote a common AA phrase) "turn it over to a Power greater than themselves," and thus allow the problem to dissipate by a nonrational means.[7] At a much deeper level the alcoholic *koan* involves a desperate and often denied need for direct spiritual contact coupled with an almost constitutional inability to allow that need to be fulfilled. Alcoholics are like devout priests who suddenly find themselves unable to believe in God (also not a rare species) — theirs is a special kind of living hell. This religious need is perhaps also manifested by the drive many alcoholics appear to have for *peak experiences,* which can definitely be provided by alcohol and other psychotropic drugs. On the other hand, this probably also reflects a need to escape from constant and

[7]As any recovered alcoholic can tell you, it is not will power that enabled him to "overcome" the disease, but unconditional *surrender* to the hopelessness of the situation and reliance upon what is commonly referred to as a "Higher Power" — a concept not necessarily at all well defined or understood. One recovered alcoholic described his "conversion" experience as follows:

I had been on an uncontrolled drinking spree for several days, during which I had rolled and severely damaged my car (one of the few episodes of that interval which I do recall). When I "came to" I was lying deathly sick in my bed, shaking uncontrollably and lapsing in and out of consciousness. I desperately needed medical attention, but I lacked the strength to get out of bed and go to the phone. I remained in that state for several days (I believe four) before I was able to summon help. I recall very little of that time, but one event is still emblazened vividly in my mind. As I lay there in the most profound despair I have ever experienced, agitated and shaking terribly, a deep tranquility and blissful serenity descended suddenly upon me, and I knew in a way that I had never known anything with such certainty before, that my ordeal was over and that I would never have to take another drink again in my life. Just like that, and my alcoholism was cured! And I have been happily sober since.

pervasive feelings of dysphoria which are so common among alcoholics. And in the case of certain personality disorders it is undoubtedly based upon underlying impulsive and hedonistic patterns. The foregoing may offer some explanation for why Alcoholics Anonymous has found reliance upon a Higher Power and commitment to spiritual growth to be so necessary and so effective in the recovery from alcoholism. It is precisely what is needed! I should add such a spiritual program of recovery by no means implies that recovered alcoholics are suddenly transformed into hymn-singing goodie-two-shoes. They are very earthy people, indeed, as attendance at almost any AA meeting will demonstrate. There, one will encounter language and gut-level discussions of visceral living problems scarcely to be found in the average church setting.

Alcoholism is also a disease of ambivalence. Many alcoholics appear to be unable to screen out collateral or extraneous information, a feature which is related to their inability to repress unwanted subconscious impulses and thoughts, and which may result from both physiological deficits in the lower forebrain, as well as from the presence of obsessional-compulsive neurotic traits. For practically any thought or emotion that appears, the opposite response will also follow almost immediately, just as any statement automatically implies its opposite. For example, it is impossible to conceive of *good* except in the context of *evil* against which to juxtapose it. Similarly *black* cannot exist without *white, matter* without *emptiness, up* without *down,* and so forth. And this is not merely a matter of being philosophically or semantically cute — it is an immutable and fundamental physical law of the Universe. *Self* cannot exist except within the context of *non-self.* Alcoholics often find it difficult to love without simultaneously experiencing hate, for example, because these two reactions are just different sides of the same emotional coin.[8] They tend to see every side of most questions all too clearly, and it is their emotional and intellectual undoing. They may be introspective enough to recognize their dilemma on a conscious level, or they may have little insight and be simply plagued by strong but vague, ill-defined doubts and fears. I believe this condition exists in many alcoholics prior to the onset of pathological drinking and that it is the dynamics of seeing too much at one time that, at least in part, causes the high levels of anxiety and tension so common to this group. Alcohol helps the alcoholic to blot out some of this extraneous input and to focus upon a single aspect of the issue at hand. The alcoholic can thus, at least for a while, experience love for someone without also having to handle feelings of anger and resentment. He can be noble and good without having to cope with also feeling like a pariah. He can feel brave without having to acknowledge his cowardice. And life becomes more or less manageable until the drug wears off.

The progressive nature of alcoholic deterioration is very well known and

---

[8]Love and hate are not opposites at all. Both are different manifestations of extreme *attachment,* and one expression can readily become transformed into the other. The opposite of love-hate is *indifference.*

widely documented. With continued alcohol consumption over time the consequences become ever worse, never better, although there may be temporary respites in this pattern. One of the most bizarre and least understood aspects of the disease is the apparent progression that occurs *even in the complete absence of alcohol intake.* It is not at all uncommon for alcoholics to achieve a fairly longstanding abstinence only to suffer a relapse after perhaps several years or more. It has been observed by both medical and lay people that such persons do not regress to their former level of alcoholic deterioration, but to the level they would have reached had they never stopped drinking in the first place (Fig. 1). It appears that the disease will run its course no matter what, and it only requires the consumption of alcohol for the signs and symptoms to become manifest. This may underlie the phenomenon described earlier that some persons who refrain from drinking until later in life develop an extremely rapid onset of far advanced alcoholism. Some of the factors behind this are almost surely constitutional. Others may well be psychological, however, as seen in the sudden worsening of alcoholic drinking commonly encountered following exposure to one or several AA meetings. This is well recognized in AA circles, as is evidenced by the saying, "Once you've been around these tables, you may decide not to stay — but we guarantee to screw up your drinking."

WHO IS SUSCEPTIBLE?

Any attempt to estimate the number of alcoholics in a given population is fraught with a great many uncertainties and requires a number of assumptions which may not be valid. Not the least of those problems is an adequate working definition of what constitutes alcoholism. In fact, this consideration is a difficulty of nearly every scientific attempt to investigate the disease. Such studies commonly deal with extremely advanced and severely debilitated alcoholics, often from the skid row sector, and they are not necessarily representative of early and middle-stage pathological drinkers. In the 1940s, Jellinek introduced his famous equation which relates the total number of alcoholics in a large population to the general mortality from Laënnec's liver cirrhosis as determined by autopsy. Laënnec's cirrhosis is strongly associated with alcoholism (although it is not exclusive to it) and the Jellinek formula assumes a constant relationship between this disease (cirrhosis) and alcoholism. His equation as currently expressed is:

$$A = \left(\frac{PD}{K} \right) \bullet R$$

where A = all alcoholics, P = percentage of deaths from cirrhosis due to alcoholism, D = total deaths from cirrhosis in a given year, K = the total number of alcoholics with complications dying of liver cirrhosis, and R = an assumed ratio between all alcoholics and those with complications. The absolute value of P has fluctuated over time (see Keller 1962), but the ratio between the sexes has remained constant, with $P♂ \div P♀ = 2.9$. K was assigned a value of 0.693 based on autopsy reports, and R was set equal to 4 on the assumption that there are three alcoholics without complications for every one with complications.

A major problem with the Jellinek formula is that R and K are frequently underestimated in many areas where autopsies are more casually performed and reported. There have also been criticisms of the assumptions underlying the presumed constant value of P relative to D, which suggest that the Jellinek formula would tend to underestimate the total number of alcoholics by from 18 to 56 percent, depending upon the "corrections" introduced. Jellinek himself long ago advocated that his formula be discontinued even in its revised versions. However, it continues to be widely employed by many agencies, including WHO, which cite evidence that estimates based on this method are at least approximately correct. In the United States there are some 8 to 10 million alcoholics at the present time, and this assessment is very likely a conservative one. Estimates of the ratio of male to female alcoholics based upon the Jellinek equation have remained fairly constant at 5 or 6 to 1 for almost half a century (these values are a function of, but are not identical with the respective values of P). Similar results were obtained in the United Kingdom (Madden 1979), with male alcoholics outnumbering females by approximately 7 or 8 to 1. One study showed 46 percent of the brothers of alcoholics to have alcoholism themselves, as compared to 5 percent of the sisters (Winokur et al. 1970). However, recent estimates indicate that the number of women alcoholics is rising rapidly, and a survey of one New York neighborhood indicated a ratio of male to female alcoholics of only 3.6 to 1 (Bailey et al., as cited in Madden 1979). A 1974 survey by Alcoholics Anonymous revealed that one of every three members was a woman, and a *Time* magazine report (April 22, 1974) indicated that 50 percent of the alcoholics in Dade County, Florida were women!

Whatever the actual figures, the rates of alcoholism in the United States are enormously high and are probably on the order of 10 percent of the adult male and 3.3 percent of the adult female population (Schuckit 1979). This means some 10 million alcoholics out of a drinking population of about 100 million. Scarcely a family has not been touched by this disease, and every alcoholic severely impacts against five or six other people, bringing the total number of persons affected by this disorder to a staggering 50 to 60 million! On the other hand, five different countries in Europe show alcoholism rates of about 3-5 percent for males and 0.1-1 percent for females. Given the tendency of these countries to keep good records, these figures probably reflect real differences in the alcoholism rates. Alcoholism must be distinguished from *heavy drinking*. More men (20%) are heavy drinkers than women (8%), and heavy drinking is more common among the lower, less-educated classes.[9] It is not rare for long-term heavy drinkers to become moderate drinkers or teetotalers in later years (Goodwin & Guze 1979). In addition, about one-third of young male drinkers have transitory problems with alcohol involving social and/or legal difficulties, but these remit with no further pathological involvement (Schuckit 1979).

Alcoholism constitutes the third leading cause of death in the United States after heart disease and cancer, and it contributes to the latter two as well, as we shall see in the following section. Moreover, alcohol addicts are usually also caffeine and cigarette addicts, which further increases their liability to heart disease and cancer. According to the National Institute on Alcohol Abuse and Alcoholism (NIAAA), alcohol is involved in one-fourth to one-third of all suicides, and in 50 percent each of all homicides, fatal automobile accidents, and all injuries from all causes. In addition, nearly 13,000 people die from liver cirrhosis each year in this country, and alcoholism takes an average of 15 years off the life of each of its victims (Schuckit 1979). Because of medical complications due to long-term alcohol abuse and injuries due to drunkenness, 20 to 40 percent of *all* hospitalized patients are alcoholic (Vaillant 1978; Schuckit 1979). The overall cost to the nation during 1974 in lost production, medical expenses and time lost from work due to alcoholism was a stupendous $25 billion, and in 1975 the figure rose to $42.75 billion!

A number of studies have shown that alcoholism rates are higher in the cities than in rural areas, but it is difficult to assess the significance of this finding. It may reflect a greater stress level and impersonal social milieu for city-dwellers as some sociologists have suggested, although no correlation between externally-generated stress and alcoholism has ever been demonstrated. I think it much more likely that a greater tendency for rural abstinence from alcohol for religious and cultural reasons masks the presence of latent alcoholism. Rates of alcoholism go up where social cohesiveness is disrupted, such as occurs in aboriginal societies undergoing "assimilation" or among socioeconomically-deprived groups such as American ghetto blacks with high rates of alcoholism. However, alcoholism rates among rural blacks are not known and one cannot separate the biological from the environmental variables, despite the superficially "apparent" sociological implications. For example, higher alcoholism rates among inner city residents and skid row inhabitants may reflect the fact that alcoholics and individuals with other psychopathologies tend to migrate to depressed and socially lower communities. More schizophrenics, for example, are found in inner city and slum areas than elsewhere, despite a clear indication of strong genetic predisposing factors in this disease. This is due to a "downward drift" to a low socioeconomic status because of the general debilitation resulting from this illness (Goodwin & Guze 1979).

---

[9]Cahalen et al. (1969) report that 77 percent of American men and 60 percent of the women drink at least once a year. Of those drinkers, 28 percent of the men and 8 percent of the women are heavy drinkers (*in* Corrigan 1980).

Alcoholics do tend to come from pathological and disrupted family backgrounds, and this is often cited as evidence that poor parenting and inadequate adult role models are involved in the development of the disorder. Yet many people from broken and severely pathological homes do not develop alcoholism. Furthermore, a high level of neuroticism is not correlated with increased alcoholism. This is evidenced in Jewish populations which have significant rates of neurosis,[10] but very low rates for alcoholism. It has been suggested that this may due to the ritual use of wine for religious purposes coupled with severe social disapproval of public drunkenness among Jews. But this by no means rules out the possibility that Jews as a group have a low incidence of the genes for alcoholism. They certainly exhibit other genetic distinctions, for example Tay-Sachs disease, which is found almost exclusively among Jewish infants.

A series of genetic studies in Denmark (the reader is referred to Volume 4 of this series which discusses these and other studies in detail) compared the biological sons having at least one alcoholic parent (the probands) which had been adopted from early infancy into foster homes with a control group of sons similarly adopted but which did not have a biological alcoholic parent. The foster families in both groups were similar, although those of the control group showed slightly higher rates for alcoholism. If environmental circumstances played a significant there, one would expect both adopted groups to show similar rates of alcoholism. In fact, the adopted probands showed *four times* the rate of alcoholism as compared with the controls. Clearly, a strong genetic component is revealed by these studies. Furthermore, some of the adopted probands had older siblings which had been raised by the biological parents. (The parental alcoholism had not yet progressed to the point when the older children were born to cause them to be placed into foster families.) The rates for alcoholism between the adopted proband and their older brothers who had been raised in their biological, alcoholic family *were identical.* Environment does not appear to play a *major* role in the etiology of alcoholism.

Studies on identical and fraternal twins raised apart have likewise shown the former to have vastly higher *concordance*[11] rates for alcoholism. In fact, very recent studies of a number of identical twin pairs raised apart since infancy (often in totally different environments),[12] have shown a startling number of similarities in the details of their personalities and lifestyles, even to the types of

---

[10]This may be merely a function of the fact that psychoneurosis is more prevalent in the uppermost socioeconomic and educational classes (Kaplan et al. 1980, vol. 3), groups in which Jews are greatly overrepresented in proportion to their percentage in the general population. Furthermore, members of these classes are less prone to regard psychiatric consultation as stigmatic and are thus more likely to seek treatment and thus add to statistical compilations.

[11]The occurrence of a given genetic trait in both members of a twin pair.

[12]Perhaps the most dramatic example is seen in Oskar Stohr and Jack Yufe, an identical twin pair raised, respectively, in Nazi Germany as a Catholic and Nazi youth, and in the Caribbean as a Jew. The similarities in their personalities, mannerisms, tempos, profiles on psychological tests are very striking.

jewelry chosen and the manner in which it is worn, the names of their spouses, children and pets, their occupations, and the kinds of cars that they drive (Holden 1980). The implication is that genetics may play a greater role in human behavior than has ever been suspected, although the case is by no means proven. In fact, Drs. C. J. Lumsden and E. O. Wislon (the latter is a renowned sociobiologist) have just published a new book, *Genes, Mind, and Culture* (1981), in which they propose that most presumed *cultural* differences between societies and ethnic groups are genetically based, as well. Needless to say, this book has already stirred up considerable controversy, and the initial feeling among most scientists able to comment authoritatively is that many of the authors' premises are based on assumptions that are not demonstrated as fact, their mathematical formulations do not always match the conclusions presented in the text, and they appear to have carried their case much too far and their interpretations are too incautious to suit most reviewers. Nevertheless, it is becoming increasingly clear that genetic and constitutional predisposing factors play a major role in who we are and what we become. For example, studies of adoptees similar to those described above for alcoholics show that the sons of criminal fathers reared in noncriminal foster homes had twice the rate of criminality as did the biological sons of noncriminal fathers raised with criminal foster fathers (Horn 1978). When adoptees with criminal biological fathers were raised with criminal foster fathers, the rate of criminality was three times that of controls. It seems apparent that environmental factors can exacerbate preexisting genetic traits, but they are not a major factor in the absence of such biological predeterminants, at least in some disorders.

Although alcoholism occurs throughout all social, occupational, and financial groups, it is more common in lower socioeconomic levels and among Catholics. Individuals, particularly males, coming from families with one or more alcoholic members are themselves at high risk for the disease.[13] More surprisingly, epidemiological studies have also shown that persons whose spouse or one of whose direct in-laws is an alcoholic are also at risk. Males of French, Irish, Polish, or Russian extraction are especially vulnerable to alcoholism, whereas Chinese, Dutch, and Jewish groups have very low incidences of alcoholism. Persons from teetotaling families are at risk should they begin to drink at any time during their lives. American blacks and Chicanos have a high incidence of alcoholism, and the extreme rates of florid alcoholism among American Indians and Eskimos is legendary — and also accurate.[14]

The greater incidence of male alcoholics relative to women has already been mentioned. It has been suggested that this represents a sex-linked genetic characteristic, although the increasing rate of alcoholism among women tends to

[13]Being at risk does not mean that the person will *necessarily* develop the disorder; it simply means that such persons are statistically far more likely to manifest the disease.

[14]But not universal. Not all tribes are equally afflicted. (Goodwin & Guze 1974).

cast doubt on this hypothesis. This subject is treated in some detail in a subsequent volume. The psychological factors are somewhat different between men and women in this disorder. The general age-range at risk for onset of alcoholism in men is from 20 to 45; women usually develop alcoholism later in life. Alcoholism is generally much more severe in women than in men. They usually exhibit more serious psychopathology and recovery is correspondingly more difficult. Profound depression plays a major role and hysterical personality a minor role in the development of alcoholism in women. Nearly all studies concur that in most women, alcoholism is secondary to preexisting psychiatric disturbance (Burns 1979). Women begin drinking later in life, but the progression of their alcoholism tends to be faster and they are hospitalized for complications at about the same age as men. Women also exhibit more polydrug abuse and use more prescribed and over-the-counter medications than do men (Gomberg 1979). (The reader is referred to Volume 4 of this series of a detailed discussion of alcoholism in women.)

The majority of men appear to have no obvious predisposing psychopathology (but see Volume 3 of this series on psychodynamics) and thus fit the concept of primary alcoholics. However, about one-fifth of male alcoholics are also sociopaths and many of them are severely depressed. The depression in male alcoholics is not as obvious as it is in their female counterparts, but it is often there and it can be very debilitating. Profound depression in this context means that due to a *primary affective disorder,* which is approximately equivalent to what used to be termed manic-depressive psychosis. *All* alcoholics are depressed to one degree or another, and episodic major depressions frequently partially remit into a less severe, but often chronic *dysthymic disorder.* These depressions typically appear during recovery after the alcoholic has stopped drinking. Alcohol serves as a self-administered medication to relieve the distress of severe depression, and when the drug is withdrawn the full depressive syndrome often nearly paralyzes the sufferer.

Until fairly recently two types of depression were generally thought to exist: *neurotic depression* (dysthymic disorder of current usage) which was believed to arise primarily from characterological deficits and environmental circumstances such as early parental loss, whereas *psychotic depressions,* also known as *endogenous depression,* derives mainly from genetically-inherited biochemical imbalances in the brain. The terms "neurotic" and "psychotic" were also formerly believed to reflect the relative seriousness of the two types of depressive syndromes. The current psychiatric consensus is that both syndromes lie along a depressive continuum from relatively mild to severely incapacitating with a high likelihood of suicide attempted or carried out. Under our current understanding of the affective states, all depression, whether so-called neurotic (dysthymic) or endogenous, is regarded fundamentally as a biologically-inherited disorder and is generally very effectively managed with antidepressant medications. The concept of *depressive-spectrum disease* refers to depression in any individual from a family in which alcoholism and/or sociopathy is also present in one or more members. There is no question that a clear relationship exists between primary affective disorder and alcoholism, with female relatives of both alcoholics and depressives more commonly exhibiting depression, and male relatives of both groups showing a greater tendency to alcoholism.

Well controlled studies of the biological offspring of both alcoholic and depressive parents (by the principal investigator for the other adoptive studies described above) raised from early infancy in nonalcoholic foster homes show very strong genetic factors linking severe alcoholism (that requiring hospitalization) to depression, but no such correlation existed between depression and milder alcoholism (that not requiring hospitalization) or problem drinking (Goodwin 1976). The implication is that severe alcoholism is essentially a genetically-transmitted disease with environmental factors exerting a minor influence, whereas so-called "milder" cases of alcoholism appear to be largely psychosocially generated. This complex and often confused issue is discussed in much greater depth in the fourth volume of this series. The important point here is that persons coming from families in which one or more close relatives (particularly female relatives) have a history of major depression are at risk for developing alcoholism and/or depression. The converse is also true: persons coming from families exhibiting depression and/or alcoholism are at risk for developing a major depressive disorder at some time in their lives.

Cross-cultural studies (Horton 1943) have suggested that high levels of cultural anxiety play an important role in the etiology of alcoholism, and that cultures with high stress loads tend to have high rates of alcoholism. However, this concept has been seriously challenged (Field 1962) and the evidence for such a view is not compelling.

The rest of this volume is devoted to the general chemistry and metabolism of alcohol and the effects of alcohol abuse upon the body, in particular the liver. Volume 2 of this series presents a detailed discussion of the human nervous system and the effects alcohol has upon discussion of the human nervous system and the effects alcohol has upon it. Volume 3 treats alcoholism in women, at least insofar as it is understood today, polydrug abuse, genetic factors, and human embryogenesis and fetal alcohol syndrome. And Volume 5 addresses codependency and its role in the addictive process, issues in recovery, and the role of professional caregivers in the recovery process. There the reader will find a complete description of the various biological and psychological systems possessed by human beings and the effects of alcohol abuse upon those systems. Treatment issues are dealt with in great depth, and the appropriateness of multiple treatment modalities and psychotropic medications are examined. I believe that this series discusses this disorder more holistically and in greater detail than any other eclectic work on this subject to date.

The reader is referred to those volumes to obtain as complete a picture of alcoholism as it is currently possible to present.

SUMMARY

Alcoholism is a complex medical disorder with a multifactorial etiology. It is characterized by a subtle and usually insidious onset and, like most chronic diseases, inevitably becomes progressively worse over time. Whenever an individual experiences significant impairment or deleterious consequences in any sphere of his or her life — marital, social, legal, financial, occupational, or medical — as a result of drinking alcohol, and that person continues to drink in the face of those consequences, then that person is considered to be an alcoholic. The overwhelming burden of the evidence indicates that alcoholism, when once present, cannot be "cured" in the sense that an alcoholic individual cannot safely return to social drinking once a remission has been established. The insistence in some professional quarters that alcoholics can and should be returned to social drinking is utterly without merit. On the basis of the medical consequences alone resulting from long-term alcohol abuse, any attempt to return an alcoholic to drinking is grossly irresponsible.

Alcoholic progression can usefully be divided into four main stages. The prealcoholic phase is characterized by subtle and inconspicuous, occasional relief drinking. This soon develops into constant relief drinking, accompanied very quickly by an increased tolerance to the effects of alcohol. This involves increased metabolic clearance of the drug from the body, adaptation of central nervous system membranes to the fluidizing effects of alcohol, and, to a lesser extent, learned adaptation. The prodromal phase of alcoholism is usually ushered in by the onset of alcoholic memory blackouts. There is now increasing reliance upon alcohol and preoccupation with drinking. Feelings of guilt about drinking appear, often associated with surreptitious drinking.

Crucial alcoholism is initiated by a sudden loss of control of drinking and the results of drinking. Once drinking is begun the alcoholic cannot predict the outcome: he may or may not become uncontrollably drunk, and there may or may not be serious consequences from the alcoholic episode. He simply has no control over things once he begins to drink. By now there are numerous consequences of his alcoholism, including marital discord, loss of jobs, arrests for drunk driving or other criminal behavior while drunk, and increasing social ostracism as he alienates friends and family. Denial is extreme and often flies in the face of obvious reality. The individual's alcholism is now obvious to everyone. Impotence and frigidity, if not previously present, now constitute a major source of anxiety, guilt, and self-loathing. Increasing paranoid jealousy may lead to overt violence. Pathological drunkenness is now common and characterized by grandiose and aggressive behavior. Family patterns are seriously disrupted and pathological, and the co-dependent significant others are completely caught up in the alcoholic's drinking and behavior. Family members may even be sicker psychologically than the alcoholic himself, and without knowing it they typically feed into the alcoholic conspiracy and further enable the alcoholic's drinking.

Chronic alcoholism is characterized by regular morning drinking and alcoholic binges lasting more than twenty-four hours. Physical addiction is now far advanced and tremors, hallucination, and delerium may develop when alcohol is completely or partially withdrawn. Intellectual and moral deterioration are often severe, and there may be irreversible brain or other medical damage. Unless recovery occurs, the end result of this level of physical and mental decompensation is usually death.

Primary alcoholism constitutes a major psychiatric and medical disorder in itself. It does not require the presence of another underlying or predisposing disorder, although they may also be present. It has now been compellingly demonstrated that primary alcoholism has a fundamentally genetic or hereditary basis. The biological offspring of alcoholic parents are much more likely to become themselves alcoholic in later life than are children of nonalcoholic biological parents, regardless of the environment in which they are raised. Biological siblings raised apart also show similar rates for alcoholism relative to normal controls.

Secondary alcoholism appears to arise in response to one or more other, previously existing, psychiatric disorders. It is frequently seen in schizophrenic patients, bipolar patients with strong manic features, and in many sociopaths. It is not by any means always clear whether one is confronting primary or secondary alcoholism in a given individual. Just because schizophrenia or sociopathy is present does not rule out the possibility that primary alcoholism may also coexist independently. Otherwise remitted sociopaths who continue to drink pathologically probably have primary alcoholism in addition to sociopathy. Those whose alcoholism also remits along with their sociopathy probably have secondary alcoholism as a function of their personality disorder.

Many authorities have commented that there is no such thing as an "addictive personality" and that alcoholics cannot be distinguished from nonalcoholics prior to the onset of their alcoholism. While this is essentially true, several distinctions about them can nevertheless be made. As a group they are more depressed, neurotic, hedonistic, both extraverted and shy and retiring, hedonistic and nonconforming, even as children, than their nonalcoholic counterparts. They were frequently sexually more explorative at an earlier age than other children. They usually have experienced a major narcissistic shock early in life such as the loss of a parent or parent-figure from death, abandonment, or divorce. Both as children and adults they tend to be orally fixated, dependent or counterdependent, passive-aggressive, narcissistic, grandiose, ambivalent about nearly everything (but especially about authority), and unable to appropriately express anger and aggression. Depression is always a major feature in all alcoholics, and while not all depressed patients are alcoholic by any means, *all alcoholics* are depressed. Depression is also now understood to be fundamentally a biologically inherited disorder involving specific neurotransmitter deficits in the brain. The earlier distinctions between endogenous or biological and reactive or "neurotic" depressions have been abandoned. Depressive spectrum disease is a diagnostic entity referring to any depression in an individual from a family in which alcoholism and/or sociopathy is also present in one or more members. Nearly all depression can be effectively treated with modern antidepressant medications. While these drugs have no effect upon active alcoholism (and are very dangerous if taken together with alcohol), they can and are being used very effectively in treating the severe depressions so common in abstinent, recovering alcoholics.

Alcoholism is also a spiritual disease and this dimension is critical to effective treatment. Alcoholism has much in common with Zen *koans*. Alcoholics cannot drink and they cannot not drink, and they are in a state of perpetual spiritual crisis. They have unusually deep spiritual needs and yet they are unable to even partially accommodate those needs. Instead of having faith and a sense of well-being and wholeness, they are bereft and overwhelmed with fear and foreboding. Because alcohol so completely erases all traces of this existential anxiety and global uneasiness (something it does not do for nonalcoholics) it is hardly surprising that they eventually become totally dependent upon it. At least early in the course of their illness it solves all their problems exceedingly well. As their deterioration progresses these unfortunate people cannot comprehend why their old friend alcohol, who has always seen them through life's many crises, has turned so viciously against them.

Section 2

PHARMACOLOGY AND METABOLISM OF ALCOHOL

ALCOHOL AND THE BODY: AN OVERVIEW

GENERAL CHEMISTRY

ALCOHOLS are those compounds in which an oxygen-hydrogen combination or *hydroxyl group* (—OH) is attached to an *aliphatic hydrocarbon* (an organic compound formed solely of hydrogen and carbon atoms). They are represented by the general formula, R—OH, in which the R stands for the aliphatic hydrocarbon attached to the hydroxyl group — it may represent a very short, simple side chain or denote a complicated organic structure with multiple aromatic rings and attached side chains (see for example Fig. 3). In one sense, alcohols are derived from water, H_2O, or more properly, HOH (hydrogen hydroxide). Water, however, is not an alcohol because the —OH group is attached to inorganic hydrogen instead of an organic (i.e., carbon-containing) group. In another sense alcohols are derived from the aliphatic hydrocarbons, and they have properties in common with both water and the hydrocarbons. Alcohols containing up to three carbon atoms are completely soluble in water, but that solubility decreases in proportion to any additional carbons above that number. As alcohols become less soluble in water, they become correspondingly more soluble in fatty substances.[15] There may be more than one —OH group in an alcohol. Ethyl alcohol or ethanol, CH_3CH_2OH, is the best known member of the general class of alcohols. It can be represented structurally as follows:

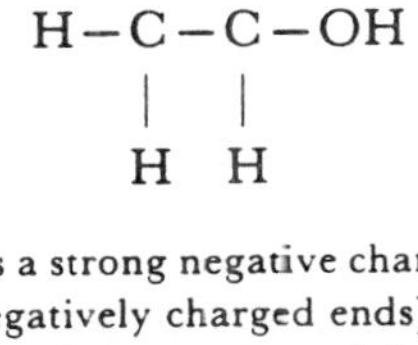

[15]The highly polar —OH group exhibits a strong negative charge and short-chain alcohols tend to have a strong *dipole-moment* (positively and negatively charged ends) due to the manner in which the shared electrons are distributed among the constituent atoms of the molecule. Polar molecules are usually highly soluble in similarly polar solvents (like water) because the forces holding the molecules of each compound together are readily replaced by the very similar forces of attraction between the *solute* (dissolved substance) and the *solvent* (medium in which it is dissolved). Nonpolar compounds are ordinarily soluble in similarly nonpolar substances (like organic liquids and fats), also because the forces holding each substance together are very similar to the forces of attraction between the two species. As the side-chains of alcohols become longer and more complex, the polar tendency of the —OH group is overridden by the stronger effect of the nonpolar, aliphatic end.

There are many more different kinds of alcohols than is generally realized, and many are constituents of compounds utilized by the body. *Glycerol,* for example, is a common constituent of *lipids,* or fats and fatlike substances. Glycerol has the structural formula:

$$\begin{array}{l} CH_2-OH \\ | \\ CH\ -OH \\ | \\ CH_2-OH \end{array}$$

Such an alcohol with more than one hydroxyl group is called a *polyhydric,* as contrasted with a *monohydric* alcohol. Fat molecules (triglycerides) are formed by joining three fatty acid molecules (complex hydrocarbon chains containing carboxyl groups ($-COOH$) formed from both a hydroxyl and a *carbonyl* [$C=O$; see Fig. 2] group) to one glycerol molecule. In this process (known as *esterification*), the $-OH$ groups of the glycerol molecule and the hydrogen atoms from the hydroxyl portion of the carboxyl groups on each of the three fatty acids are removed, forming three water molecules.

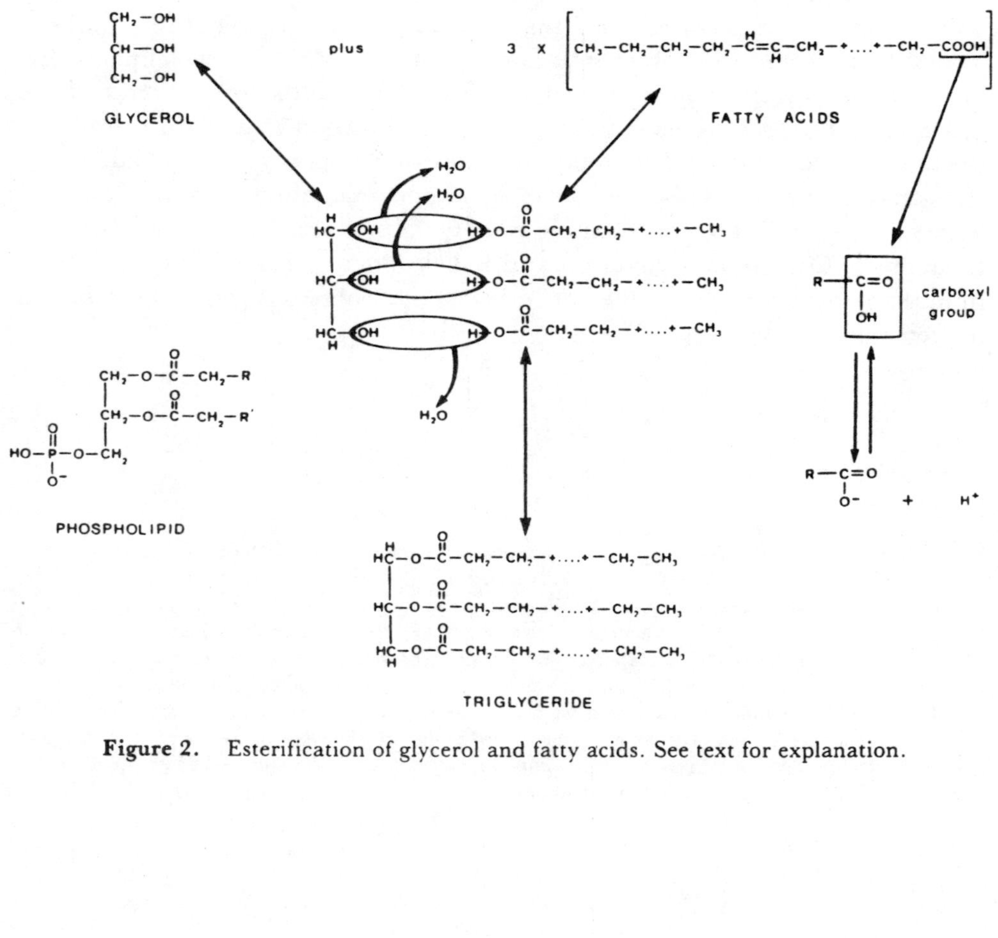

Figure 2. Esterification of glycerol and fatty acids. See text for explanation.

Sterols or steroid alcohols are very complex alcohols formed when an $-OH$ group is attached to a *steroid nucleus* or *hydrogenated cyclopentophenanthrene-ring* (see Fig. 3). Cholesterol is such a sterol which is found in cell membrane systems and which serves as a precursor molecule from which such biologically important steroids as cortisone and testosterone are synthesized. Cholesterol has the following structural formula, where each of the corners in the ring systems is occupied by a carbon atom (notice the $-OH$ group in the lower left-hand corner):

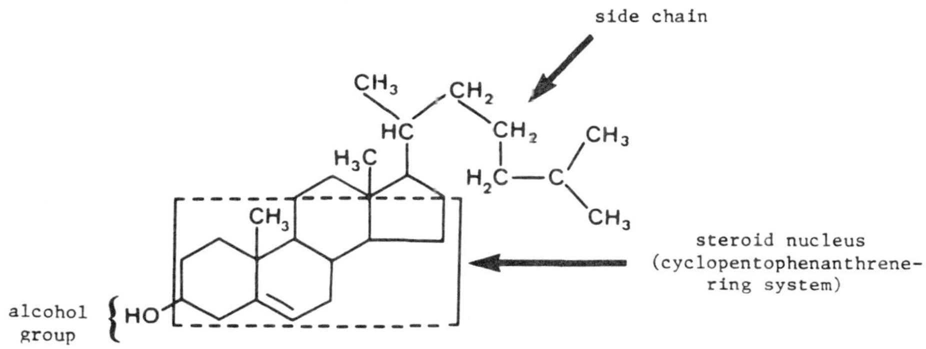

Figure 3. Structural formula of cholesterol, a complex alcohol.

Alcohols undergo two major types of chemical reactions: (1) those involving the breaking of the $O-H$ bond similar to the types of reactions found in water chemistry, and (2) those involving cleavage of the $C-O$ bond similar to typical hydrocarbon reactions. The latter reactions require an acid or a halogen[16] intermediate, and it is the former type of reaction that is of metabolic significance in human beings. For example, the first stage in the metabolism of ethanol is its oxidation to acetaldehyde, $CH_3HC=O$, by the removal of two hydrogens, one from the $-OH$ group and one from the attached carbon atom, resulting in the formation of a *carbonyl group* ($C=O$; see also Fig. 2). In this carbonyl group, the carbon and hydrogen are joined by two bonds instead of one, because of the extra *valence* or attachment site left on the carbon by the removal of one of its hydrogen atoms. Such reactions require the presence of special proteins called *enzymes,* which are catalysts allowing the process to occur in the very low temperatures (for many chemical reactions) of the human body. Enzymes and their analogous *coenzymes* or *cofactors* (catalysts which are not proteins) work by accelerating or retarding a reaction while remaining essentially unchanged them-

[16]An element of the seventh periodic group, including iodine, flourine, chlorine, and bromine, which normally exist in the free state as diatomic molecules and which combine with metals to form a *halide,* or salt-like compound (e.g., common table salt, NaCl).

selves. Thus, a more complete way of writing the oxidation of alcohol into acetaldehyde is:

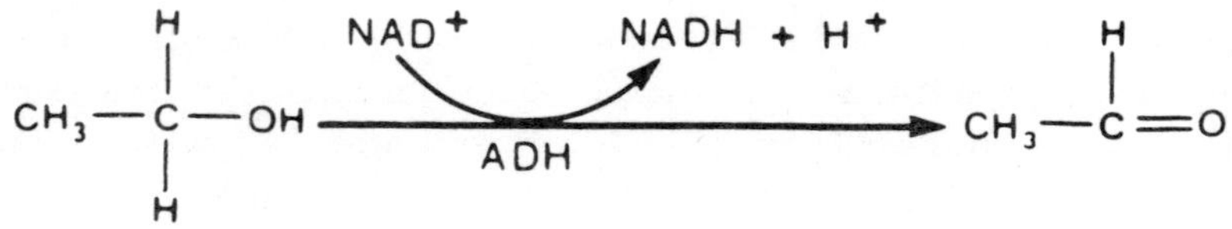

In this reaction, ADH stands for the enzyme *alcohol dehydrogenase,* so-called because it facilitates the dehydrogenation or removal of hydrogen atoms from the alcohol molecule. ADH is very common in living systems, and it is involved in a great many reactions other than the one just illustrated, as we shall see. NAD stands for the cofactor *nicotinamide adenine dinucleotide,* which takes up one of the two hydrogens removed from the ethanol, thus becoming reduced to NADH (or NAD with an attached hydrogen) plus a free hydrogen ion (H^+). Thus:

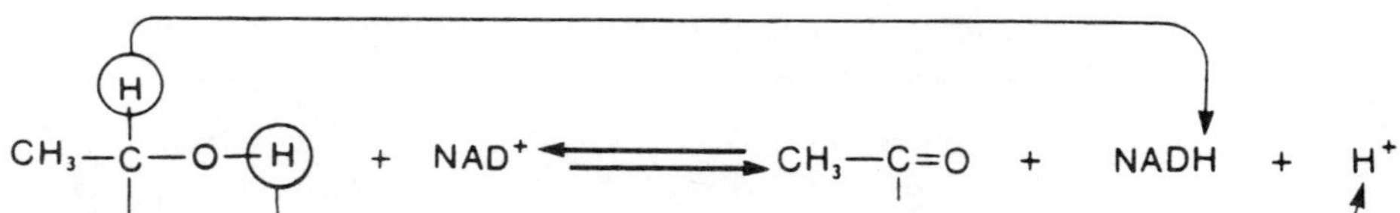

One of the methylene ($-CH_2$ group) hydrogens is transferred to NAD^+ in the form of a *hydride* ion ($:H^-$); the other hydrogen is removed from the $-OH$ group and given off into the medium as a hydrogen ion (H^+). The ADH remains completely unchanged in this reaction, and although the NAD^+ becomes converted into its reduced form, NADH, its essential nature remains the same and it is readily reoxidized back into NAD^+. Figure 4 illustrates how enzymes and their cofactors are thought to facilitate metabolic reactions by bringing the interacting substrate and cofactor(s) together onto a template. The close proximity of the susceptible bond of the substrate and the *active site* or recating group of the cofactor greatly enhances the likelihood and rate of the interaction. However, this stereochemical proximity is not in itself sufficient to account for the known increase of reactivity induced by enzymes, which must also play an active role in the reactive process itself in ways that are still poorly understood.

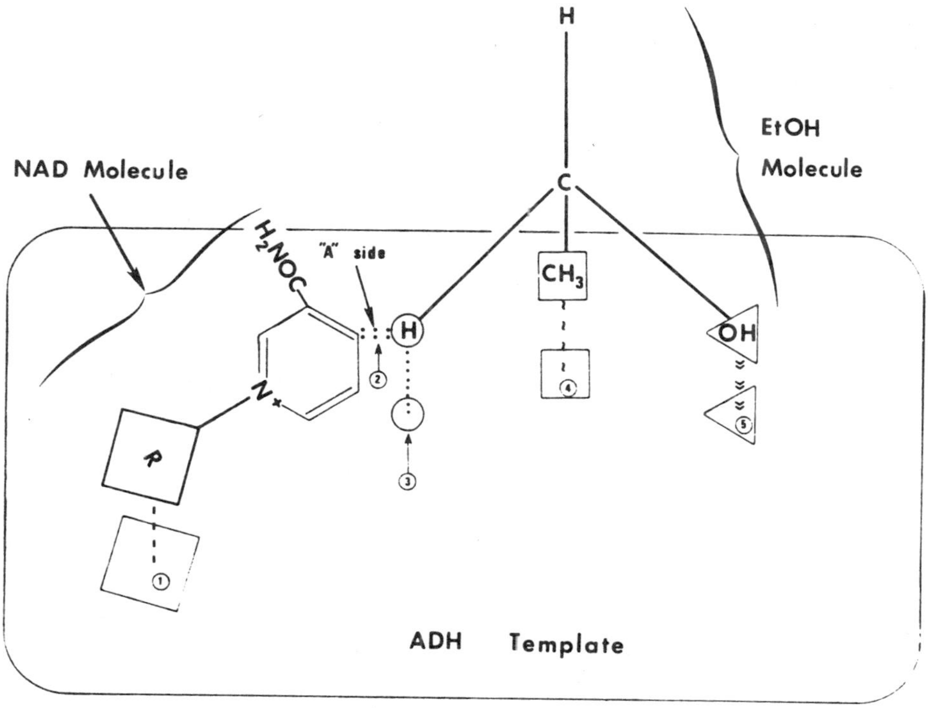

Figure 4. Stereochemical action of alcohol dehydrogenase.

The three-point attachment model of the substrate (ethanol) with the enzyme alcohol dehydrogenase (ADH) accounts for the stereospecific removal of hydrogen by the cofactor NAD^+. ADH always conveys the *same* reducing equivalent upon oxidation of the alcohol; similarly, when the substrate is reduced, a hydrogen is transferred back to the same site on the alcohol molecule. When this hydrogen atom is removed from the ethanol molecule, the methylene carbon is left with an unattached valence bond and the bonding configuration of the ethanol molecule becomes unstable. The disengaged carbon bond immediately connects to the oxygen atom, forming a strong $-C=O$ bond. This breaks the much weaker $-O-H$ bond, causing the hydroxyl hydrogen to be ejected. This oxidizes ethanol into acetaldehyde and reduced NAD^+ into NADH and H^+.

Ethanol is bound to the enzyme very precisely in a lock-and-key fashion at three attachment sites at the methyl ($-CH_3$), hydroxyl ($-OH$), and a specific hydrogen of the methylene groups. When the ethanol is thus bound to ADH, only *one specific* methylene hydrogen is appropriately positioned to be captured by the NAD^+molecule (which is also stereochemically bound to the ADH by its R-group). In reality, only the methyl and hydroxyl groups need be so bound to explain this stereospecificity.

1 = attachment site on the ADH template for the R-group of NAD^+; 2 = binding site on NAD^+ for the methylene hydrogen; 3 = ADH attachment site for the methylene hydrogen; 4 = ADH attachment site for the methyl group; 5 = ADH attachment site for the hydroxyl group. Modified from Segel 1975, Figures 1-4, page 11.

In any chemical reaction, a certain minimal amount of energy known as the *activation energy* must be introduced to initiate the reaction at any specified

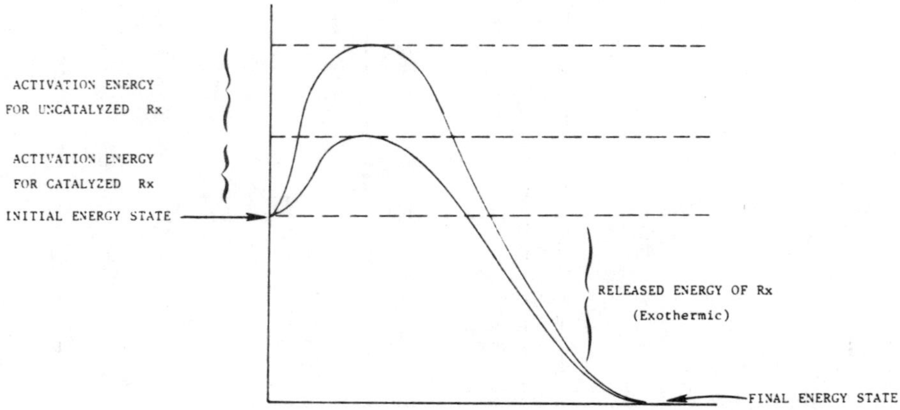

Figure 5. Enzyme reaction energies.

temperature. Enzymes, being catalysts, lower the required activation energy for a given reaction at that specified temperature. As previously mentioned, this allows many biochemical processes to occur at the relatively low body temperatures of living cells which would otherwise be energetically prohibited. This is illustrated in Figure 5.

The oxidation of ethanol to acetaldehyde represents a typical *oxidation-reduction* or *redox* reaction. *Oxidation* is the process of either adding an oxygen or taking away a hydrogen, both of which result in the same chemical effort: the molecule loses an electron or so-called *hydrogen-* or *reducing equivalent. Reduction* is the opposite process of gaining an electron or hydrogen equivalent (or of losing an oxygen or gaining a hydrogen). Because redox reactions really represent transfers of electrons, they can occur without the participation of oxygen or hydrogen. Oxidation and reduction always occur together in a redox reaction, since the hydrogen given up by one molecule is accepted by another. In the particular example given above, the generation of excessive reducing or hydrogen equivalents by both the oxidation of ethanol to acetaldehyde and the subsequent oxidation of acetaldehyde into its breakdown products is responsible for many of the serious medical complications of chronic alcohol abuse. This will become very apparent as we proceed.

In order to understand the role ethyl alcohol plays in nature, it is necessary first to discuss briefly the basic energy requirements underlying all living systems (see Fig. 6). By the process of *photosynthesis,* chlorophyll-containing green plants convert radiant energy from the sun into energy-rich carbon compounds, which when metabolically broken down again by living cells release their stored energy to drive the machinery of life. Discrete packages of light energy called *photons* are captured by photosynthesizing plants and the energy thus obtained is used to split water molecules into their constituent hydrogen and oxygen atoms. Electrons are then stripped away from the hydrogen atoms and boosted by special, highly reactive chlorophyll molecules into very high energy states. These boosted electrons are then allowed to "flow downhill," releasing their accumulated energy to a special energy-accepting molecule, *adenosine diphosphate* (ADP). ADP absorbs this energy by attaching to a high-energy phosphate group and becoming converted into *adenosine triphosphate* (ATP). ATP is found in abundance in all living cells and when it is converted back into ADP by giving up one of its energy-rich phosphate units, an enormous amount of energy is released to do all sorts of work. Among many other things, the ATP formed by the first stage of photosynthesis is used in the second stage to convert carbon dioxide in a series of complicated steps into a more complex organic precursor molecule with the general formula CH_2O. From this precursor molecule, sugars, cellulose, amino acids (the building blocks of all proteins), and other compounds needed by the cell can be formed. In summary, plants convert CO_2 and H_2O into free oxygen (O_2) and energy-rich carbon compounds:

$$CO_2 + H_2O + \text{sunlight} \longrightarrow O_2 + H_2O + CH_2O.$$

Some bacteria split hydrogen sulfide (H_2S) instead of water in their photosynthetic reaction, but the end result is much the same. With the exception of a recently discovered energy source in deep-sea rift areas (such as occur in regions of sea-floor spreading, for example, off the Galápagos Islands) dependent upon nonphotosynthesizing, lithophagic ("rock-eating"), sulfide-reducing bacteria, all life on earth depends upon photosynthesis. Animals ultimately must derive their energy from eating green plants or from eating other animals which eat green plants.

However, in order for the sugars and other energy-rich carbon compounds to be utilized by the living cell, they must be further broken down by a process called *glycolysis* (Greek: glyco = sugar; lysis = to split apart or dissolve). In glycolysis, glucose, a sugar composed of 6 carbon atoms plus hydrogen and oxygen, is oxidized anaerobically (i.e., in the absence of free, molecular oxygen) into a 3-carbon compound, *pyruvic acid* or *pyruvate,* in a series of complex steps here much simplified (see also Figs. 6 and 25):

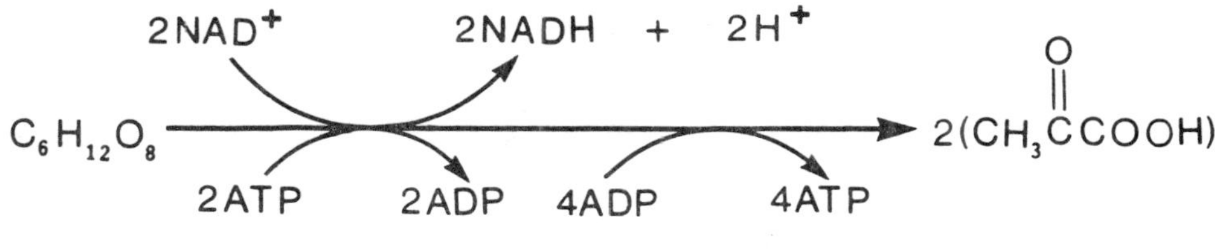

In this process, a 6-carbon ring is broken down into two 3-carbon pyruvate molecules. This is an oxidation process even though it occurs in the complete absence of free oxygen, because some hydrogen equivalents have been given off with the corresponding reduction of NAD^+ to NADH. Notice that although energy has been used up in this process (2 ATPs converted into 2 ADPs), even more energy has been generated (4 ADPs converted into 4 ATPs). There is thus a net gain of energy.

In all higher organisms, this pyruvate is further oxidized into *acetyl coenzyme A* (or more simply, *acetyl co-A*),[17] a molecule with which we shall become very familiar when we examine how ethanol is metabolized in the liver. Thus:

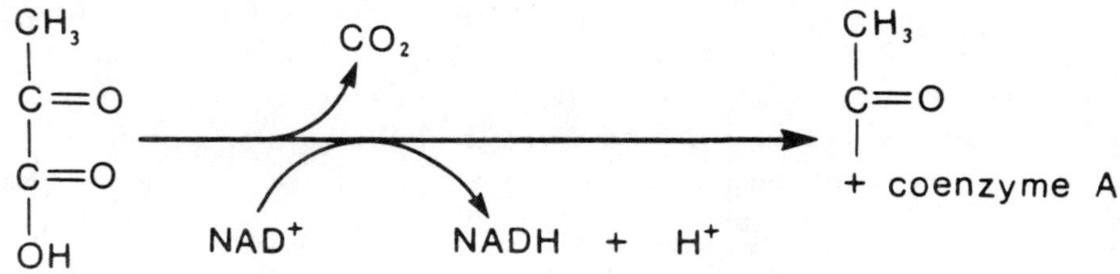

pyruvate acetyl co-A

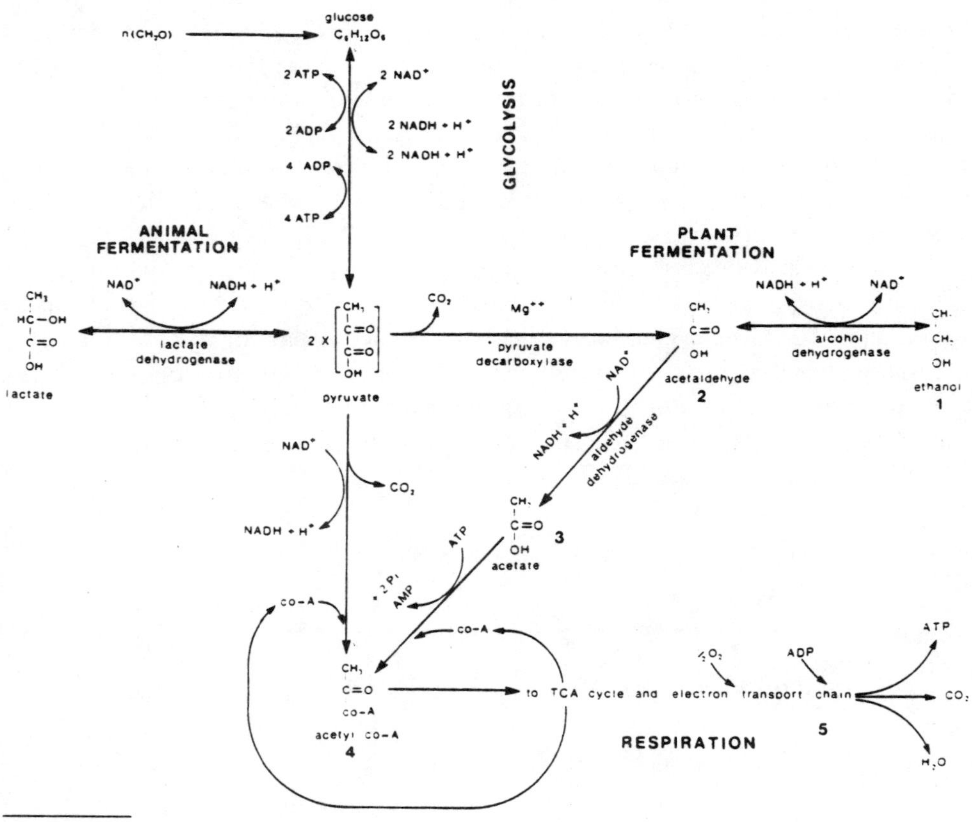

[17]See Figures 6 and 23.

This is the final step in glycolysis.

The next step is *respiration*. Biologically speaking, respiration has two meanings: (1) the usually understood process whereby oxygen is taken into the organism and exchanged for carbon dioxide, and (2) cellular respiration, the free-oxygen-requiring stage in the processing of carbon-containing fuel molecules and the corresponding release of energy to do the vital work of the cells (this process occurs in all higher plants and animals). In cellular respiration, the 2-carbon acetyl group and its attached co-A molecule enter an extremely complicated sequence of reactions known variously as the *Krebs cycle, tricarboxylic acid* (TCA) *cycle,* or *citric acid cycle*. In the Krebs cycle, the acetyl group and attached co-A combine with a 4-carbon compound, *oxaloacetic acid,* to yield a 6-carbon compound, *citric acid* (Fig. 7). In the process the co-A group is given up and leaves the Krebs cycle and is again available to combine with a new acetyl group and re-enter the cycle. The citric acid is oxidized into the 5-carbon-containing *ketoglutaric acid,* which then undergoes several more steps to be converted back into oxaloacetic acid, and the whole cycle begins anew. Throughout this cycle, carbon dioxide is given off, ADP is converted into ATP, and NAD^+ is reduced to NADH. There are also eight electrons in a very high

---

Figure 6. Glycolysis, fermentation and respiration. By the process of photosynthesis, green plants convert sunlight and CO_2 into organic molecules containing energy-rich carbon bonds with the general formula $n(CH_2O)$, such as glucose ($C_6H_{12}O_6$). Glucose is then broken down into pyruvate by a process known as glycolysis (also referred to as the Embden-Meyerhof pathway; see Figure 26). The energy contained in the carbon bonds is extracted and stored as ATP molecules which are thus available to drive the various energy-requiring biochemical processes of the body. The earliest organisms that evolved on this planet extracted this energy via two consecutive anaerobic processes: (1) glycolysis, in which one 6-carbon glucose molecule is broken down into two 3-carbon pyruvate molecules; and (2) plant fermentation, in which pyruvate is first converted into acetaldehyde by giving off a CO_2 molecule, and the acetaldehyde is then reduced into ethyl alcohol by the enzyme alcohol dehydrogenase. Fermentation is the reverse of the process by which consumed ethanol is oxidized by human beings and other animals. In fact, the reason why we possess the necessary enzymes at all is because glycolysis and fermentation were among the very first biochemical pathways to evolve. By the combined processes of glycolysis and fermentation, the earliest and most primitive organisms were able to convert one molecule of glucose into six or eight (depending upon the particulars of the specific reactions involved) molecules of ATP.

As free, molecular oxygen resulting from photosynthesis accumulated in Earth's primitive atmosphere, another, much more efficient system of extracting energy from glucose evolved. In this process, known as respiration, pyruvate resulting from glycolysis is routed through the tricarboxylic acid (Krebs) cycle acid and the electron transport chain (see Fig. 7). Oxidative respiration is much more efficient than fermentation and it results in a net production of 38 ATP molecules from one glucose molecule. As the original, oxygen-producing photosynthesizers poisoned themselves out of existence (see footnote 20), the way was opened for the more advanced and efficient aerobic organisms that followed.

Animals are unable to ferment acetaldehyde into ethanol and can only run this pathway towards acetyl co-A. Animal fermentation involves the conversion of pyruvate into lactate to provide energy to the muscles under anaerobic conditions.

←

energy state produced by this process. These electrons are allowed to flow downhill (energetically speaking) via the *cytochromes*[18] of the *electron transport chain*, yielding a final combustion product of water. Figure 7 illustrates the major stages of the Krebs cycle and electron transport mechanism.

The electrons flow from higher to lower energy levels, that is from NADH and reduced flavoprotein[19] to a series of cytochromes (see footnote 18) which use the released energy to convert ADP to ATP. As we have noted several times

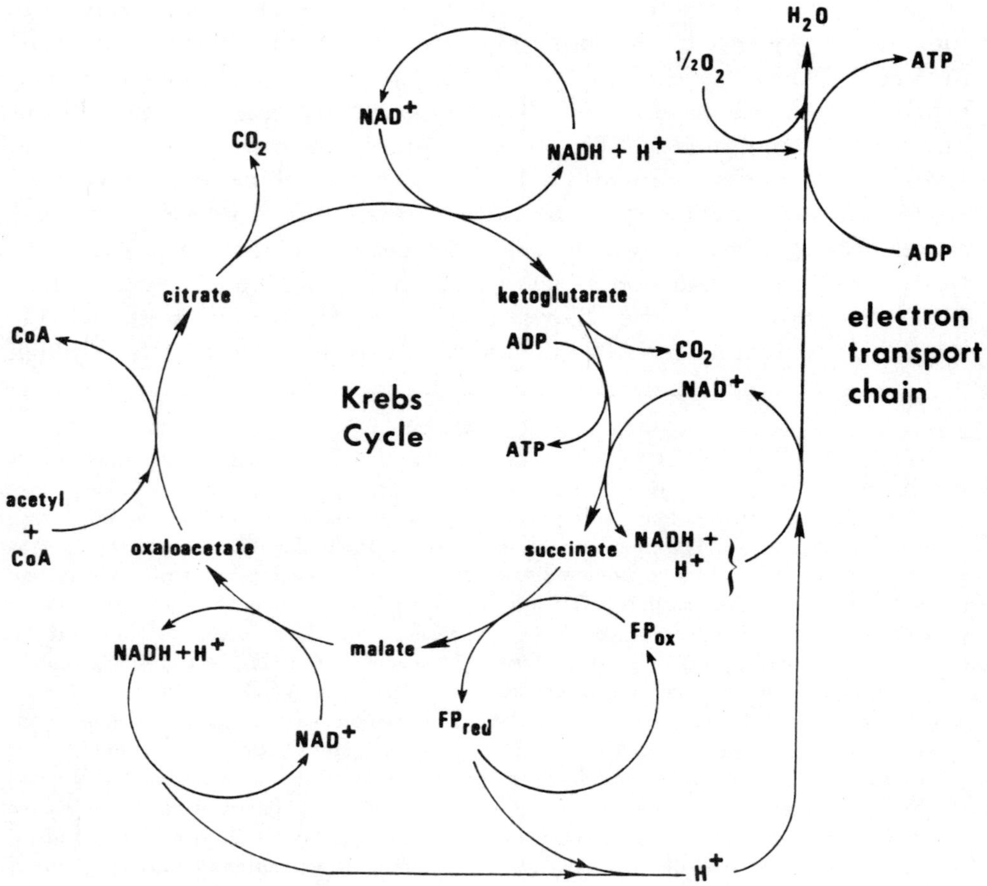

Figure 7. Krebs cycle and electron transport chain.

---

[18]Cytochromes are *heme-* (or *haeme*) containing enzymes important in all electron transfer processes which function through a reversible valency change of the heme group. A heme is an iron-containing *porphyrin-ring* — a compound ring system of four nitrogen-bearing subrings and their attached carbon atoms with the nitrogens all attached to a reactive metal (usually iron or magnesium).

[19]FPox and FPred in Figure 7 stand for a *flavoprotein* in an oxidized and a reduced state respectively. Flavoproteins are proteins with an attached pigment, *flavin*, which is readily oxidized and reduced; they are thus important in electron transport chains. These proteins are yellow when oxidized (thus their name) and colorless when reduced.

previously, the energy stored in ATP is used to drive the cellular machinery. The complete combustion of one glucose molecule, from its initial glycolysis through the respiratory cycle (the Krebs cycle and the electron transport chain), yields 38 ATP molecules. The respiratory cycle thus produces an enormous amount of energy in the form of ATP, and the final breakdown products are carbon dioxide (given off via the lungs) and water. This cycle can only occur in the presence of free, molecular oxygen (O_2), which presently makes up about 20 percent of our atmosphere. It was not always thus, however, and when life first originated on Earth some 3½ billion years ago, the atmosphere was completely devoid of free oxygen, containing instead mostly nitrogen (N_2), carbon dioxide (CO_2), hydrogen sulfide (H_2S), methane (CH_4), free hydrogen (H_2), and ammonia (NH_3). The earliest forms of life were one-celled plant-like creatures known as blue-green algae, whose metabolism was entirely anaerobic. In fact, free atmospheric oxygen would have poisoned them![20] Remember that glycolysis is an anaerobic process and it undoubtedly evolved very early under the reducing conditions of the primitive atmosphere. Even today, many organisms are able to obtain their energy entirely from glycolysis if oxygen is not available. For example, yeast cells convert the pyruvic acid formed by the first part of glycolysis into ethyl alcohol in the absence of oxygen by anaerobic *fermentation*. In this process, which includes the initial glycolysis, pyruvate is first converted into acetaldehyde along with a release of carbon dioxide and the acetaldehyde is then reduced to ethanol (see also Fig. 6).

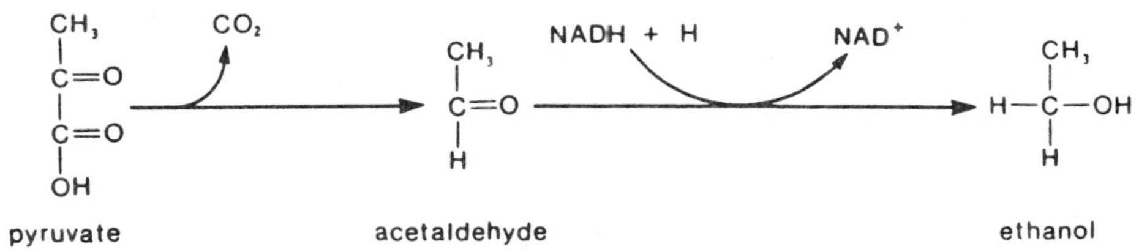

Notice that the acetaldehyde is reduced to ethanol,[21] so that cofactor NADH must be oxidized to NAD^+. The total number of ATP generated by glycolysis and fermentation from one glucose molecule is 6 or 8, depending upon circum-

[20] The source of all the oxygen in our present atmosphere comes from photosynthesis, which first occurred about 2½ to 2 billion years ago. The organisms that produced this oxygen as a metabolic by-product poisoned themselves out of existence (the original environmental polluters!), but they paved the way for more advanced, aerobic life forms.

[21] Pyruvic acid can also be reduced anaerobically in some animal tissues such as muscles during strenuous exercise (see Fig. 6); however, the product is not ethanol, but lactic acid ($CH_3CHOHCO_2H$). This allows the muscles to work even when all oxygen immediately available to them has been depleted by the exercise. Stored animal starch (glycogen) in the muscles is converted to glucose, then to pyruvate, and finally to lactic acid, resulting in an *oxygen debt* which is gradually paid off by hard breathing whereupon the lactic acid is then oxidized. This process is also sometimes referred to as fermentation.

stances. Respiration is thus far more efficient. In making wine, the yeast cells are unable to tolerate an alcohol content in excess of about 12 or 13 percent, at which point they are poisoned and die. Thirteen percent is therefore the maximum strength that can be produced in an unfortified wine. Stronger alcoholic beverages must be distilled off and concentrated or the fermented wines must be fortified by adding extra alcohol.

Strong alcoholic spirits appear to have been distilled at least 3,000 years ago in Asia and appeared in medieval Persia near the beginning of the ninth century, A. D., arriving in Italy about a century later (Bowman & Rand 1980). However, fermented ethanol probably has been used by most human cultures as an intoxicating and ritual beverage for as long as mankind has existed as such. Fermentation is common enough in Nature, and African elephants and a variety of birds are known to become grossly intoxicated at certain times of the year from ingesting fermented fruits and berries. At such times the elephants can become exceedingly dangerous — they have completely demolished native villages and occasionally trampled one or more of the inhabitants to death during drunken rampages. Ethanol is also produced in the human gut, mostly by bacterial fermentation, but the amounts generated are very small and pose no problem for the abstinent, recovering alcoholic. Such metabolically-produced alcohol is oxidized as it is produced and it never builds up into significant amounts in the bloodstream (about 0.3 milligram-percent).

Those water soluble alcohols with short (less than three carbons) hydrocarbon side chains, for example, methyl or wood alcohol (CH_3OH) and ethylene glycol (automobile antifreeze) also can cause intoxication when consumed. However, they produce very highly toxic by-products (formaldehyde, in the case of methanol or methyl alcohol) and they can cause permanent injury and death in even moderate doses.[22] Methanol is oxidized via the same metabolic pathway as is ethanol, that is, involving the enzyme alcohol dehydrogenase and the reduction of the cofactor NAD^+ to NADH. However, since the substrate (methanol) is slightly different chemically, the oxidation product is formaldehyde (HCHO) instead of acetaldehyde, and the formaldehyde is subsequently oxidized to formic acid, instead of acetic acid as in the case of acetaldehyde. Both formaldehyde and formic acid are extremely poisonous and it is these two by-products that produce the severe effects of methanol poisoning. Because ethanol is metabolized about nine times more rapidly than methanol (Cornish 1980), the former is preferentially oxidized via the ADH pathway when both alcohols are present. Therefore, the treatment for methanol poisoning consists of administering large doses of intravenous ethyl alcohol for several days. This ethanol is metabolized in preference to the methanol, and the latter is slowly

[22] Methanol poisonings show an increased incidence whenever access to ethanol is curtailed, such as occurred during the Prohibition Era in the United States (Casarette & Doull 1980). About one-third of these cases recover completely, one-third suffer permanent, partial or total blindness, and one-third die.

excreted from the body via the breath and urine without being oxidized into its dangerous metabolites. Once blood methanol levels are negligible, the ethanol can be safely withdrawn, although the ensuing hangover is not likely to be soon forgotten. This treatment is also effective against antifreeze poisoning for the same reason.

EFFECTS OF ETHANOL ON THE BODY

Ethanol belongs to that class of drugs known as *sedative-hypnotics,* and thus shares with Librium® and Valium® the characteristic features of alleviating anxiety and inducing sleep. In strong enough doses, all of these drugs cause the typical manifestations of "drunkenness," including blurred vision, slurred speech, and loss of inhibition and coordination. In spite of their similar effects in human beings, alcohol and the other sedative-hypnotics are not related pharmacologically and their chemical structures are quite different. Alcohol and the barbiturates exert their effects on the central nervous system (CNS) by altering the configuration of the membranes surrounding the nerve cells and thereby affecting the transmission of nervous impulses. They also enhance the inhibitory effects of GABA.[23] Benzodiazepines act primarily on benzodiazephine-GABA receptor complexes.

All of the drugs in this class are potentially addictive when abused for any substantial period, and they can all induce increased tolerance to the effects not only of the drug being used (or abused), but also to all similar acting drugs, a phenomenon known as *cross-tolerance* or, less commonly, *pan-tolerance.* Tolerance, in which increasing doses of a drug are required to obtain a given effect, occurs in two ways: (1) *metabolic tolerance* involves more rapid clearance of the drug from the body due to physical changes in the liver cells resulting in faster metabolism of the drug (see the discussion below on the mixed-function oxidase system); (2) *pharmacodynamic tolerance* results from changes in the target tissues upon which the drug acts, usually in the CNS. Heavy drinkers (not necessarily only alcoholics) show an increased tolerance to alcohol and also to many so-called *minor tranquilizers,* (including Chlordiazepoxide or Librium, Diazepam or Valium, and Meprobamate or Miltown®, and Equanil®) and the *hyponotics,* including the barbiturates (e.g., Pentobarbital or Nembutal®, Secobarbital or Seconal®, and Phenobarbitol), and the barbiturate-like drugs (e.g., Methaqualone or Quaalude®).

Ethanol is rapidly absorbed from the entire gastrointestinal tract (stomach, small and large intestines) directly into the bloodstream, although the rate at

[23] Many authorities object to the term "sedative", and refer to this class of drugs simply as "hypnotics." Benzodiazepines, such as Valium, also appear to act upon specific postsynaptic receptors in the CNS, and both the benzodiazepines and the barbiturates enhance the CNS-inhibiting effect of the neurotransmitter gamma-aminobutyric acid (GABA).

which this happens can be altered by a number of factors. Absorption from the stomach is very rapid at first, but subsequently allows to a very slow rate even in the continued presence of high-alcohol concentrations. High concentrations of alcohol may cause a spasmodic contraction of the *pyloric sphincter* so that the stomach contents cannot be emptied into the small intestine (Goodman & Gilman 1975). This results in a decrease in absorption of ingested alcohol after an initial rapid rate because of the astringent properties of the alcohol which causes a shut-down of blood supply to the stomach. The presence of food in the stomach also inhibits absorption as do certain *congeners* (fusel oils and other flavoring substances) found in many alcoholic beverages, especially those in beer. Once alcohol reaches the small intestine aborption is extremely rapid, and this is unaffected by the presence of food or the continued presence of alcohol.

Ethyl alcohol is 30 times more soluble in water than in lipids (Madden 1979) and it accumulates in those tissues with the highest water content (Erickson 1979). It is thus rapidly transported to all parts of the body via the bloodstream where it is fairly evenly distributed in the body fluids. Alcohol is also highly volatile and it is readily absorbed through the lungs — in fact, fatal intoxications have occurred via this route (Goodman & Gilman 1975). The *volume of distribution* of a drug is the volume of fluid a drug would occupy if the total amount present in the body were at the same concentration as it is in the plasma. This volume is given by the formula: $V_d = M/C$, where M = the total amount of drug in the body and C = the plasma concentration of the drug in mg/liter (Bowman & Rand 1980). Values of V_d in the range of 0.06 liters/kg of plasma indicate a drug which is tightly bound to circulating plasma proteins; V_d values in the range of 0.2 liters/kg are typical of a drug which passes readily through capillary walls but which cannot pass through the lipid layer of cell membranes — such a drug is found throughout the extracellular fluid volume. Drugs exhibiting V_d values around 0.6 liter/kg (for example ethanol) readily pass through cell membranes and are lipid soluble as well as water soluble. Such a drug is found throughout the body water, both the intracellular and extracellular fractions, and is not selectively bound to any body tissue. The volume of distribution of ethanol is 0.68 liter/kg for males and 0.60 liter/kg for females. This slight discrepancy results from the fact that women have more body fat as a secondary sexual characteristic than do men, the total body water being 50 percent in women and 60 percent in men.

The distribution of drugs is also a function of the relative degrees of perfusion of blood to the various tissues. Perfusion to various tissues is as follows (data from Bowman & Rand 1980).:

Tissue	*Blood Flow (l/kg tissue per min)*
abdominal viscera & liver	0.75 (portal venous flow)
kidneys	4.5

Tissue	*Blood Flow (l/kg tissue per min)*
heart	0.70
brain	0.55
liver	0.20
resting muscle	0.03
connective tissue	0.01
adipose tissue	0.01

Blood perfusion rates are highest for the brain, kidneys, liver and other abdominal viscera and the lungs, and drug equilibrium between those tissues and blood concentrations occurs rapidly. Muscle and adipose tissue are much more slowly perfused and equilibrium distributions are built up only slowly. Final drug distributions are also dependent upon the water content of the various tissues within the body. Typical tissue water content values are (data from Bowman & Rand 1980):

Tissue	*Water in Tissue (l/kg)*
blood	0.830
brain	0.748
liver	0.683
other abdominal viscera & the lungs	0.745-0.795
muscle	0.756
adipose tissue	0.1

The equilibration of ethanol in the brain, kidneys, liver and other well-perfused tissues with plasma concentrations is essentially complete in one passage of the blood. Slowly perfused tissues like the adipose reserves (comprising 20% or more of the total body weight), muscle tissue (normally about 40% of total body weight), and connective tissue will only attain saturation values of water soluble drugs after a number of passages of the blood through the body. Because of its enormous total mass, muscle tissue can sequester large amounts of ethanol if sufficient time is allowed for its relatively low perfusion rates. Although the water content of fat is low (0.1 l/kg), ethanol is also very lipid soluble and the adiopose reserves can pack away large amounts of this drug in the lipid fraction. Depending upon the proportion of total body weight represented by the fat tissues in a given individual, the amount of ethanol that can be thus sequestered is very considerable. As a consequence of the foregoing dynamics, a blood alcohol level *overshoot* is typically seen on the rising part of the BAL curve as drinking progresses. This overshoot later falls off because of the delayed sequestering of ethanol in muscle and fat tissues, thus lowering the blood alcoholic concentration below that accounted for by metabolic clearance alone. The phenomenon of BAL overshoot and subsequent sequestration of ethanol and the ensuing drop in blood ethanol concentration is partly responsible for the fact that intoxication and its manifestations are most pronounced on the rising part of the BAL curve.

Because of the vast blood supply to the brain and central nervous system, alcohol levels in those sites rapidly attain values similar to those of the bloodstream, a fact of major importance in view of the profound effects of this drug on the CNS. Many drugs (for example, antibiotics) and other substances, especially those that are not soluble in lipids, are excluded from the brain by a mechanism called the *blood-brain barrier* which either prevents or significantly retards the rate at which they are absorbed from the blood into the tissues of the brain and spinal cord. Water, CO_2, and oxygen traverse this barrier readily. Glucose is taken up more slowly, and many important *ions* (electrically charged atoms) can cross only from 3 to 30 times more slowly than they enter other cells and intercellular fluids (Ganong 1973). Many substances are almost completely excluded, except for minute traces, and the blood-brain barrier provides a vital stabilizing mechanism for maintaining a constant cellular environment within the CNS.

On the other hand, any CNS-depressant or other mind-altering drug must cross this barrier to be effective, and all such agents must be lipid soluble at least to some degree in order to penetrate the membranes of the CNS. Most researchers believe that the blood-brain barrier poses no obstacle whatever to ethanol (Erickson 1979), and this molecule is taken up by the CNS essentially without resistance. The primary site of action by alcohol and many other sedative-hypnotic agents on the CNS is on the membranes surrounding the *neurons* or nerve cells. All animal cells are surrounded by such a cell or plasma membrane.[24] Such membranes are composed of a double layer of *phospholipids* (molecules in which two fatty acids are linked to a glycerol frame, with the third methylene group of the glycerol being occupied by a highly polar phosphate group (see also Fig. 2). The polar phosphate heads of the phospholipids are readily attracted to the equally polar water molecules in the cellular and intercellular media, whereas the nonpolar fatty-acid tails are repelled by the water. This results in their spontaneous arrangement into two layers with the polar heads directed outwards towards the watery environment and the nonpolar, hydrophobic tails pointing inward. Scattered within this double-layered matrix are various globular proteins which function as enzymes, structural units, or which serve as carrier molecules in the *active transport* of other molecules across the membrane (transport against a concentration gradient requiring energy). This is illustrated in Figure 8.

Active transport across the cell membrane of a molecule against its own concentration gradient is accomplished by *carrier proteins* which engage the molecule to be transported in a lock-and-key manner much like that described for

[24] Plant cells are surrounded by *cell walls* constructed of elongated cellulose fibers embedded in a polysaccharide matrix.

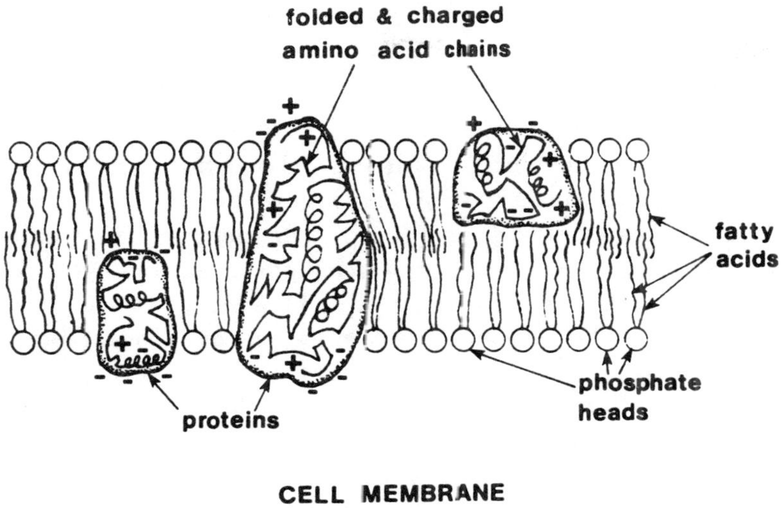

Figure 8. Structure of the cell membrane. The proteins consist of the folded amino acid chains; the sac-like envelopes are for graphic clarity only.

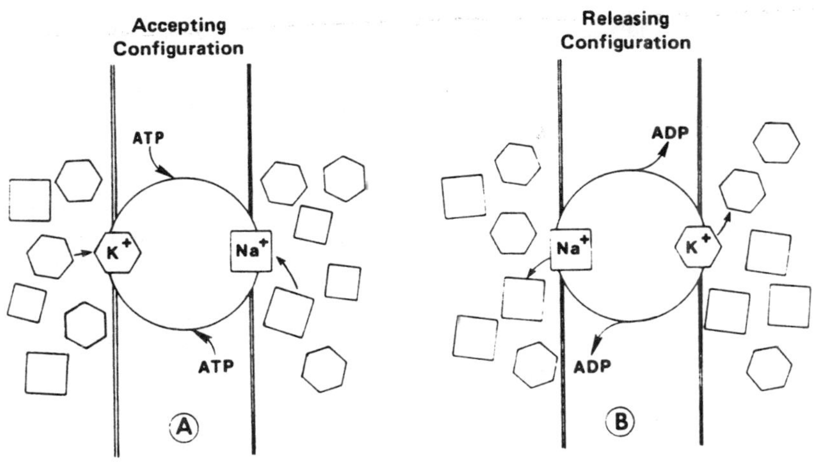

Figure 9. Active transport mechanism.

enzymes and their substrates (Fig. 9). When the molecule to be transported is combined with the carrier protein, a change in charge or configuration of the carrier activates ATP which gives up its energy to the system by being converted into ADP. This energy causes the carrier and attached molecule to be transported to rotate 180°, transporting the substrate across the membrane system whereupon it is released. In contrast to active transport whereby substances are concentrated as much as 1,000 times that of the surrounding medium, many substances such as water, oxygen and CO_2 tend to move in and out of cells along a gradient by *osmosis* or diffusion — a process termed appropriately enough, *passive transport.*

The neural membrane in the normal or resting state is polarized, that is, there is a net positive charge on the outside of the membrane relative to the inside. This results from sodium ions (Na^+) being concentrated in the extracellular medium outside the membrane, which is only slightly permeable to those ions. There is a similar concentration of potassium ions (K^+) inside the neural membrane within the cytoplasm or cell sap of the neuron. The membrane is very highly permeable to K^+, however, which tends to leak out of the cell down the concentration gradient. However, an ATP-dependent active transport mechanism known as the *sodium-potassium pump* returns the escaping K^+ back inside almost as fast as it leaks out. But because more K^+ is constantly escaping, a small (about -70 millivolts) but constant K^+ deficiency exists within the neuron relative to the Na^+ in the exterior. The resulting net polarity is called the *resting potential.* A nervous impulse is generated when an appropriate stimulus causes the neural membrane suddenly to become completely permeable to Na^+, which immediately rushes in through the now open "gates" in the membrane. These mechanisms and the details of nervous transmission are discussed fully in the second volume dealing with the nervous system.

Ethanol causes changes in the structural integrity of the neural membranes by packing into the phospholipid bilayer and distorting the membrane architecture. As these membranes swell and become more "fluid," the component phospholipids and embedded proteins become more disordered, the ionic gates through which Na^+ and K^+ pass during the transmission of a nervous impulse are similarly distorted and no longer function to permit such ionic passage. This directly results in suppression of nervous function and is the primary mechanism by which ethanol depresses the central nervous system. As neural transmission is progressively inhibited by increasing concentrations of alcohol, consciousness becomes increasingly clouded, and stupor and coma eventually ensue as alcohol intake continues. The other general anaesthetics and sedative-hypnotic agents likewise cause the central neural membranes to swell and become more fluid, due to the general solubility of such substances in the lipid fraction of the membranes. Pharmacodynamic tolerance to alcohol occurs as neural membranes become hyperrigid in response to the drug's fluidizing effects. It then takes more alcohol to achieve the same state of intoxication. As alcohol abuse progresses, the membranes become so rigid that it now requires the *presence* of alcohol in order to function at all. Physical tolerance has become physical dependence.

The higher portions of the brain are the first to be affected by alcohol and other hypnotic agents. This includes the cerebral cortex which exerts an inhibitory control on the lower, more primitive portions of the brain involved in emotional response, fear and aggression. The ensuing release of inhibition upon the lower brain centers causes a so-called *paradoxical excitement* in which the drinker subjectively feels and appears more stimulated, voluble, and clever. In fact, this response is actually due to the depressant effect of alcohol (or other sedating drug), which allows the normally suppressed responses of the lower brain regions to bubble over into conscious awareness and overt behavior. Sexual feelings may similarly appear to be aroused, but they are also manifested for the most part because of the loss of normal inhibition and control over one's behavior and emotional responses. There is some evidence, however, that alcohol in small amounts can have a direct excitatory on neuronal activity, whereas larger amounts of the drug suppress such effects. This phenomenon may also contribute to the paradoxical excitement phase of early intoxication.

As drinking progresses, emotional responses often become more labile and inappropriate because of the increasing reduction of normal censoring mechanisms upon the lower brain. When such emotions are not subjected to conscious filtering and interpretation, they may spontaneously spill over into overt behavior as silliness, giggling, and as inebriation progresses, fits of crying, rage, or other responses with little relevance to the actual circumstances in which the individual finds himself. The cerebellum soon becomes affected, and as this center for motor coordination and modulation of spinal impulses to the brain is depressed, the drinker begins to stagger and lose coordination. As drinking and consequent CNS depression progress, obvious stupor sets in and the drinker will finally pass out or become comatose when blood alcohol levels become sufficiently high. A drinker who has passed out is quite literally in a surgical coma. Unfortunately, he or she is also very close to death because of the concomitant profound depression of respiration and other vital functions. The effective dose for inducing general anaesthesia by ethanol is also dangerously close to the lethal dose. For this reason it is no longer used for such purposes.

Alcohol also induces sleep because of this depressant action, but like all such chemical hypnotics, it also reduces the amount of time spent in *rapid-eye movement* (REM) sleep. REM sleep is associated with dreaming states and appears to be essential to the maintenance of physical and mental well-being.[25] When alcohol or any other hypnotic drug is withdrawn after a period of such artificially reduced REM sleep, a *rebound effect* is usually observed in which subsequent sleep is marked by significant increases in REM sleep over the normal or baseline amount. When REM sleep has been chemically suppressed for long periods, as in alcoholic binge-drinking or when the use of such agents has been protracted, the rebound may be drastic and prolonged. Sleeping in alcoholic persons is fitful at best and they tend to suffer from major sleep disorders and chronic insomnia long after alcohol has been

[25]All vertebrates appear to need sleep. Even elasmobranchs (sharks and rays) and bony fishes are known to sleep at regular intervals, including those pelagic sharks that were once thought to require continual swimming in order to breathe.

withdrawn, sometimes for many years. This may be due in part to chronic psychological depression (which, in turn, is at least partly organically-based) and perhaps also in part to more or less permanent neurological deficits due to long-term insult by ethanol.

Normally, all but about 2 percent of the alcohol ingested is oxidized in the cells of the liver, but when large amounts have been consumed this figure may reach 10 percent. Very minute traces of alcohol can be found in the sweat, tears, saliva, and other bodily secretions, but essentially all of the unoxidized alcohol is excreted via the lungs as exhaled air and from the kidneys in the urine. Unlike most substances, alcohol is metabolized at a constant rate and this rate is not increased by increased levels of the drug. Alcohol acts as a *diuretic* by suppressing the production of antidiuretic hormone or *vasopressin* from the pituitary gland.[26] But even the resulting production of extra urine does not cause an increase of alcohol excretion via this route because the alcohol concentration in the urine remains only very slightly higher than that in the blood; one would essentially have to urinate away nearly the entire liquid portion of the body's blood supply in order to sober up by this method (Goodman & Gilman 1975).[27] The remaining 90-98 percent of the alcohol ingested is oxidized in the *hepatocytes* or liver cells, mainly via the alcohol dehydrogenase (ADH) pathway we have already encountered and with the concomitant reduction of NAD to NADH. There are very small amounts of ADH in some other tissues, notably in the brain and testes of the male. Although trace amounts of ethanol are oxidized in these other ADH-containing tissues, the quantities thus metabolized are negligible.

EFFECTS OF ALCOHOL ON THE GASTROINTESTINAL TRACT

One gram of alcohol will generate 7.1 kilocalories or nutritional "calories" upon metabolism, and one pint of 86-proof whiskey contains one-half of the daily caloric requirement for an average adult. As a result, heavy drinkers often fail to eat adequately since they consume most of their daily calories as alcohol and are rarely hungry for other food. However, alcohol contains only so-called *empty calories* which are entirely devoid of necessary vitamins, minerals, or proteins. Worse, alcohol causes direct irritation and inflammation

[26]The production of vasopressin causes the walls of the collecting tubules of the kidney to become permeable to water; this water is then absorbed back into the kidney because of the very high salt concentration in that organ. When vasopressin is suppressed, the collecting tubules become water impermeable and a high volume of hypotonic or dilute urine is produced.

[27]The circulating blood volume normally equals about 8 percent of the total body weight, or about 5,600 ml in a 70 kg man (Ganong 1973). Of this total blood volume, only 55 percent, or about 3,000-3,500 ml, consists of the *plasma* or liquid portion. The rest is made up of a large variety of plasma proteins and so-called *formed elements*, including *erythrocytes* (red blood cells), the different kinds of *leukocytes* or white blood cells, and *platelets* (small circulating bodies involved in clotting).

of the lining of the stomach and intestine, as well as to the pancreas,[28] even when taken only occasionally in modest amounts. This can result in impaired absorption of what food that is eaten, especially in the case of chronic heavy drinkers. Alcohol also damages liver cells in a variety of ways, as we shall see, resulting in inadequate assimilation of vitamins and amino acids (this also occurs with only small amounts of alcohol). Indeed, abnormal intestinal absorption is seen in approximately 50 percent of all hospitalized alcoholics, whether or not they also have liver cirrhosis (Shaw & Lieber 1979). Ethanol has a strong tendency to preempt other food items in the metabolic pathways of the liver, especially in the Krebs cycle (see Fig. 6), because it is energetically easier to oxidize than are many other carbohydrates. As a result, even absorbed and assimilated food is incompletely utilized by the liver. Malnutrition is thus actually promoted by alcoholic intake above that due merely to the dietary replacement of "rich" calories in real food by the "empty" ones in ethanol.[29] When severe malnutrition is seen in alcoholics, the alcoholism is usually far advanced.

Vitamin deficiencies are commonly seen in alcoholics, both with and without adequate food intake. These deficiencies can occur from several causes (Glass et al. 1979): (1) inadequate diet due to high caloric intake with excessive drinking, as just discussed; (2) decreased absorption of vitamins due to damage to the intestine and pancreas by alcohol; (3) decreased ability of the liver to convert vitamins into the active cofactors needed by the body because of liver damage; (4) increased requirements for certain vitamins because of the induced increase of enzymes using these vitamins as cofactors resulting from the excessive amounts of alcohol that must be metabolized. The most frequently seen vitamin deficiencies among alcohol abusers are due to poor intestinal uptake of *thiamine* (vitamin B_1), *cyanocobalamin* (vitamin B_{12}) and *folate* or *folic acid.*

Thiamine deficiency is associated with *beriberi,* a disorder involving degeneration of the nerves and muscles, particularly the heart muscle. In symptomless patients it may be manifested by reduction or loss of the tendon reflexes, especially in the legs (Madden 1979). Thiamine deficiency is also responsible for the symptoms seen in the Wernicke stage of Wernicke-Korsakoff syndrome, previously mentioned. Wernicke's encephalopathy is characterized by a pervasive and global confusional state in which the victim is disoriented with respect to space and time, is unable to recognize family and friends, cannot carry on coherent conversation, and is apathetic. The following are also prominent features: *nystagmus* or rapid involuntary shifting of the eyeballs and

[28]The pancreas is a complex glandular organ lying between the stomach and the liver which secretes protein-splitting, fat-splitting, and carbohydrate-splitting enzymes into the small intestine to aid in digestion; it also secretes two hormones important in the regulation of blood-sugar levels: *insulin* and *glucagon.*

[29]Some alcoholic beverages do contain protein and carbohydrate as congeners. An example is beer with about 500 kilocalories per liter, of which 250 kilocalories consist of protein and carbohydrates.

paralysis of the eye muscles, both due to lesions in the *oculomotor nuclei*[30] of the brainstem; *polyneuropathy* or multiple inflammation of the nerves involving pain and weakness, especially of the arms and legs;[31] and *ataxia* or loss of motor coordination resulting from lesions in the cerebellum. If such patients are given prompt thiamine therapy, most of the more dramatic signs and symptoms will clear in two or three weeks (Butters & Cermak 1980); failure to provide large doses of thiamine may result in fatal brain hemorrhages. Very few Wernicke patients recover completely, however, and most of them enter a chronic Korsakoff stage characterized by both anterograde and retrograde amnesia and the ensuing confabulations as discussed previously. The profound memory disorder is associated with lesions in the *thalamus* and *mamillary bodies* of the brainstem.[32] Thiamine deficiency has also traditionally been invoked as the cause of Korsakoff's psychosis, but no permanent memory disorders are known to result solely from thiamine deficiency (Butters & Cermak 1980). Moreover, thiamine therapy does not clear up the amnesic and confabulational states in Korsakoff patients. It appears that thiamine deficiency can cause Korsakoff-type symptoms *only* in alcoholic individuals, and alcohol very likely has a necessary and direct toxic role in the development of this disorder.

Both vitamin B_{12} and folic acid are required for formation and maturation of the red blood cells, and they are both also necessary for general cell replication. Folic acid is also needed in the synthesis of DNA, the carrier of genetic information in the cell nuclei (see footnote 30). Deficiencies in these two vitamins cause severe anemia due to reduced red blood cell counts. This anemia is often complicated by a coincident iron deficiency resulting from acute bleeding of the upper stomach. Alcohol directly disrupts the membrances of the cells in the stomach lining or *gastraic mucosa* and dissolves away the protective mucous lubricant secreted by the mucosal *epithelial cells*. Not only are hemorrhagic lesions directly formed in the stomach lining by alcohol-induced damage, but the removal of the protective mucous coat allows the hydrochloric acid normally present in the stomach for digestive purposes to attack the stomach wall. Alcohol additionally stimulates excess production of HCl, (by promoting gastrin release) and in high concentrations, delays emptying of the stomach contents. In

---

[30]The term *nucleus* has two major meanings in biology: (1) the subcellular, membrane-enclosed organelle found in all higher plants and all animal cells containing the genetic material, *deoxyribonucleic acid* (DNA) and which serves as the organizing center for the cell; (2) a general term for specialized groups of nerve cell bodies located within the CNS which coordinate a specific nerve or nerves; the oculomotor nuclei innervate the eye muscles and are responsible for their functioning.

[31]A common sign of Wernicke's encephalopathy is a characteristic limp drooping of the wrist and/or foot.

[32]The thalamus functions as the main relay and processing center between the cerebellum and brainstem and the higher cortical portions of the brain; it is also involved in language and long-term memory. The mammillary bodies are paired nuclei located at the base of the hypothalamus which function together with the nearby hippocampus in short-term memory. These and other neural structures are discussed in greater detail in volume two of this series.

high doses it also delays absorption from the stomach into the blood stream, probably by inhibiting gastric motility (Lieber 1983). All of these factors prolong the corrosive effect of both alcohol and hydrochloric acid upon the stomach mucosa. Furthermore, the accompanying deficiency of folic acid inhibits the cell division necessary for the repair of such damage.[33] Gastritis and atrophy of the gastric mucosa are frequently seen in alcoholics. Massive hemorrhages of the upper gastrointestinal tract are a life-threatening emergency not uncommon in chronic alcoholics — upper G. I. bleeding is often precipitated by the combined heavy intake of both alcohol and aspirin, the latter often taken for hangovers.

Folic acid deficiency can itself further decrease intestinal uptake of vitamins and proteins (Baraona & Lindenbaum 1978), and some investigators believe that folate deficiency due to inadequate dietary intake is the major factor behind decreased intestinal absorption seen in alcoholics. Ethanol itself is known to depress intestinal uptake of some substances, but not of others; it may be that *active* transport mechanisms are impaired in man, whereas nutrients that are passively diffused across the intestinal mucosa are unaffected or even enhanced (Baraona & Lindenbaum 1978). It is fairly well established that ethanol and folic acid deficiency act synergistically to depress intestinal uptake of nutrients.

Nicotinic acid or *niacin*[34] (vitamin B_3) is used by the body in forming our old friend NAD, which is a necessary cofactor in the dehydrogenation of many substances, including alcohol as we have seen. Nicotinic acid is absorbed in the upper intestinal tract, and the disruption of this organ due to alcohol abuse makes niacin deficiency a common medical problem in chronic alcoholics. *Pellagra* is the condition resulting from niacin deficiency. It is characterized clinically by the classical three D's — *dermatitis, diarrhea,* and *dementia.* The dermatitis occurs on those areas of the skin exposed to sunlight and involves redness and thickening of the skin, followed by *keratosis* or increased horniness and callousness; in advanced cases chronic inflammation and swelling of the underlying tissues occur followed by scaling and flaking of the skin. There may be alternating areas of pigmented and depigmented skin along with the formation of fibrous tissue with scarring. The mucous membranes of the mouth may become swollen and ulcerated and the tongue red and swollen. Ulcerations and lesions similar to those seen in the skin occur throughout the intestinal tract, but are particularly prominent in the esophagus, stomach, and colon. They cause the watery diarrhea and occasionally bloody stools seen in this disorder. Dementia (intellectual deficit, confusion, and disorientation) accompanies the

[33]Under normal circumstances, the gastric mucosa is completely regenerated about every three days. This prevents ulceration due to the constant corrosive effect of HCl.

[34]*Nicotinamide* or *niacinamide* refers to the amide form of nicotinic acid in which the hydroxyl group is replaced by a amine group ($-NH_2$). Niacin is frequently given in its amide form to reduce unpleasant gastrointestinal side effects.

degeneration of certain cell bodies of the brain and nerve tracts within the spinal cord. Signs and symptoms of CNS involvement include headache, dizziness, and insomnia, depression, memory impairment, and in severe cases, dementia or mental deterioration, delusions, and hallucinations. The mental aspects of this condition superficially resemble a schizophrenic state, and this gave rise in the 1960s to the now discredited theory that schizophrenia arises from niacin deficiency, and that it could be cured by massive doses (3 grams per day!) of the vitamin along with ascorbic acid or vitamin C (the so-called *megavitamin therapy* of the *orthomolecular school*[35] of psychiatry). Pellagra has traditionally been associated with poverty-level groups in the southern United States whose diets are largely pork and hominy grits made from corn (which has a low tryptophan and niacin content), as well as in parts of Mexico, the Middle East, and Africa with largely maize diets. Pellagra has now disappeared from the United States, except among alcoholics (Beeson & McDermott 1975).

Finally, it should be noted that the entire complex of vitamins B are mutually synergistic and interdependent. A deficiency in any one of them may cause a relative insufficiency in one or more of the others. They are important as cofactors in carbohydrate metabolism, particularly in the tricarboxylic acid or Krebs cycle, and as precursors for the formation of nicotinic acid in NAD. Deficiencies in vitamins B are often seen in alcoholics because of the increased activity of enzymes requiring these cofactors induced by the metabolism of chronically excessive alcohol concentrations. The common major effect of such depletion is damage to the nervous system.

Most of what we eat is absorbed through the walls of the small intestine. The main function of the large intestine or colon is to resorb water from the undigested residue of the ingested food to prevent dehydration. About 2-3 liters of water from the body fluids enter the stomach and small intestine during digestion. Some of this is absorbed in the small intestine, but the bulk of it is taken back up by the colon. When this process is disturbed, diarrhea and resulting dehydration can occur. The large intestine also provides for bacterial breakdown of undigested food residue and prepares it for elimination in the feces.

The small intestine is about 9 feet long in a living adult human.[36] The inner lining or mucosa bears innumerable tiny fingerlike projections known as *villi* (singular, *villus*) which protrude into the central cavity or *lumen* (Fig. 10). These small projections greatly increase the surface area available for absorption of

[35]Adherents of this school believe that all mental disorders can be effectively treated by adjusting the concentration of substances normally present in the body, such as vitamins. These substances, though manufactured in the laboratory, they believe are superior to "unnatural" chemicals such as antipsychotic drugs. This approach has few adherents in mainstream psychiatry, however.

[36]The often quoted figures of 5-7 meters (15-21 feet) for the length of the small intestine come from dissections of cadavers. The small intestine in living humans is always in a somewhat contracted state and is thus shorter than it is shortly after death (Ganong 1973).

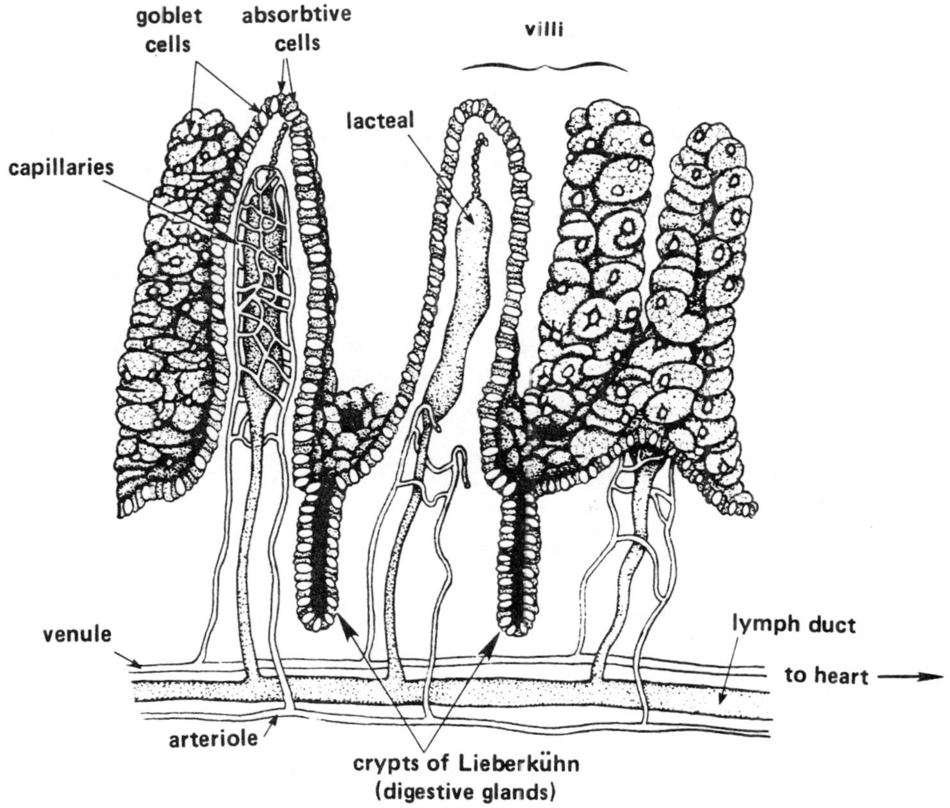

Figure 10. Structural details of intestinal wall.

food. In addition, the cells of the mucosa each bear even smaller projections of the cell membrane and included cytoplasm (not shown here), called *microvilli,* which further augment the surface area. The total surface area of the intestinal lining is about 5 times that of the external body surface represented by the skin (Johnson et al. 1977). Specialized *goblet cells* secrete *mucin,* a protective lubricant coating the intestinal lining. Many substances such as sugars, amino acids (the building blocks of proteins, and thus also their metabolic breakdown products), minerals, and water-soluble vitamins (like B-complex and vitamin C) enter the capillaries of the circulatory system in the villi. From there they are transported to the liver for further processing. *Triglycerides*[37] are neutral fats consisting of three fatty acids esterified to glycerol (see Fig. 2). These are

[37]This term is technically incorrect. According to strict and standardized modern usage as dictated by the International Union of Pure and Applied Chemistry and The International Union of Biochemistry, fatty acid esters of glycerol are termed *acylglycerols* and not *"glycerides."* Triglycerides are thus correctly called *triacylglycerols.* "Triglyceride" is a commonly used term, however, even in the current literature, and it is retained here for the sake of convenience and clarity.

hydrolyzed (the opposite process from esterification) into free fatty acids (monoglycerides) in the upper intestine. Short-chain fatty acids (containing fewer than 10-12 carbon atoms) are absorbed directly into the capillaries of the villi and transported to the liver. Long-chain fatty acids (longer than 12 or so carbon atoms) are re-esterified into triglycerides in the intestinal mucosa, and combined with several other small molecules (lipoproteins, cholesterol esters and phospholipids) to form small fat droplets called *chylomicrons (chylomicra)*. These chylomicrons are taken into the lymph vessel or *lacteal* found in each villus and from there are transported via the lymphatic system to a point where they enter the bloodstream in the left subclavian vein. They are then deposited into various fat depots of the body, including the inner linings of the arteries where they cause atherosclerosis. Free fatty acids are released into the bloodstream from the storage depots as needed and oxidized for energy by a variety of cells and tissues.

As it does in the stomach, ethanol dissolves away the protective mucin coat and produces a variety of ultrastructural abnormalities in the cells of the intestinal lining, even in the presence of a nutritionally adequate diet (Baraona & Lindenbaum 1978).[38] Such changes include distortion of the *mitochondria*[39] and disruption of the *endolplasmic reticulum* (ER)[40] and the *Golgi apparatus* (see Fig. 12).[41] In addition, ethanol in doses found in many alcoholic beverages causes a shortening of the intestinal villi and produces hemorrhagic lesions at the tips of those structures (Glass et al. 1979). All of these effects cause serious disturbances in the absorption and transport of food and nutrients to the body.

In addition to damaging the stomach and small intestine, prolonged heavy alcohol intake can cause direct irritation of the mouth and esophagus. Cancer of the mouth and esophagus are statistically correlated with the use of both alcohol and tobacco. Esophageal cancer is 25 times more common among heavy drinkers and six to seven times more frequent among all types of tobacco users than in controls. Since most alcoholics are also tobacco addicts, their risk is compounded for such cancers. *Acute hemorrhagic pancreatitis* is a common condition

---

[38] By now the reader is surely aware that the concept of a "drinking man's diet" in which one can drink to one's heart's content as long as he or she eats a nutritionally balanced diet is totally without any scientific or medical foundation.

[39] Smaller granular organelles found in all cells which are the main sites of ATP generation from the oxidation of food; they contain the enzymes of the Krebs cycle as well as those of the respiratory pathway (electron transport chain).

[40] A lybyrhinthine network of double membranes found throughout the cytoplasm of most cells. This system may contain *ribosomes* (rough ER), small bodies where proteins are manufactured, or ribosomes may be lacking (smooth ER). A variety of enzymes are located in the ER and many metabolic processes are carried out there.

[41] Complexes of flattened membranes stacked together which concentrate substances produced in the ER and which package many of them into membrane-lined vesicles or *vacuoles* for transport to other parts of the cell. They are involved in wrapping many substances, notably fats and sugars, with a protein coat to aid in transportation.

among chronic alcoholics, particularly in middle life. This is a first-order medical emergency of life-threatening proportions. It is characterized by a sudden onset of intense pain in the abdominal area which resembles acute appendicitis. This is a recurrent condition, and such an abrupt onset of an "acute abdomen" usually follows soon after a very large meal or an alcoholic binge. In many cases this is followed by peripheral vascular collapse with profound shock having a 20 to 50 percent mortality rate! In the later stages of this disorder, multiple and profound metabolic disturbances are seen, including diabetes, *steatorrhea* (fatty stools) and *azotorrhea* (excessive nitrogen loss in the stools).

This dangerous complication is caused by massive cell death within the pancreas due to massive release of *lysing* (tissue dissolving) enzymes by that organ. Alcohol causes increased secretion of hydrochloric acid in the stomach (see above), which in turn promotes increased production of *secretin,* a hormone put out by the mucosa of the *duodenum* (the first 10 inches or so of the small intestine). Secretin is normally produced in response to the presence of the acidic, gruel-like food or *chyme* entering the duodenum from the stomach through the pyloric sphincter.[42] This hormone induces the pancreas to secrete its *pancreatic juice* containing acid-neutralizing bicarbonate plus a complete complement of digestive enzymes capable of splitting carbohydrates *(maltase),* proteins *(proteases),* lipids *(lipase)* and nucleic acids *(ribonuclease and deoxyribonuclease).* This induced hypersecretion of pancreatic enzymes by alcohol is thought to result in attack upon that organ by its own lysing enzymes, with ensuing tissue destruction and necrosis (Robbins 1974). This pancreatic necrosis appears to be exacerbated because of partial obstruction of the pancreatic sphincter by alcohol, causing these enzymes to remain within that organ for protracted periods and causing even greater damage.

Such chronic relapsing pancreatitis events invariably damage this gland due to recurrent fat necrosis, edema, and calcification. The normal cells of the pancreas are gradually replaced by fibrous tissue and late in the disease, pancreatic juice secretion is severely restricted. The *islet cells* or *islets of Langerhans*[43] contained within the pancreas are similarly destroyed. These cells secrete two hormones important in blood-sugar regulation (see also footnote 28): *glucagon* is secreted by the *alpha cells* of the islets of Langerhans and it promotes the conversion of *glyogen* or *animal starch* (a stored form of glucose in the liver) into glucose

[42]Acidity in the stomach may reach *p*H values as low as 1; by the time the chyme has passed the duodenum, the bicarbonate from the pancreas has neutralized this acidity to *p*H 6.0-7.0. Acidity and alkalinity are measured in *p*H units on a logarithmic scale ranging from 0 to 14, with 7.0 being the neutral point. In any solution, the $pH = -\log[H^+]$, where $[H^+]$ = the concentration of the *hydrogen ion* in moles/liter. Each unit decrement downwards from $pH = 7$ equals a tenfold increase in acidity; each unit increase upwards from 7 equals a tenfold increase in alkalinity.

[43]The pancreas is simultaneously an *exocrine* or duct-bearing gland and an *endocrine* or ductless gland. The pancreatic juice with all of its enzymes and the bicarbonate fraction are secreted by the exocrine portion via the pancreatic duct into the small intestine. The islet cells comprise the endocrine portion and secrete their hormones directly into the bloodstream for action at distant target cells or tissues.

in the blood stream; *insulin* is released by the *beta cells* within the islets of Langerhans in response to excess blood-sugar levels. If islet cell destruction progresses too far, frank diabetes mellitus will develop. A great many recovering alcoholics suffer from recurrent attacks of *reactive hypoglycemia* which results from an initial delayed release of insulin in response to a meal and the consequent rise in blood-sugar levels. This is followed one or two hours later by a sudden overreaction on the part of the beta cells to elevated blood glucose levels, and the injection of massive amounts of insulin into the bloodstream. The ensuing rapid fall in blood-sugar levels causes the abrupt onset of hypoglycemic symptoms and signs.[44] The clinical signs and symptoms of an acute hypoglycemic or low blood-sugar attack can include several or all of the following: sweating, weakness, shakiness and tremor, rapid heartbeat (tachycardia), headache, fatigue and lethargy, agitation and restlessness, anxiety, apprehension, blurred vision, excessive yawning, mental confusion, anger (may include overt rage reactions) and irritability, and visual disturbances. These features arise from both the activation of the autonomic nervous system with the release of epinephrine (adrenaline), and impaired metabolism of the brain cells which require adequate amounts of glucose for fuel. Reactive hypoglycemia is very commonly involved in the so-called *dry drunks* experienced by many sober alcoholics, although there are also concomitant psychological factors involved in these disturbances. This syndrome is discussed in some detail in the last volume of this series, which deals with the problems faced by recovering alcoholics (see also footnote 46).

Steatorrhea, or malabsorption of fat and its excretion in the feces, also results from chronic relapsing pancreatitis because of damage to the exocrine portion (see footnote 43). It results in part from *lipase* (fat-splitting enzymes) deficiency, but fat absorption by the small intestine is also inhibited because of the reduction in bicarbonate output by the pancreas with an ensuing failure to neutralize the acidic chyme coming in from the stomach. Fats are normally emulsified into very fine droplets called *micelles* in the upper intestine by the detergent-like action of *bile salts* put out by the liver and stored in the gall bladder for use when a meal containing fats is eaten. Because of the relatively acid conditions in the small intestine due to impaired bicarbonate secretion from the damaged pancreas, fats and fatty acids are prevented from forming micelles with the bile salts and glycerides; they are therefore not well absorbed by the intestine and they pass out in the stools. This deprives the body of calories and contributes to the malnutrition seen in alcoholics.

Pancreatic cancer is now the fourth leading cause of death among all types of cancer in this country (Beeson & McDermott 1975). The three most commonly

---

[44] *Symptoms* are the subjective experiences felt by a patient resulting from his disease or condition — they cannot be objectively perceived by an observer (examples: headache or feelings of giddiness or nausea); *signs* are the objective evidence of a disease state perceived by the examining physician (examples: fever, rash, and elevated blood pressure).

cited causes in the development of this disease are: chronic pancreatitis, chronic alcohol abuse, and diabetes mellitus. It is especially difficult to detect until it is too late for effective treatment, and it affects twice as many males as females.

EFFECTS OF ALCOHOL ON THE LIVER AND METABOLISM

The wedge-shaped, reddish-brown liver or *hepar* is the largest gland in the body and it weights 1.8 kilograms in a typical adult. It is located in the upper right portion of the abdominal cavity and its domed upper surface fits snugly against the underside of the diaphram, partly covering the stomach (Fig. 11). The sac-like, dark green *gallbladder* is nestled within the lobes of the liver; the

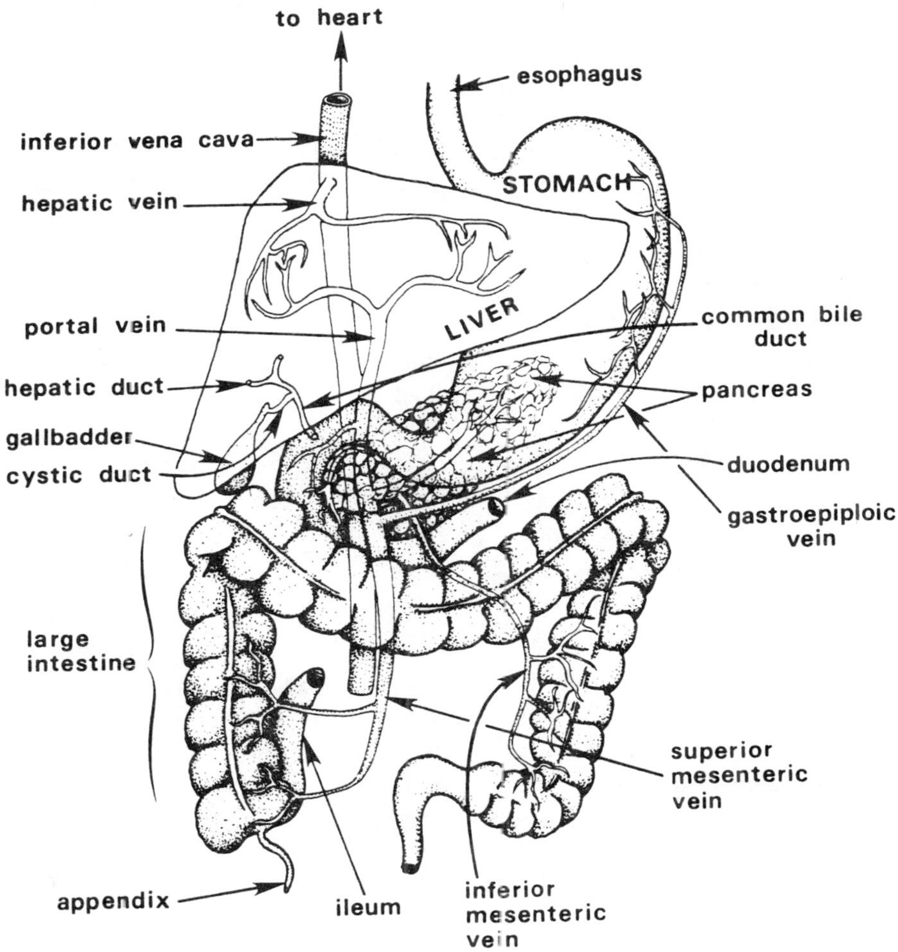

Figure 11. Relationship of viscera to hepatic portal system.

cystic duct connects the gallbladder to the *hepatic duct* coming from the liver, and both empty into the small intestine through the *common bile duct.* Bile is released from the liver and stored in the gallbladder to be used in the digestion of fats, as just discussed. Blood containing the products of digestion is taken from the intestine to the liver via the *hepatic portal vein* for further processing. This blood is then distributed throughout the liver by a highly complex system of *hepatic sinuses,* a capillary network which evenly spreads the products of digestion into close proximity with the individual liver cells or *hepatocytes* for further processing. The spent, deoxygenated blood is then passed out of the liver via the *hepatic veins* and collected into a single large vessel, the *posterior* (or *inferior*) *vena cava,* which transports all of the blood coming from the body region lying below the heart back into the heart for transport to the lungs and reoxygenation, and subsequent redistribution throughout the body via the arterial system. In this way, each individual hepatocyte is brought into intimate contact with one or more hepatic sinuses, so that the products of digestion are completely absorbed into the liver for further metabolism (see also Fig. 19).

The liver has multiple metabolic functions. Its role in bile secretion has already been discussed. Glucose from the blood is converted into glycogen by the hepatocytes in which form it is stored until needed as fuel by the body. Proteins are completely broken down into their basic building blocks, the 20 *amino acids,* by proteolytic enzymes in the stomach and small intestine. These amino acids are used by the body to synthesize new proteins specific to the organism under the direction of the genetic blueprint, DNA (see footnote 30). Unlike lipids and carbohydrates, proteins are not stored in the body. Excess amino acids are *deaminated* or stripped of their amine groups ($-NH_2$) by the liver cells:

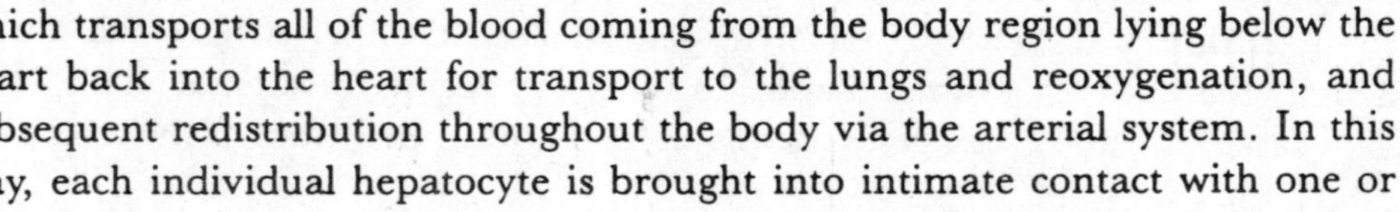

In the deaminative process, NAD^+ is reduced to NADH and the amino acid is oxidized into its corresponding *keto acid* (a compound containing both the C=O and COOH groups)[45] and ammonia. Most of the NH_3 thus formed is converted into urea by the liver for elimination from the kidneys in the urine; a very small amount of ammonia is converted into urea in the brain.

Amino acids are also synthesized into glucose *de novo* by the hepatocytes in a

[45]Pyruvic acid is an example of a keto acid; the COOH group is more accurately represented as:

```
-C=O
 |
 OH
```

process called *gluconeogenesis*. This involves the deamination of the amino acid and its conversion into pyruvic acid, either directly (as in the case of alanine) or indirectly by entering the Krebs cycle at one of several points, depending upon the particular amino acid involved. The pyruvate thus formed is then converted into glucose by going backwards through the glycolytic pathway (see Fig. 26). This process is severely impaired in both acute (see Fig. 27) and chronic alcoholism and is responsible for the severe hypoglycemia often seen in emergency wards. Such acute hypoglycemia is probably responsible for many of the unexplained deaths that occur among arrested alcoholics "sleeping it off" in drunk tanks.[46]

In addition to the foregoing functions, the liver is responsible for detoxifying a number of substances into inactive, harmless compounds via the *mixed function oxidase* or *microsomal enzyme oxidizing system,* which we will discuss shortly in some detail. It produces vital clotting substances and many other plasma proteins needed by the blood and it is the site where vitamins A, D, and B_{12} are stored. Finally, the liver and spleen are the site of red blood cell destruction. *Bilirubin,* the breakdown product of hemoglobin, is metabolized by the liver into a water-soluble complex called *bilirubin glucuronide* by conjugating each bilirubin molecule to two glucuronic acid molecules. This bilirubin glucuronide is then passed out with the bile into the intestines, where it colors the feces brown and is eliminated with them. The iron released by the breakdown of hemoglobin is retained in the liver to be used in the synthesis of new hemoglobin.[47]

It is apparent from the foregoing discussion that the liver plays a great many vital roles necessary to life itself, and severe damage to this organ results in a life-threatening situation. Fortunately, the liver has enormous powers of regeneration and it can tolerate substantial abuse. It can also maintain much of its function even when major portions have been destroyed, as long as some tissue remains intact. Nonetheless, there are finite limits and even this organ can be damaged to the point of total failure, with death being the swift and inevitable consequence.

We have seen that ethanol is oxidized almost wholly in the cells of the liver, primarily by the enzyme alcohol dehydrogenase, into acetaldehyde with the accompanying reduction of NAD^+ to NADH. This process occurs in the *cytosol* or *cell sap* of the hypatocytes (Fig. 12). ADH has a wide specificity for many substrates. These include most kinds of alcohols as well as many of the corre-

---

[46]The metabolic hypoglycemia discussed here is not the same as that seen in abstinent alcoholics with pancreatic impairment. Hypoglycemia has multiple causes and effects, all of which can be seen in alcoholic persons.

[47]Red blood cells or erythrocytes are produced in the marrow of the ribs and the ends of the long bones of the arms and legs at the rate of about two million per second, and they are destroyed at the same rate by the liver and spleen. If the iron were not conserved a severe anemia would soon result. Indeed, gastric bleeding caused by alcohol abuse and menstrual bleeding in women can cause anemia if the iron thus lost is not replaced in the diet.

sponding aldehydes (including acetaldehyde). It is also involved in steroid dehydrogenation and a special type of fatty acid oxidation known as *ω-oxidation or omega oxidation* which need not concern us here (Wartburg 1971; Lieber 1978). ADH is also the enzyme responsible for converting the stored form of vitamin A in the liver (an alcohol, *retinol*) into its aldehyde form *(retinal or retinene),* which can then combine with *opsin,* a protein from the rods and cones of the retina, to form the visual pigments *rhodopsin* for black-and-white and dim-light (night) vision, and *photopsin* and related pigments for color and bright-light vision. ADH is also present in the testis of the male and is needed for the synthesis of the *androgens* or male sex hormones. Finally, ADH metabolizes the aldehyde breakdown products of certain brain neurotransmitter substances into their respective alcohols in the CNS.

The immediate oxidation product of ethanol, acetaldehyde, is extremely toxic and it must be rapidly detoxified to prevent damage to the organism. Although alcohol dehydrogenase can oxidize acetaldehyde, most of it is metabolized by another enzyme, *acetaldehyde dehydrogenase* (AcDH)[48] into *acetic acid or acetate,* again with the reduction of NAD^+ to NADH:

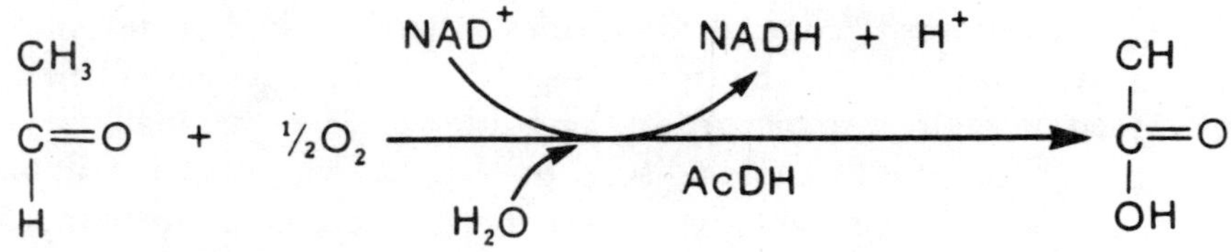

This process takes place primarily in the mitrochondria where about 80 percent of the AcDH activity is located [see Fig. 16] (Lieber & DeCarli 1978), although some AcDH activity is known to occur in the cytosolic and *microsomal* (or smooth endoplasmic reticulum) (see footnote 40) fractions of the hepatocytes. The acetate thus produced is combined with coenzyme A to form acetyl co-A, which then enters the Krebs cycle (see Fig. 7) to be converted into water, CO_2 and energy in the form of ATP. About 50-80 percent of the acetate derived from ethanol oxidation is handled outside the liver (Madden 1979; Lieber 1982). The bulk of acetaldehyde oxidation to acetate (90-95%) occurs in the liver, and the rate of its oxidation is very close to that of ethanol oxidation (Weiner 1979).[49] It was formerly thought that the level and activity of aldehyde

[48]This enzyme is actually a general one for all aldehydes, and it is perhaps more correctly termed *aldehyde dehydrogenase;* the present usage is retained for clarity and because of its general prevalence in the ethanol research and general literature.

[49]But see Casarett & Doull 1980:478. These authors report that AcDH has 4 to 5 times more activity in the liver and kidney than does ADH; thus acetaldehyde does not tend to build up in the blood.

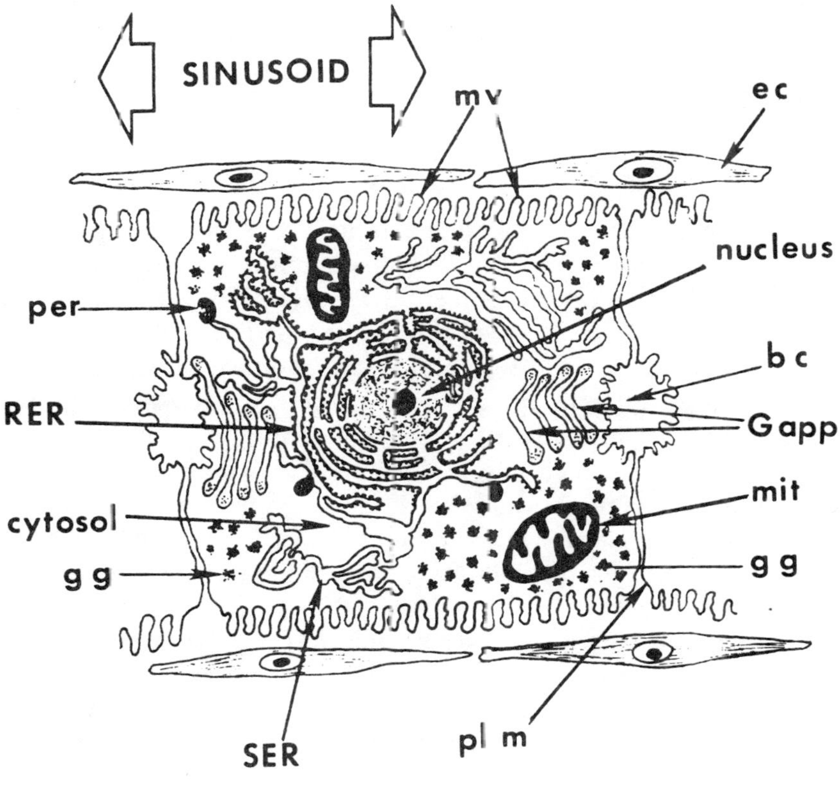

Figure 12. Ultrasturcture of hepatocyte. Subcellular structures not drawn to scale. e c = epithelial cell lining sinusoid; b c = bile canaliculus; G app = Golgi apparatus; g g = glycogen granules; mit = mitochondrion; mv = microvilli; per = peroxisome; pl m = plasma membrane; RER = rough endoplasmic reticulum; SER = smooth endoplasmic reticulum.

dehydrogenase was the rate-limiting factor in this oxidative pathway, but the rate of conversion of reduced NADH back to NAD^+ is now known to be the limiting determinant.

Acetaldehyde is also oxidized to a small extent in the other tissues, notably the brain, heart and other musculature; in fact, some level of AcDH activity can be found in almost all tissues. The acetaldehyde metabolized by the brain is potentially of great importance in view of the severe toxicity of this compound. Nearly all of this acetaldehyde appears to be oxidized as it crosses the blood-brain barrier, so that none is found in the brain tissues themselves except when the cerebral blood acetaldehyde levels are extremely high (Weiner 1979). Similarly, AcDH activity in the human placenta and fetal liver adequately protects the fetus from the toxic effects of acetaldehyde, although this may not be the case during the critical first trimester of pregnancy. It thus appears that acetaldehyde is not involved in the etiology of fetal alcohol syndrome.

Antabuse or *disulfiram* has the chemical formula $C_{10}H_{20}N_2S_4$, or more accurately,

$$(C_2H_5)_2-N-\overset{\overset{\displaystyle S}{\|}}{C}-S-S-\overset{\overset{\displaystyle S}{\|}}{C}-N-(C_2H_5)_2$$

It is often used by physicians in treating chronic alcoholics. As long as the drug is present in the body, drinking even a small amount of alcohol can produce an extremely unpleasant and often dangerous reaction. If a person taking disulfiram does drink, within about 10 or 20 minutes the face will become hot and flushed to a scarlet color due to a general vasodilation which soon spreads over the body. Difficulty in breathing, heart palpitations, profuse sweating, pounding headache, chest pains, nausea, and severe vomiting soon follow. There is a drop in blood pressure which may lead to cardiovascular shock, cardiac arrhythmias, and even to myocardial infarction, congestive heart failure, convulsions, and death. The risk for this reaction can last for several days after discontinuing disulfiram. A small minority of individuals do not develop the disulfiram-ethanol reaction.

Disulfiram appears to act by outcompeting NAD for the active sites of aldehyde dehydrogenase, thus blocking the oxidation of acetaldehyde and causing a rapid buildup of that substance. The severe reaction described above is thought to be due largely to the direct toxic effects of acetaldehyde itself. However, not all of the effects of the disulfiram-ethanol reaction can be explained solely by this mechanism, especially since acetaldehyde given experimentally results in a *rise* rather than a fall in blood pressure. In addition, a number of studies have shown that chronic alcoholics tend to develop higher blood acetaldehyde levels when drinking (in the absence of disulfiram) than do nonalcoholic control subjects without showing obvious signs of the disulfiram-ethanol response. Disulfiram is also known to inhibit the transformation of *dopamine* into *noradrenalin (norepinephrine)* by blocking the action of the enzyme involved, *dopamine-beta-hydroxylase.* The combination of direct acetaldehyde toxicity coupled with the induced noradrenalin deficit causing decreased heart and arterial *tonus* (contractile tension) and an ensuing drop in blood pressure appears to be the best explanation for the overall disulfiram-ethanol reaction.

Disulfiram metabolism appears to involve the following two steps (Faiman 1979): (1) disulfiram is reduced to *diethyldithiocarbamate,* which in turn is converted into (2) *diethylamine* and *carbon disulfide,* by reduction of the nitrogen atom and oxidation of the carbon atom, respectively.

The reduced disulfiram (diethldithiocarbamate) is able to form mixed disulfides between its SH group and the sulfhydryl groups of aldehyde dehydrogenase. The affinity of hepatic aldehyde dehydrogenase for disulfiram is 46 times greater than that for the cofactor NAD, and about 350 times greater than

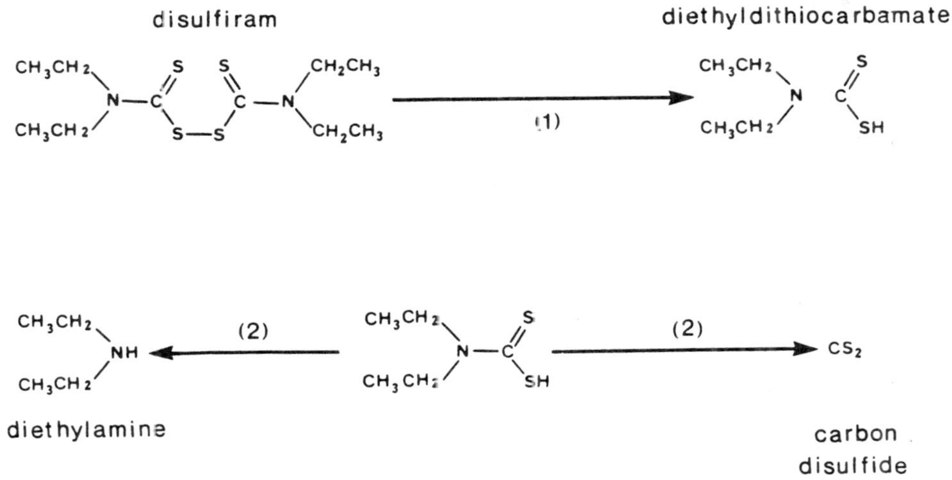

that for acetaldehyde (Faiman 1979). The inhibition of aldehyde dehydrogenase by disulfiram is irreversible and recovery from the effect depends upon the synthesis of new enzyme. The administration of cycloheximide, a potent inhibitor of protein synthesis, prevents the renewal of aldehyde dehydrogenase activity.

Disulfiram nonspecifically inhibits a variety of enzyme systems. Its effect upon dopamine-beta-hydroxylase by chelating[50] the copper (Cu^{2+}) prosthetic group[51] of the enzyme has already been mentioned, Disulfiram also nonspecifically inhibits a number of microsomal drug metabolizing enzymes, including cytochromes P_{450} and P_{420}, and both microsomal and plasma carboxylases[52] and cholinesterases,[53] in addition to hexokinase[54] and D-amino acid oxidase.[55] All appear to be similarly inhibited. The reduced metabolite of disulfiram, diethyl-

[50]Dopamine and noradrenalin are *catecholamines*, neurotransmitter substances derived from the amino acid precursor *tyrosine*. These substances are discussed in great detail in the volume of this series dealing with the neurobiological aspects of alcohol abuse.

[51]Chelating agents form stable, water-soluble complexes with metal ions. A prosthetic group is a non-protein, accessory complex or cofactor which is strongly bound to the protein moiety of an enzyme, and which is essential to its functioning.

[52]Carboxylesterases hydrolyze carboxylic acid esters into carboxylic acid and the corresponding alcohol.

[53]Cholinesterase hydrolyzes the neurotransmitter acetylcholine into choline (one of the vitamins B) and acetic acid; it also hydrolyzes other acylcholines into choline and carboxylic acid.

[54]Hexokinase catalyzes the phosphorylation of glucose into glucose-6-phosphate; metabolically important sugars must first be thus phosphorylated before they can be metabolized. See also footnote 89.

[55]D-amino acid oxidase (also termed D-amino acid dehydrogenase) is an FAD-linked enzyme in the liver and kidneys which oxidatively deaminates the D- or dextro-amino acids (those which rotate a beam of polarized light in a right-handed or clockwise direction.

dithiocarbamate, appears to be the active form in all of these inhibitory effects, and the mechanism is the same as that whereby it inhibits aldehyde dehydrogenase — *viz.* by tying up the sulfhydryl groups of these other enzyme systems (Faiman 1979).

Disulfiram occurs naturally in an edible fungus, *Coprinus atramentarius,* and eating this fungus results in a pronounced intolerance to ethanol (Bowman & Rand 1980). Because of the dangerous effects of this drug in combination with alcohol, disulfiram is rarely used in alcoholic patients with ischemic heart disease, severe liver or brain damage, epilepsy, asthma, diabetes, mental incapacity, or in persons over age 60. Several other agents also produce a disulfiram-like reaction when combined with ethanol. *Thiram* is a closely related compound to disulfiram and it is similarly used in the rubber industry as a vulcanizing agent and polymerization accelerator. In thiram, the ethyl groups ($-CH_2CH_3$) are replaced by methyl groups ($-CH_3$); workers exposed to this agent have become ill when they drink beverage alcohol (Bowman & Rand 1980).

Certain sulfonurea derivatives used as oral hypoglycemic agents in the treatment of diabetes also produce the disulfiram-ethanol reaction, but the response is less severe and does not last as long. *Tolbutamide* and *Chlorpropamide* are among the most prominent of these agents, and they appear to noncompetitively inhibit aldehyde dehydrogenase (Faiman 1979; Bowman & Rand 1980). *Metronidazole* or *Flagyl®* is an antiprotozoal agent which is very effective in treating *trichomoniasis* (a protozoan which infects the vagina in females, and the bladder and urethra in males), amoebic dystentery, and *lambliasis* (an intestinal infection by a flagellate protzoan, *Giardia lamblia,* causing protracted diarrhea and malabsorption). In some individuals Flagyl produces a disulfiram-like effect when alcohol is consumed, and it has been used occasionally as an aversion therapy for alcoholism. Its effects are controversial, and it is said to inhibit both alcohol dehydrogenase and aldehyde dehydrogenase (Bowman & Rand), which may account for its less potent effect since less alcohol would be oxidized into acetaldehyde. However, other workers have shown that Metronidazole has no inhibitory effect upon either enzyme (Faiman 1979). A severe psychosis can result when Metronidazole is used in combination with disulfiram (Bowman & Rand 1980), and its use for treating alcoholics is of very dubious value. Finally, *citrated calcium carbimide* ($Ca=N-C\equiv N$) is also reported to produce a disulfiram-like reaction with alcohol.

Both the oxidation of alcohol to acetaldehyde and the subsequent oxidation of acetaldehyde to acetate produce a massive buildup of hydrogen equivalents because of the corresponding reduction of NAD^+ to NADH plus H^+ when ethanol is consumed in large amounts. This increase in hydrogen equivalents causes a major shift in the redox state in the cells of the liver and of many other organs, which disrupts a number of important biochemical pathways. NAD^+ is reconsituated from NADH in a complex series of redox reactions in the mitochondria which convey the hydrogen equivalents away from the NADH; if this system becomes saturated with hydrogen, as happens when large quantities of alcohol are consumed, then oxidized NAD^+ cannot be regenerated and all reactions depending upon its reduction to NADH (including alcohol metabolism) are blocked. This change in redox balance is responsible for the majority of pathological changes and medical complications seen in long-term alcohol abuse. This redox shift will be encountered frequently in our discussion of ethanol's effect upon the various systems, organs, and tissues of the body.

There are two other biochemical pathways in the hepatocytes by which alcohol is oxidized (Fig. 13): (1) the *mixed function oxidase* (MFO) *system,* also called the *cytochrome P_{450} containing monooxygenase*[56] or the *microsomal enzyme oxidizing system* (MEOS) located in the *microsomal fraction*[57] or endoplasmic reticulum (ER) of the liver cells (see also footnote 40); (2) the *catalase* pathway found in the *peroxisomes* (see below), mitochondria (see footnote 39), and to a very small extent, in the *microsomes.*[57] The MEOS plays a significant role in the oxidation of ethanol, although it is not nearly as important as the ADH pathway; the catalase system is of very minor importance, and at the outside does not account for more than about 5 percent of the non-ADH mediated metabolism of consumed alcohol (Lieber 1978).

The microsomal enzyme oxidizing system is very important in the metabolism of foreign compounds of all types. It is the system by which almost all drugs and toxic substances are rendered harmless. In some cases, however, relatively harmless precursor molecules may be biotransformed by the microsomal monooxygenases into biologically-active and highly toxic metabolites capable of causing severe tissue damage to certain organs or of inducing cancers. For example, the barbiturates are metabolized by this system into nontoxic substances that are readily excreted, whereas the extreme toxicity of carbon tetrachloride (CCl_4) is due to its biotransformation into a highly reactive compound ($\cdot CCl_3$) by the microsomal monooxygenases, which combines with and destroys lipid membranes, thus killing the hepatocytes.

The mixed function oxidase system, of which the *microsomal ethanol oxidizing system* (also designated by the acronym MEOS in the alcohol literature) is a part, is a membrane-bound system of oxidases or oxidizing enzymes which facilitate the transfer of electrons or hydrogen equivalents between compounds.

---

[56] Monoxygenases are enzymes which transfer only one oxygen atom from molecular oxygen (O_2) to each molecule of substrate being oxidized; the other oxygen is reduced to water (see Fig. 13).

[57] The endoplasmic reticulum cannot be isolated intact from living cells. However, when cells are subjected to *differential centrifugation* (i.e., undergo extremely high centrifugal forces in a rapidly spinning device known as a centrifuge) the different components of the cells sediment out in the test tube at different rates because of their differing densities. The continuous, double-membrane ER complex which is distributed throughout the cytosol (see Fig. 12) is fragmented by centrifugation into numerous small, membrane-lined vesicles, the microsomes. Those microsomes of the smooth endoplasmic reticulum contain the mixed-function monoxygenases.

These enzymes act largely on lipid-soluble molecules which can penetrate the membrane system of the ER and they convert them into more polar substances; these polar metabolites are thus more water-soluble and able to be excreted via the kidneys in the urine. Alcohol is both water and lipid soluble and can thus be acted upon by the MEOS.

The MEOS is dependent upon the conversion of reduced *nicotinamide adenine dinucleotide phosphate* (NADPH) to its oxidized form, $NADP^+$, which is none other than NAD^+ with an attached phosphate group (Fig. 13). Two electrons are transferred from NADPH, converting a flavoprotein, *cytochrome c reductase* (also termed *NADPH-cytochrome P_{450} reductase;* see also footnotes 18 and 19), from the oxidized to the reduced state. Cytochrome P_{450} is so named because when combined with carbon monoxide and analyzed in a spectrophotometer, it shows maximum absorption of light at a wavelength of 450 nannometers (450×10^{-9} meters or 4500 Angstrom units) — about midway between the violet and blue regions of the spectrum. When a foreign substance (i.e., a drug or alcohol) is metabolized via the MEOS, it combines with cytochrome P_{450}, whose heme group (see footnote 18) is in the maximally-oxidized or *trivalent* state — i.e., the iron atom carries three plus charges (or lacks three electrons) and is in the *ferric* charge state. The drug-cytochrome P_{450} complex that results (drug-$[Fe^{+++}]/P_{450}$; see Fig. 13) is then reduced to the *ferrous* or *divalent* charge state (drug-$[Fe^{++}]/P_{450}$ of Fig. 13) by the transfer of an electron (e^-) from the reduced flavoprotein, $FADH_2$. The ferrous cytochrome P_{450}-drug complex then splits molecular oxygen (O_2) by receiving a second electron plus two protons (hydrogen ions) from the NADPH-cytochrome c reductase-flavoprotein donor system in a series of poorly understood steps. The molecular oxygen is reduced to water and a charged radical of "active" oxygen (O•). This active oxygen then combines readily with the drug, oxidizing it to its metabolite.[58] Ethanol is oxidized via this system to acetaldehyde, yielding $NADP^+$ and water. Thus (Fig. 13).

The microsomal ethanol oxidizing system becomes more significant at higher blood alcohol concentrations. This is because the *Michaelis-Menten constants* or *Km* values of alcohol dehydrogenase and the MEOS are 0.26-2 mM and 8-10mM, respectively. In order to adequately understand the significance

---

[58]Although most substances are deactivated and rendered less harmful than the parent compound via the cytochrome P_{450} pathway, some agents such as the polycyclic aromatic hydrocarbons (compounds formed in the distillation of coal tar) are transformed into active and toxic substances with strong cancer-causing properties by a closely-related monoxygenase within the MFO system, *cytochrome P_{448}*. Many industrial chemicals such as most pesticides and the chlorinated biphenyls (PCBs) so ubiquitous in the environment undergo a *mixed type* of oxidation in the microsomes involving both cytochromes P_{450} and P_{448}. Most substances that are metabolized by themicrosomal enzymes are capable of markedly increasing the activity of those monoxygenases, a process known as *induction.* There are over 300 compounds now known to cause such microsomal induction (Casarett & Doull 1980). Interestingly, there is a much higher level of cytochrome P_{450} activity in males than in females (at least in the rat), and the difference appears to be androgen-related (see also footnote 72).

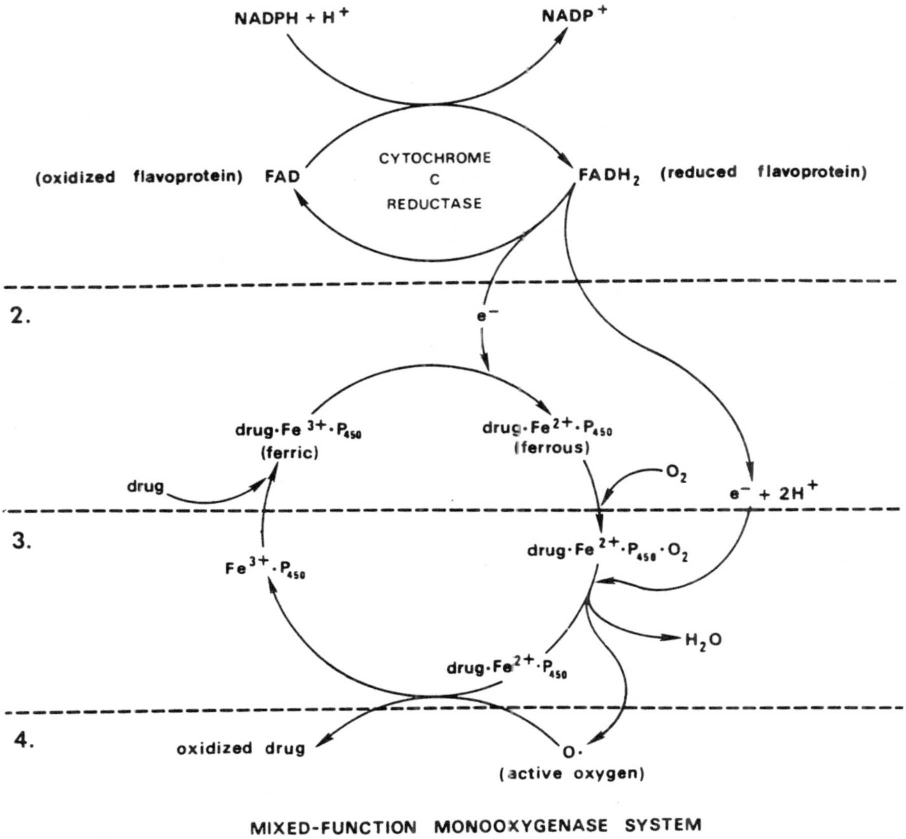

Figure 13. Mixed-function monoxygenase system (Microsomal Enzymes). See also footnote 72.

of these figures, it is necessary to discuss briefly the basic concepts of energy kinetics involved in enzyme reactions (see also Fig. 5).

Most enzymatic reactions are *first-order reactions* and go to completion at a rate proportional to the concentration of only one of the reacting substrates. Reactions may also be *zero-order,* in which case they proceed at a rate that is independent of the concentration of any to the reactants. *Second-order* and *third-order* reactions proceed at a rate proportional to the product of two or three reactants, respectively. Third-order reactions are very rare. Both the ADH and MEOS pathways represent first-order kinetics at low ethanol concentrations ($<$10-20 mg-percent[$=$10-20 mg ethanol per 100 ml blood]); above that range the rate of clearance is independent of the ethanol concentration and zero-order kinetics obtain. When a simple first-order reaction is considered:

$$A \longrightarrow B$$

the rate of reaction at time $t = \frac{-d[A]}{dt} = k[A]$ where *[A]* is the molar concentration of substrate A and $-d[A]/dt$ is the decreasing concentration of A; $k=$ the *rate constant.* Figure 14 shows the plot of a first order reaction:

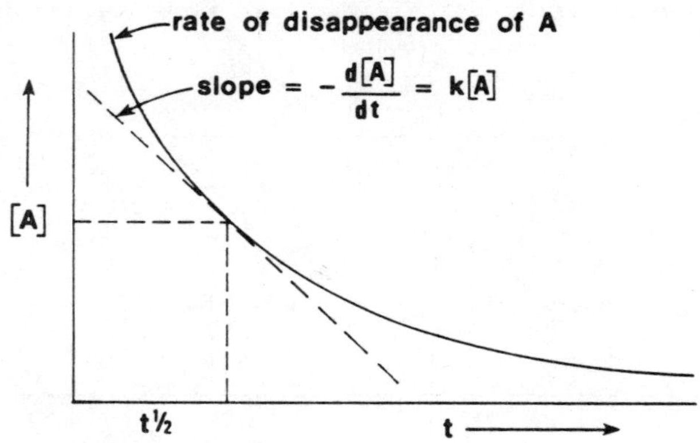

Figure 14. First-order enzyme kinetics. See text for details.

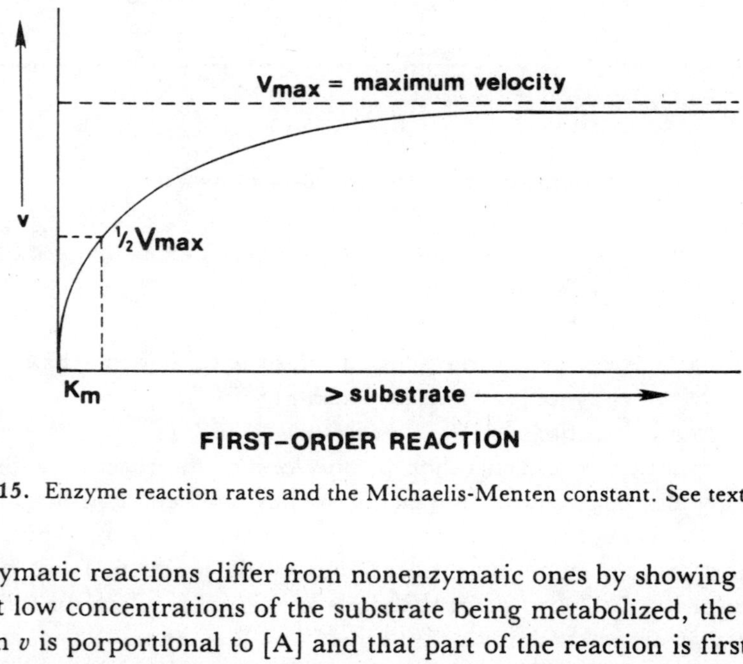

Figure 15. Enzyme reaction rates and the Michaelis-Menten constant. See text for details.

Enzymatic reactions differ from nonenzymatic ones by showing a *saturation effect:* at low concentrations of the substrate being metabolized, the velocity of reaction v is porportional to [A] and that part of the reaction is first-order. As the concentration of the substrate increases, the reaction rate increase is diminished, and is no longer exactly proportional to the concentration of the substrate. The reaction in this region is *mixed-order.* Finally, as the substrate concentration increases still further, the reaction rate becomes asymptototically constant and is now zero-order, being independent of the substrate concentration.

According to enzyme kinetic theory, the enzyme E first reacts with a substrate S to form an enzyme-substrate complex ES. This complex then undergoes a second reaction to form a free enzyme and a product or products P:

equilibrium
usually much faster Rx

$$E + S \underset{k_2}{\overset{k_1}{\rightleftharpoons}} ES$$

$$ES \underset{k_4}{\overset{k_3}{\rightleftharpoons}} E + P$$

usually slower
rate-limiting step

These reactions are reversible and k_n = the specific rate constant for the reaction indicated. When the reaction system is in equilibrium, that is, when the complex ES is being formed at the same rate that it is broken down and its net concentration remains constant and equal to that of the substrate, then:

$$\frac{[E]\bullet[S]}{[ES]} = \frac{k_2 + k_3}{k_1} = Km, \text{ or the Michaelis-Menten constant.}$$

It so happens that when $v = \frac{1}{2}\,Vmax$, *Km* (the combined constant) is equal to the substrate concentration at which the reaction velocity is exactly half of maximum (see Fig. 15). Thus, the higher the value of *Km,* the higher must be the concentration of the substrate for the reaction to proceed at 50 percent of maximum velocity. Therefore, the microsomal ethanol oxidizing system is relatively insignificant at low concentrations of the substrate ethanol, and the ADH pathway assumes the paramount role. However, as blood alcohol levels climb, the MEOS takes on an increasingly important role in the oxidation of ethanol. It will also be recalled that the MEOS pathway is NADPH-dependent (see Fig. 13), and as the concentration of reducing equivalents increases due to the oxidation of greater amounts of alcohol and acetaldehyde via the ADH and AcDH pathways, the redox state is shifted in favor of inducing oxidation through the microsomal monoxygenase system.

The rise in MEOS activity induced by chronic high blood alcohol levels can account for one-half to two-thirds of the observed increase in blood ethanol clearance reported in alcoholics exhibiting metabolic tolerance (Lieber 1978). The one-third to one-half increase in alcohol clearance from the blood not accounted for by increased MEOS activity may actually be due to a secondary increase in ethanol oxidation via the ADH pathway. As we have been, this pathway is limited by the rate at which NADH is reoxidized to NAD^+; since the MEOS is driven by oxidizing reduced NADPH to $NADP^+$, which in turn appears to derive some of its hydrogen equivalents from reduced NADH,[59] the enhanced operation of the MEOS would have the effect of reoxidizing both NADH and NADPH and generating additional NAD^+ cofactors to run the ADH and AcDH oxidizing pathways.

A class of very small microorganelles known as *peroxisomes* (see Fig. 12) are found in close association with the endoplasmic reticulum of all mammalian cell types, except for red blood cells. These bodies contain a number of oxidases important in the degradation of amino acids and purines and which yield hydrogen peroxide (H_2O_2) as a by-product. Since H_2O_2 is quite toxic, the peroxisomes also contain *catalase,* an enzyme which catalyzes its degradation to H_2O and O_2. Catalase has been shown to oxidize ethanol to acetaldehyde in the presence of H_2O_2, yielding water as a by-product. The role of peroxisomal catalase in the peroxidation of ethanol is minimal, however, and is limited by the amount of independently generated hydrogen peroxide. It accounts at best for less than 2 percent of the total *in vivo*[60] oxidation of ethanol, since the physiological rate of H_2O_2 generation does not exceed 2 percent of the total rate of ethanol oxidation and not all of that H_2O_2 can be used by the liver peroxisomes to peroxidize alcohol (Lieber 1978). Moreover, the *Km* value of alcohol for catalase is 25mM (Lehninger 1970), more than double that of the MEOS, and it can only come into play at fairly high blood alcohol concentrations. The consumption of large amounts of ethanol in itself can lead to increased levels of hydrogen peroxide by inducing enhanced activity of NADPH-oxidase secondarily due to the excess of reducing equivalents from ethanol oxidation via ADH:

$$NADPH + H^+ \xrightarrow[\text{NADPH-oxidase}]{} NADP^+ + H_2O_2$$

Ethanol itself can thus indirectly furnish some of the H_2O_2 needed for the peroxidation of ethanol by catalase. However, the hepatic oxygen concentration is less than 50 uM[61] — far too inadequate for significant production of

[59]NADH itself appears to serve directly as a partial electron donor for the MEOS via transhydrogenation (Lieber 1978), and the two systems are also otherwise linked, despite the fact that NADPH normally is generated primarily by the hexose monophosphate shunt (see also Fig. 26).

[60]*In vivo* means occurring inside the living organism, in contrast to experiments performed *in vitro,* or in an artificial culture medium outside the organism.

[61]M stands for *molar solution,* or moles per liter. One mole of a substance or compound is equal to its molecular weight in grams; mM = millimoles (10^{-3} moles) per liter, and uM = micromoles (10^{-6} moles) per liter.

H_2O_2, which has a *Km* of 100 mM for oxygen (Lieber 1978). Finally, the use of catalase inhibitors has shown that no observable change in ethanol metabolism occurs when this pathway is suppressed, either *in vivo* or *in vitro* (Cornish 1980). In summary, the amount of ethanol peroxidized by the catalase pathway is insignificant.

The chronic ingestion of significant amounts of ethanol results in a marked increase in microsomal monoxygenase activity, as we have seen. This is accompanied by a proliferation of the membranes of the smooth endoplasmic reticulum (SER) which is readily observable under the electron microscope. This proliferation of SER is certainly partly responsible for the increased tolerance to various drugs typically shown by alcoholics.[62] Alcoholics and heavy drinkers show enhanced blood clearance rates for a number of drugs which are oxidized via the microsomal cytochrome P_{450} pathway. Likewise, the dangerous effects of carbon tetrachloride which result from its biotransformation by cytochrome P_{450} into a toxic metabolite (see above) is greatly exacerbated in alcoholics. However, such increased metabolic clearance of microsomally oxidized agents only occurs in the absence of significant concentrations of ethanol – i.e., in "sober" or abstinent alcoholics. When these drugs are taken concurrently with alcohol, the oxidation of the former is usually considerably reduced due to competitive displacement of the drug from the cytochrome P_{450} binding sites by ethanol, and high levels of the drug are maintained in the blood for protracted periods. This phenomenon appears to be at least partially responsible for the enhanced effect that two or more sedative-hypnotic agents have on the organism. All of the sedative-hypnotics *potentiate* the depressive effects of alcohol on the CNS.[63] This combined effect which occurs when agents like the benzodiazepines (Valium®, Librium®, Dalmane®) or the barbiturates are taken together with alcohol may cause a fatal respiratory depression.

It has been suggested that ethanol acts to suppress the metabolism of other drugs by a nonspecific disturbance of the microsomal membranes, resulting in their expansion and enhanced fluidity (Khanna et al. 1980). This would result in decreased binding and hence oxidation of those drugs. These authors further believe that ethanol does not displace other drugs from the cytochrome P_{450} binding sites, and that alcohol does not even induce enhanced microsomal enzyme activity. They assert that catalase peroxidation plays the most important role in the non-ADH medicated oxidation of ethanol. However, the evidence clearly indicates that catalase plays only an insignificant role and that the induction of the MEOS or cytochrome P_{450} monoxygenases accounts for the vast

---

[62]This enhanced tolerance to other drugs is also due to CNS adaptation. However, increased blood clearance is also a major factor since decreased drug sensitivity occurs *prior* to CNS tolerance.

[63]Two drugs acting in concert are *additive* when their combined effect is proportional to their respective concentrations [i.e., 1 + 1 = 2]; they are *synergistic* or *potentiate* each other when their combined effect greatly exceeds that to be expected from their respective concentrations [i.e., 1 + 1 = 5].

majority of non-ADH medicated oxidation of ethanol. This latter view is also accepted by the majority of investigators in the field. The fact that the metabolism of other drugs is reduced in acute intoxication but enhanced in abstinent alcoholics strongly suggests that competition for cytochrome P_{450} binding sites is the major factor. Nonetheless, ethanol has been clearly shown to generally alter membrane fluidity, but the role of such membrane disruption in altered microsomal drug metabolism is not clear.

Membrane disruption due to chronic alcohol abuse does result in severely disorganized liver cell mitochondria and this is associated with an impaired ability to oxidize acetaldehyde, which occurs primarily in those organelles. This may be exacerbated by impaired reoxidation of NADH to NAD^+ which is rate limiting for both alcohol and aldehyde dehydrogenase activity, and which is also dependent upon intact mitochondria.[64,65] This phenomenon is undoubtedly related to the fact that alcoholics consistently show elevated blood acetaldehyde levels over nonalcoholic controls at any given blood concentration of ethanol (Lieber 1978). These high blood acetaldehyde levels in alcoholics are probably augmented by increased microsomal ethanol oxidation resulting in still more acetaldehyde. Both chronic alcohol insult and high acetaldehyde levels cause mitochondrial membrane disruption and impairment of the processes occurring there. The resulting inhibition of acetaldehyde metabolism further increases the already high blood acetaldehyde concentrations, which further injures the mitochondria, and so forth in a "vicious cycle" (Lieber 1978).

Figure 16 shows the relationships between the various ethanol oxidizing pathways in the liver cells as they are presently understood.

LIVER PATHOLOGY DUE TO CHRONIC ALCOHOL ABUSE

The basic anatomical relationship between the liver cells, their blood supply and the bile system was first described in 1833, and these relationships were presumed to represent the basic functional unit of the liver. The terminology

[64]A mixture of chloral hydrate [$CCl_3CH(OH)_2$] and ethanol; the *Mickey Finn* or *knockout drops* are popularly thought to be extremely toxic and to produce almost instant coma in rather small amounts. Although the two are at least additive (and probably synergistic – Goodman & Gilman 1975) when mixed, controlled studies have shown that the combination is not potent enough to produce the effect described in popular lore. Death and serious CNS depression can occur from mixing these two drugs because of the synergy between them, but they constitute no more effective a knockout potion than does any other combination of powerful CNS depressants. Interestingly, chloral hydrate, itself an alcohol, is not oxidized by the microsomes, but competes with alcohol for the ADH-pathway.

[65]The shuttle system by which hydrogen equivalents are transferred from one cofactor to another are dependent on the mitochondria; the electron transport chain (see Fig. 7) where these hydrogen equivalents are utilized in *oxidative phosphorylation* – the process whereby ADP is converted to ATP – is also located in the mitochondria.

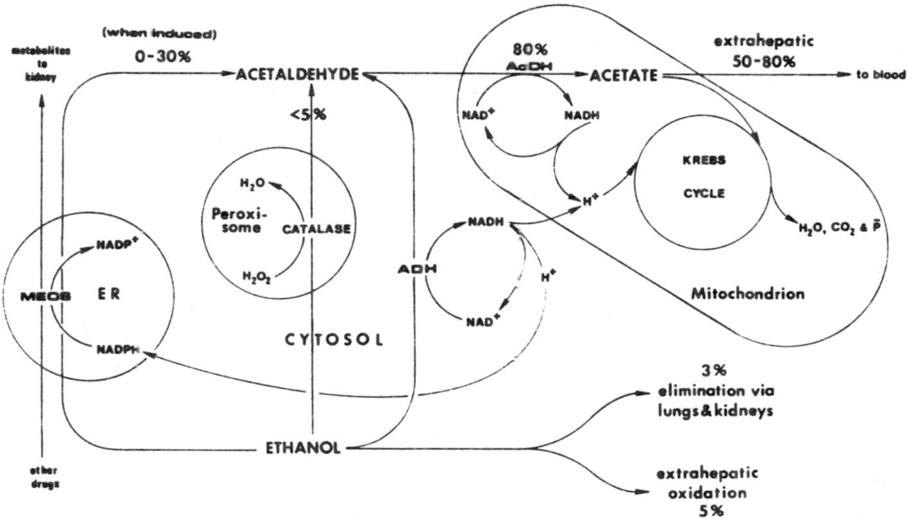

Figure 16. Oxidative pathways for ethanol metabolism. Percentages indicate relative fraction of *in vivo* metabolized ethanol. Adapted from Lieber and DeCarli 1978 and Higgins 1979.

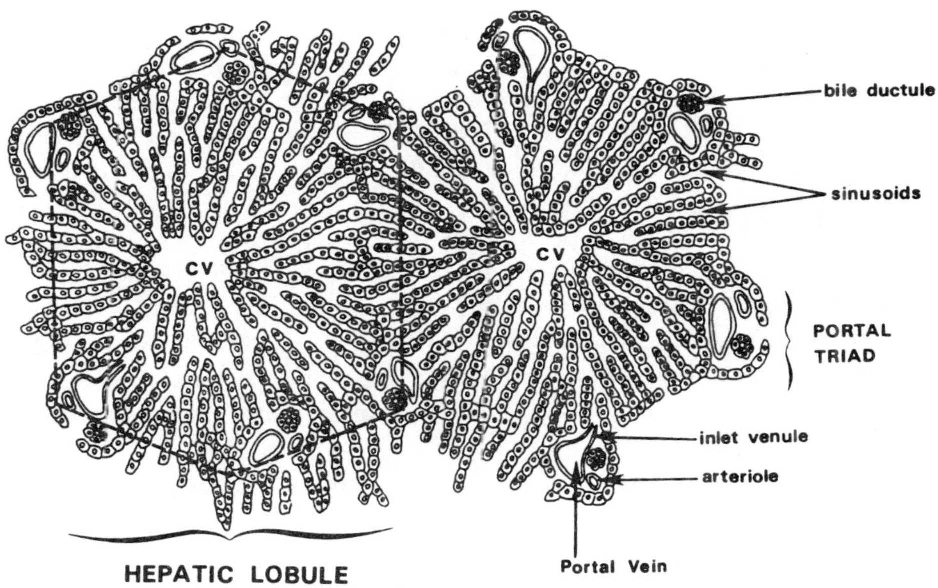

Figure 17. Classical hexagonal structural hepatic lobule. CV = central hepatic vein.

associated with hepatotoxicity was derived from this classical anatomical model of the basic liver unit, and this terminology is still widely employed at the present time. However, recent investigations have shown that the true functional relationships of the liver components do not correspond to the classical structural model as it was originally proposed (and as it is still presented in a great many "current" textbooks). Because the disparity between the presently understood functional liver unit and the still-employed terminology based upon the classical anatomical model are often confusing, it is necessary to present a brief discussion of both approaches in an attempt to integrate them. A cross reference to Figures 11 and 12 and the corresponding text sections will help to make the concepts presented here more comprehensible.

According to the classical model, the liver is composed of a vast number of hexagonal (in cross section) *hepatic lobules,* each about 1 mm in diameter and consisting of a centrally located *hepatic venule* or *central vein* (a tributary of the hepatic vein, see Fig. 11) and several peripheral *portal triads* (Fig. 17). Each portal triad contains a distributary branch of the portal vein, a *hepatic arteriole,* and a *bile ductule.*[66] Although in man and most other mammals these lobules are not anatomically separated from each other, in the pig (commonly used for anatomical studies) each hepatic lobule is separated from its neighbors by fibrous *septa* or partitions; such fibrous connective tissue would be evidence of a pathological liver cirrhosis in most other mammalian species, including man. The classical hepatic lobule represents the functional unit of the liver from the perspective of flow *out from* the liver via the hepatic vein system as the central structure.

In the physiologically more accurate model the functional hepatic unit is the *liver acinus* or *portal lobule* (Fig. 18), which consists of a now centrally placed portal triad where three adjacent hepatic lobules unite, along with two or more peripheral hepatic venules and the contained liver *parenchyma* or cellular mass. Actually, the acini are irregularly polygonal in shape and they lie between two or more terminal hepatic venules. The "hexagonal lobule" does not really exist as such (Rappaport 1975). There is likewise no physical separation between adjacent liver acini, and they represent merely a functional unit based upon the perspective of flow *into* the liver via the portal vein and the arterioles. The classical anatomical model is based upon the terminal hepatic venule (still termed the *central vein* by many authors, including frequently this one) as the central structure, whereas the portal lobule or liver acinus is based upon a centrally located portal triad.

The hepatocytes are arranged as a series of laminae or plates one cell thick forming a continuous network throughout the liver. Histological sections through hepatic lobules (Fig. 17) with their apparent "rows" of cells radiating from the hepatic venule really represent cross sections through these laminae (Fig. 19).[67] Blood laden with the products of digestion is conveyed from the

---

[66]Arterioles, venules and ductules are merely very small branches of arteries, veins, and ducts, respectively.

[67]These cells do not really radiate out in straight lines, but wander somewhat irregularly because of the branched and anastomosing nature of the laminae.

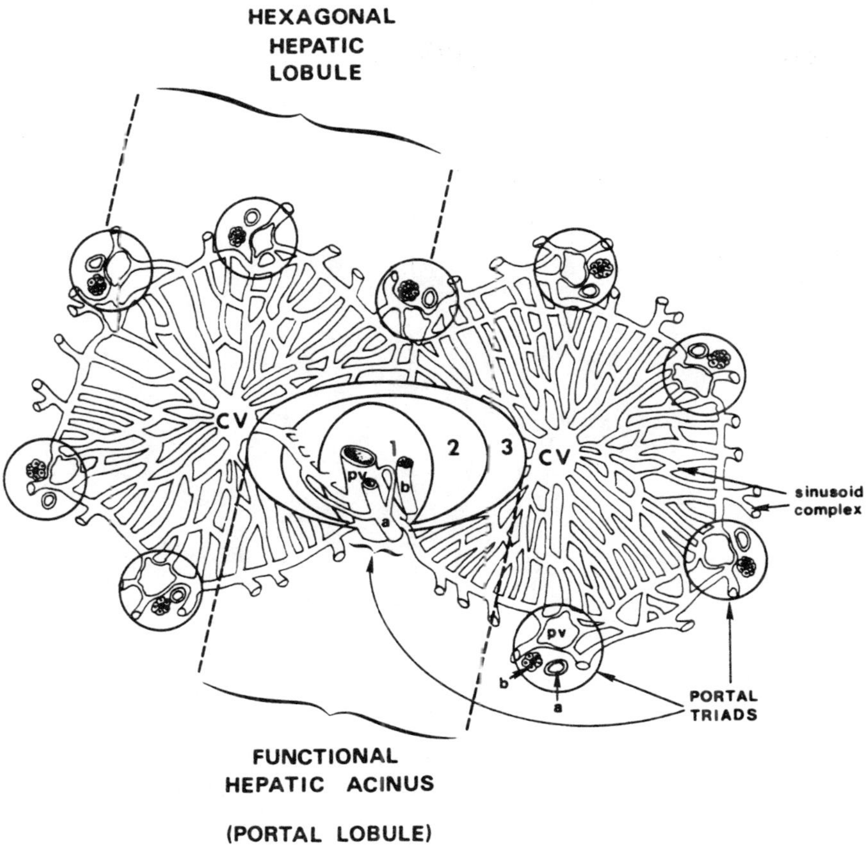

Figure 18. Functional hepatic acinus (portal lobule). CV = central vein; pv = portal vein; a = arteriole; b = bile duct; the numbers 1-3 refer to circulatory zones: zone 1 shows maximum activity of respiratory (mitochondrial) enzymes, whereas zone 3 shows maximum microsomal activity. Adapted and modified from Scheuer 1980 and Casarett & Doull 1980.

small intestine to the liver via the hepatic portal vein (Fig. 11). In the liver the portal vein divides and subdivides into innumerable branches called *inlet venules* (Fig. 19) which enter the hepatic lobules and become continuous with the sinusoids (part of the hepatic sinus complex) lying between the hepatic laminae. The digestive products are taken up by the individual hepatocytes for further metabolism and waste products are excreted by the hepatocytes into the blood. This "spent" blood is then transported by the sinusoids to the hepatic venules (central veins), which join together into larger *sublobular veins,* which in turn coalesce into the hepatic veins draining the blood into the inferior vena cava for transport to the heart (see Fig. 11). The tiny *bile canaliculi* (see also Fig. 12) surround each hepatocyte on those surfaces not juxtaposed to the venous sinusoids (Fig. 19). The bile canaliculi are located close to the Golgi bodies within the

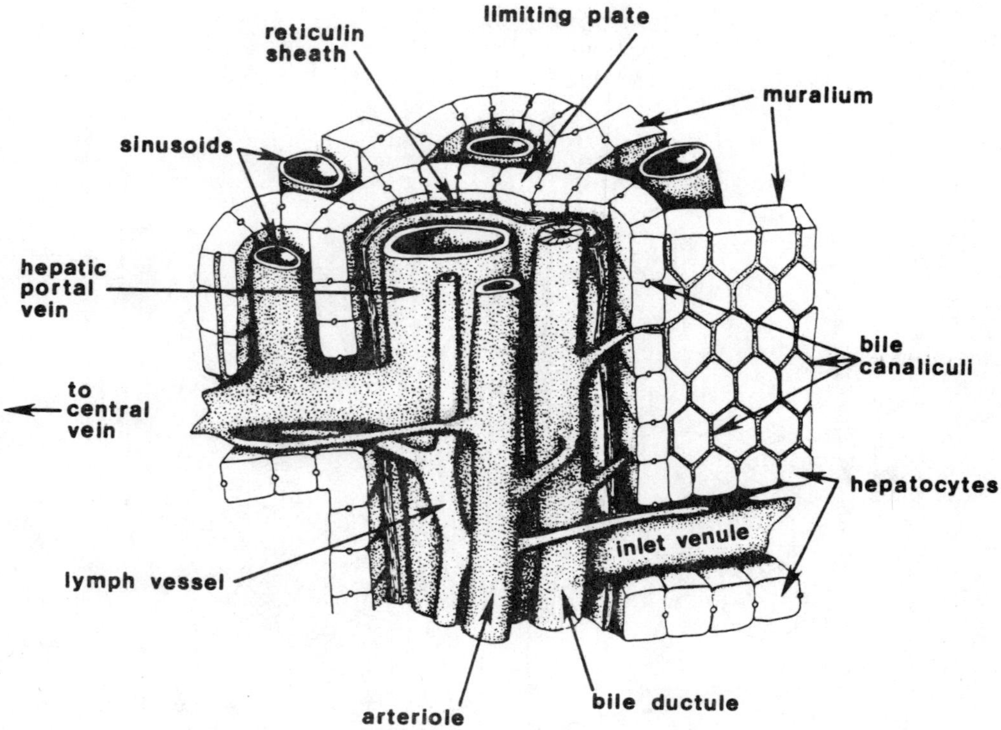

Figure 19. Three-dimensional view of liver structure. The single-thickness "wallwork" of hepatocytes is collectively termed the *muralium;* where this wallwork surrounds a portal triad it is called the *limiting plate.* The portal triad is surrounded by a sheath of connective tissue — *reticulin* or *type III collagen.* Such a sheath is absent from around the central veins. Deoxygenated blood laden with digestion products flows from the gut into the liver where it comes into direct contact with the hepatocytes. It flows out of the liver via the hepatic vein into the inferior vena cava and thence into the heart. The hepatic arterioles bring freshly oxygenated blood from the lungs and heart into the hepatic acini (see Fig. 18), each arteriole supplying its own limited acinus. The liver sinusoids thus carry both oxygenated and deoxygenated blood to the central veins whence it passes into the hepatic veins. This results in a series of graded circulatory zones (see Fig. 18) of differing oxygen tensions and enzyme activities. After H. Elias and A. M. Rappaport. Adapted and modified from Warwick & Williams 1973 and Scheuer 1980.

liver cells (Fig. 12), and they drain the bile salts secreted by these organelles into the bile ductules located within the *portal canals* as part of the portal triad. The bile is then taken to the gallbladder (see Fig. 11) via the hepatic and cystic ducts where it is stored until needed to emulsify fats in the intestine. The hepatic arterioles within the portal canals give rise to branches entering both the inlet venules and the venous sinusoids. The sinusoids thus carry both deoxygenated venous blood and oxygenated arterial blood which feeds the hepatocytes. The hepatic arterioles also supply oxygenated blood to the portal canal structures. Each portal triad, consisting of the portal venule, bile ductule, and the hepatic arteriole and their respective distributaries, supplies its own limited region — the portal lobular area or hepatic acinus — and there are usually no interconnections between adjacent acini (Fig. 18). In contrast, the hepatic or central veins form a complex anastomosing network which freely crosses over from one hepatic and/or portal lobule to another. Because mixed venous and arterial blood from the portal triad are received by the peripheral[68] liver cells first and only subsequently by the parenchyma adjacent to the central or hepatic venule, an uneven distribution of oxygen and digestive substrates is found within the lobules and the most *hypoxic* (low oxygen) conditions occur around the hepatic venule.

The portal lobule or acinus thus consists of a concentric series of circulatory zones (see Fig. 18), each showing a graded differential in enzyme activities. Zone 1, lying next to the portal canal, exhibits the highest activity of respiratory (mitochondrial) enzymes, including those of the Krebs cycle and the electron transport mechanism. This corresponds to the relatively higher degree of oxygenation in that zone. Zone 3, lying most distant from the portal triad and immediately adjacent to the hepatic venule, shows the highest microsomal enzyme activity. Notice that zone 1 corresponds to the "peripheral" region of the classical anatomical liver unit (the hepatic lobule) and zone 3 is located "centrally." Because of this, lesions[69] of the liver parenchyma found in zone 3 are traditionally termed *centrilobular* even though they lie peripheral to the *de facto* physiological or "functional" unit, the portal lobule or liver acinus. Lesions in zone 1 are called *periportal* (around the portal) and those in zone 2 *midzonal* lesions. The inflammations that occur in liver cells frequently lead to cell death or *necrosis*. Unicellular and very small necroses are usually randomly distributed throughout the liver and are not associated with any of the circulatory regions of the lobules. These are called *focal necroses*. More commonly, necroses are more extensive and *zonal* in distribution, and they may also be termed centrilobular, midzonal, or periportal.

Hepatotoxic agents may be classified as *intrinsic* or *host idiosyncratic*. Intrinsic hepatotoxins cause injury in nearly all individuals exposed to *threshold* or minimal effective doses, whereas host idiosyncratic hepatotoxins only induce injury in a few hypersensitive or idiosyncratically reactive individuals.[70] Carbon tetrachloride is an intrinsic hepatotoxin which produces massive liver necrosis in all individuals exposed to standard effective concentrations or doses; chlorpromazine (Thorazine®) is an example of a host idiosyncratic agent which causes adverse reactions in only a very small number of hyperreactive persons who are given the drug.

[68]That is, peripheral relative to the classical hepatic lobular model.

[69]The term *lesion* refers to any tissue abnormality or pathology of any kind.

[70]Host idiosyncratic hepatotoxicity is *not* dose-dependent and the results cannot be reliably reproduced in expermiental animals.

Intrinsic toxicants may be (1) *direct,* causing damage to tissues and organs in addition to the liver and producing injury to most or all of the subcellular organelles, or (2) *indirect,* causing liver cell damage by disrupting specific metabolic pathways. Both direct and indirect hepatotoxins are dose-dependent, but the former generally requires much shorter exposure times and the effects are more reliably reproduced experimentally. Ethanol acts both directly by damaging membranes and subcellular organelles of nearly all tissues and organs, and indirectly by disrupting selective biochemical and metabolic pathways in the hepatocytes.

Hepatotoxins may be (1) *cytotoxic,* causing focal or zonal necrosis, (2) *cholestatic,* producing bile flow obstruction or inhibition often leading to jaundice, or (3) *mixed,* resulting in both necrosis and cholestasis. Cholestatic liver disease is in itself usually relatively mild, and when unaccompanied by necrosis generally remits when the precipitating agent is removed. Necrosis is far more dangerous and when severe enough can lead to liver cirrhosis, liver failure, and death. Cholestasis is a general term referring to partial or total bile flow obstruction at any point from the hepatocyte to the common bile duct draining into the duodenum. *Extrahepatic cholestasis* is caused by stenosis or constriction of the left and/or right hepatic ducts, the common bile duct, or the *ampulla of Vater* (the enlarged chamber formed by the junction of the common bile duct and the pancreatic duct just prior to their joining the duodenum – also termed the *ampulla hepatopancreatica*). *Intrahepatic cholestasis* results when conjugated bilirubin (bilirubin glucuronide) is prevented from passing out of the hepatocyte into the bile canaliculi. Cytotoxic damage to the hepatocyte can result in reduced cellular uptake of extrahepatically generated bilirubin, causing a buildup of bilirubin in the blood *(hyperbilirubinemia).*[71] Normally the bilirubin-albumin bond of the circulating complex (see footnote 71) is broken at the surface of the plasma membrane of the hepatocyte and the bilirubin moiety then passes into the cytosol where it appears to be attached to acceptor proteins. The exact mechanism whereby this process is impaired is poorly understood, but it occurs in certain genetic disorders and toxic drug responses. Cytotoxic damage to the smooth endoplasmic reticulum of the hepatocytes can block the conjugation of bilirubin to bilirubin glucuronide by the *glucuronyl transferase*

[71]Unconjugated bilirubin is water insoluble. It is conjugated into bilirubin glucuronide (or more accurately, bilirubin diglucuronide) by the SER and is then excreted by the hepatocyte into the bile canaliculi for transport to the gallbladder. Lecithin, bile salts and acids are added by cells lining the bile ducts. About 85 percent of the bilirubin is formed by red blood cell destruction in the *reticuloendothelial system,* which consists of *phagocytes* or "eater" white blood cells *(leukocytes* and *lymphocytes)* in the bone marrow and lymph nodes and lining the sinusoids of the liver and spleen. The remainder is produced as a by-product of hemoglobin synthesis in the bone marrow and from the turnover of certain heme-bearing cytochromes and other enzymes in the liver. Extrahepatically-generated bilirubin is immediately bound to circulating *albumin* (a water-soluble, heat-coagulable protein) forming a lipid-soluble complex which allows the bilirubin fraction to pass through the cell membranes of the hepatocytes.

pathway.[72] The common result of all these conditions is *jaundice* or *icterus,* a yellowish discoloration of the skin and especially of the white of the eyes or *sclera* due to an accumulation of bilirubin in the tissues and body fluids. The sclerae are particularly prone to exhibit jaundice because of their rich abundance of elastic fibers for which bilirubin has a strong affinity. Both conjugated and unconjugated bilirubin are typically elevated in most cases of jaundice, and jaundice is observed in all types of liver insult involving severe cellular damage. Intrahepatically caused hyperbilirubinemia results from (1) impaired uptake of bilirubin by the hepatocytes, (2) diminished bilirubin conjugation by the smooth endoplasmic reticulum, and (3) impaired excretion of conjugated bilirubin across plasma membranes of the liver cells into the bile canaliculi. Extrahepatic cholestasis results from bile flow blockage due to cytotoxically induced hepatocytic inflammation and lipid accumulation (see below), as well as to obstruction of the bile passages by pancreatic inflammation and cirrhotic scarring of the liver parenchyma. The distinctions between intrahepatic and extrahepatic cholestasis and between cholestatic and cytotoxic mechanisms is rather blurred and arbitrary, and they generally occur together.

Alcohol-induced liver damage occurs in several well defined stages. Initially, a mild to severe and largely reversible *fatty liver* develops in which vacuoles of fat appear in the cytoplasm of the hepatocytes. With continued long-term heavy drinking, a far more serious and not always reversible condition known as *alcoholic hepatitis* occurs in 10-20 percent of alcoholic patients, characterized by cellular inflammation and death (necrosis) – the necrosis represents an irreversible condition, and morality rates range from 10-30 percent (Lieber and DeCarli 1978). Massive cell death results in *fibrosis* or scarring of the liver parenchyma by fibrous connective tissue, an irreversible condition known as *cirrhosis.* Far advanced cirrhosis results in distortion of the normal liver architecture (see Figs. 28 & 29), the liver develops a finely modular pattern of regenerating cells and intervening network of scar tissue (the so-called *hobnail pattern*) and the entire organ shrinks to a small, hard, fibrotic mass weighing less than 1200 grams (Robbins 1974).

---

[72]Most *xenobiotics* (foreign compounds) and endogenous substrates requiring metabolic clearance (such as bilirubin and steroids) are *lipophilic* or fat soluble and they undergo a complex detoxification process divided into two phases. Phase I involves the introduction of a highly reactive polar group into the parent compound, and the most important Phase I system is the cytochrome P_{450} pathway (see Fig. 13). Phase I reactions do render the molecule more water-soluble, but their primary purpose is to produce a *reactive intermediate* for Phase II reactions. Phase II reactions are the so-called *conjugation reactions* in which the transformed reactive intermediate is combined with an endogenous substrate such as glucuronic acid to produce a highly water-soluble metabolite that is readily excreted in the urine or bile. The synthesis of *glucuronides* (derivatives of glucuronic acid) via glucuronyl transferase is one of the major Phase II pathways. Glucuronide-substrate complexes are excreted in the bile or urine, depending upon the size of the compound and thus its water-solubility. Larger, less water-soluble substrates tend to be eliminated in the bile. Phase II enzymes may be found either in the microsomal fraction (such as glucuronyl transferase) or in the cytosol (glutathione S-transferase and sulfotransferase, for example).

FATTY LIVER

Fatty liver is defined as one having a lipid content greater than 5 percent by weight (Kulkarni & Hodgson 1980), and it represents an absolute increase in the amount of intracellular lipid. It first appears as small vacuoles of fat in the cytoplasm surrounding the nucleus of the hepatocytes, often in acinar zones 2 and 3, and as fat accumulation progresses, the vacuoles join to form large cleared spaces displacing the nucleus to one side and causing most of the rest of the cellular matrix to be eliminated. It is often accompanied by moderate to severe swelling of the hepatocyte resulting in cholestasis due to blockage of the bile canaliculi and bile obstruction in the hepatocytes. There is often associated proliferation of the endoplasmic reticulum and mitochondrial engorgement (Becker et al. 1974) due to the disrupting effect of ethanol on membrane systems. Enhanced protein synthesis is also a contributing factor. During this early stage of liver disease, the fat may appear and disappear rapidly depending upon the alcohol intake. As fat deposition becomes severe, the nuclei may be destroyed and the cells killed. Adjacent cells may rupture and coalesce to form fatty cysts known as *lipogranulomas*. Such cysts represent necrotic foci. In a small percentage of heavy drinkers, fatty liver is accompanied by periportal fibrosis accompanied by bile duct proliferation within the fibrous septa. Such portal fibrosis probably accounts for the term *portal cirrhosis* sometimes applied to advanced alcoholic liver disease. However, alcoholic hepatitis and the cirrhosis it induces begin as centrilobular lesions, and the periportal fibrosis seen with fatty liver changes appears to be due to other causes such as pancreatitis (Scheuer 1980).

With advanced fatty liver disease such as is seen in many chronic alcoholics, the liver may become grossly enlarged *(hepatomegaly)*, increasingly yellow in color and greasy in texture. In extreme cases the organ may be bright yellow and weigh up to 5 or 6 kilos (Robbins 1974).[73]

A brief discussion of the normal triglyceride or fat cycle is necessary in order to fully understand the various processes involved in the pathogenesis of alcohol-induced fatty liver disease and associated complications. A review of the treatment of triglycerides will clarify the present discussion. Triglycerides are neutral fats made up of three fatty acids (see Fig. 2) covalently bound to a glycerol molecule. Fatty acids contain both a carbonyl and a hydroxyl group, and they may be *saturated* or *unsaturated*. Saturated fatty acids have no double bonds between adjacent carbon atoms in the chain — that is, all available attachment sites on each carbon are occupied by hydrogen atoms. Fatty acids are unsaturated when all available sites on the carbons are not occupied by

[73]The normal liver is dark reddish-brown and weighs about 1½ kilos.

hydrogen atoms, resulting in double bonds between adjacent carbons.[74] The structural formula for a triglyceride is:

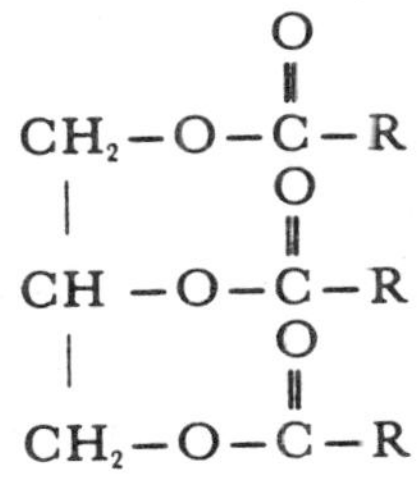

in which R, as usual, represents the side chain.

Triglycerides are hydrolyzed in the small intestine into short- and long-chain fatty acids as previously discussed. The short-chain fatty acids are absorbed directly into the blood and transported to the liver. Long-chain fatty acids are re-esterified into triglycerides in the intestinal mucosa and carried into the lymphatic system in chylomicrons and thence to all parts of the body where they are deposited out in the various fat depots by the action of the enzyme *lipoprotein lipase.* Free fatty acids are complexed to albumin (see footnote 71) and mobilized from the fat depots and adipose tissue and transported to the liver via the blood, where they may be oxidized in the TCA (Krebs) cycle or re-esterified into triglycerides. Free fatty acids, phospholipids (esters of a glycerol molecule and two fatty acids plus a phosphate group) and sterols (cholesterol derivatives, see Fig. 3, including bile acids and many hormones) all circulate in the blood bound to their respective *apoproteins* or *apolipoproteins,*[75] forming lipid-protein complexes known as *lipoproteins* which render the nonpolar and hydrophobic lipid molecules soluble in the watery blood medium. The free fatty acids, as mentioned previously, are released from the adipose depots and transported in the blood bound to albumin. The water insoluble triglycerides are combined with cholesterol esters which form a central core wrapped in an envelope composed of more polar phospholipids, cholesterol, and apoproteins. These lipoproteins exhibit different densities depending upon the amounts of lipid they contain and the relative sizes of the protein moiety. Since fat is less dense than water, the greater the lipid portion of a lipoprotein, the larger will be the volume and the smaller the density of the entire complex. Apart from the free fatty acids (FFA) and the complexes they form with albumin, there are four major classes of lipoproteins: (1) *chylomicrons,* which we have previously encountered — they are formed in the gut wall and are sometimes called *exogenous lipoproteins* because the lipid they carry is derived from dietary fat; (2) *very low density lipoproteins (VLDL or pre-beta-lipoproteins);* (3) *low density lipoproteins (LDL or beta-lipoproteins);* and (4) *high density lipoproteins (HDL or alpha-*

---

[74]This does *not* refer to the double bond in the carbonyl group, $R-\overset{\overset{O}{\|}}{C}-OH$, of the fatty acid.

[75]The protein moieties of lipoproteins; apoproteins are also called *carrier proteins.*

lipoproteins). VLDL, LDL, and HDL are sometimes referred to as *endogenous lipoproteins* because the lipid they transport is not derived directly from dietary fat, but comes from the *de novo* synthesis of triglycerides from fatty acids in the liver — involving either free fatty acids (FFA) mobilized from adipose tissue or synthesized from carbohydrate precursors. To a lesser extent, the endogenous lipoproteins are also synthesized in the gut. Those lipoproteins with the lowest densities also contain the highest triglyceride loads, and those with the highest densities bear the smallest amounts of triglyceride. As the triglyceride load decreases, the percentage composition of the other lipid constituents (phospholipids, free cholesterol, and cholesterol esters) correspondingly increases.

Chylomicrons are the largest of these complexes with diameters of 0.075-1 μm (micrometers) and they are just visible under the optical compound microscope. They also have the lowest density and the highest triglyceride content (75-90%). Very low density lipoproteins are somewhat smaller and less dense than chylomicrons, although their diameters (0.015-0.075μm) overlap those of the lower end of the chylomicron range. The amount of triglyceride carried by the VLDL is in the range of 50-56 percent. Low density lipoproteins and high density lipoproteins have diameters generally under 0.02 and 0.01 μm, respectively, and they both carry triglyceride loads of 5-9 percent.

The apoproteins associated with the lipoproteins have been classified on the basis of their molecular weight, the number of amino acids and presence or absence of carbohydrate residues, and the particular amino acid attached to the *C-terminal* position.[76] These apoproteins are named according to "ABC nonmenclature" as follows:

(1) *apoprotein A ("apo-A")* — the main apoprotein in HLD — also found in chylomicrons.
(2) *apoprotein B ("apo-B")* — the main apoprotein in LDL — also found in VLDL and chylomicrons.
(3) *apoprotein C ("apo-C")* — found in HDL, VLDL and chylomicrons.

The C apoproteins are freely transferable between VLDL and chylomicrons and between VLDL and HDL. One of them, apoprotein C-II, is a necessary cofactor in the activation of lipoprotein lipase (see below). There are several

[76]About 300 amino acids occur in nature, of which only 20 are found in the proteins of living systems. These same 20 amino acids occur in all animal, plant, and microbial forms. They are designated as alpha-amino acids because they bear a terminal carbon atom, the alpha-carbon, to which is attached an amino group and a carboxyl group. This position is known as the C-terminal position:

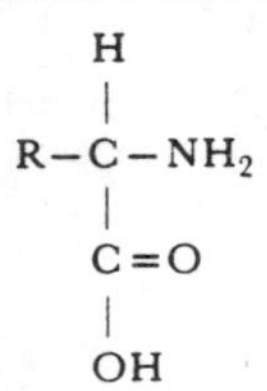

other proteins found in plasma lipoproteins whose role in triglyceride metabolism is not directly pertinent to this discussion. The protein fractions of the lipoproteins may constitute nearly 60 percent of some HDL or as little as 1-2 percent of the chylomicrons.

To summarize, chylomicrons are formed only in the intestinal wall, from which they carry triglycerides re-esterfied from dietary long-chain fatty acids via the lymphatic system into the blood stream through the thoracic duct. These triglycerides are then deposited in various fat depots throughout the body by the action of the enzyme lipoprotein lipase (a triglyceride esterase also known as *clearing factor*) upon the chylomicrons. This enzyme, located in the walls of the blood capillaries in a variety of tissues, but especially in the extensive capillaries of adipose tissue, requires the following cofactors in order to be activated: apoprotein C-II, phospholipid, insulin, and *heparin,* an anticlotting agent found abundantly in certain white blood cells (basophils) and wandering mast cells. The dietary short-chain fatty acids are taken directly into the intestinal capillaries and carried to the liver. Albumin-bound free fatty acids are constantly released from the fat storage depots and carried by the blood to the liver where they are oxidized as fuel or re-esterified into triglycerides. Triglycerides are also generated in the liver from dietary carbohydrates or from glucose mobilized from glycogen or synthesized via gluconeogenesis. These newly synthesized triglycerides are then transported in the plasma by VLDL and deposited out in the well-vascularized adipose tissue and other fat depots. As in the case of the chylomicrons, this deposition depends upon the action of lipoprotein lipase which cleaves one triglyceride molecule into one glycerol molecule and three fatty acid molecules. Two of the fatty acid molecules are incorporated into the *adipocytes* (*lipocytes,* or fat storage cells of the adipose tissue), and the remaining fatty acid is liberated into the plasma together with the glycerol molecule (Scheig 1979). In this case, too, heparin, insulin, phospholipid, and apoprotein C-II are necessary cofactors.

As triglyceride is removed from the chylomicrons and VLDL, these particles become progressively smaller and they accumulate free cholesterol and phospholipid on their surfaces. Since free cholesterol inhibits the action of lipoprotein lipase, it is converted into cholesterol ester by a second enzyme which is bound to the surface of HDL, *lecithin-cholesterol acyl transferase* or *LCAT.* The cholesterol ester thus formed is taken up by HDL and transported to the liver where it is either recycled or excreted in the bile.[77] The action of LCAT requires another activator from HDL, apoprotein A-I, and it permits the continued hydrolysis of triglyceride from the shrinking VLDL until they are reduced to

[77]HDL are synthesized both in the liver and intestine and they are thought to be the major vehicle whereby cholesterol is transported in its ester form from the extrahepatic tissues (such as in the arterial walls where it contributes to the development of atherosclerosis and coronary heart disease) to the liver for elimination. See also the discussion below on HDL heterogeneity.

small remnants about 0.03 μm in diameter.[78] By this time, apo-C has been removed from the VLDL remnants and transferred to HDL.[79] The VLDL remnants undergo final hydrolysis in the liver of the small amount of triglyceride remaining, a reaction catalyzed and still another enzyme, ***hepatic lipase.*** The final product of VLDL catabolism is LDL or beta-lipoprotein, and a portion of the VLDL apoproteins (apo-C) has been transferred to HDL for possible recycling back into chylomicrons or new VLDL. The LDL is removed from the plasma by the liver, broken down still further, and eliminated in the bile acids. The complex triglyceride cycle is illustrated in Figure 20.

A number of factors influence the rate of mobilization of FFA from adipose tissue storage depots. Stimulation of the pituitary-adrenal axis causes the release of *glucocorticoids* from the adrenal cortex and *catecholamines* from the adrenal medulla. These hormones stimulate a number of different lipases in the adipose sites into lipolytic activity, resulting in FFA liberation. Almost any physiological or even psychological stress to the organism can bring this system into play. Glucagon also promotes rapid lipolysis and FFA mobilization. The catecholamines and glucagon exert their action by stimulating the activity of *adenylate cyclase,* the enzyme that converts ATP to *cAMP* or *cyclic adenosine monophosphate,* and the increased levels of cAMP activate still another enzyme, *cAMP-dependent protein kinase,* which converts the hormone-sensitive triglyceride lipases into activated enzymes which liberate FFA from the fat stores. Other hormones which promote the liberation of FFA are *thyroid-stimulating hormone (TSH)* and vasopressin (see footnote 26). Perhaps the strongest hormone affecting lipolysis is insulin, which inhibits cAMP production and thus acts to decrease the levels of circulating FFA.[80]

The oxidation of fatty acids occurs via three pathways, of which the most important quantitatively is known as beta-oxidation (Fig. 21). It occurs only via the TCA (Krebs cycle in the mitochondria, albeit in a great many different tissues. The fatty acids are first converted into an activated enzyme called *acyl co-A* ($R-CH_2-CH_2-\overset{\overset{\displaystyle O}{\|}}{C}\cdot S-\text{co-A}$) by the enzyme *thiokinase (acyl co-A synthetase)*

[78]LCAT converts surface cholesterol and *lecithin* (a phospholipid containing choline) into cholesterol ester and *lysolecithin* (a lecithin from which the fatty acid radical has been removed from the number 2 position) by transferring the number 2 fatty acid from the lecithin to the cholesterol. Thus:

$$\text{lecithin} + \text{cholesterol} \xrightarrow[\text{LCAT}]{} \text{lysolecithin} + \text{cholesterol ester.}$$

[79]The chylomicrons also undergo a size decrease as they give up their triglyceride loads and they also transfer apo-C as well as apo-A to HDL. Chylomicron remnants also undergo a final breakdown in the liver into free cholesterol, and the remaining triglycerides are broken down into free fatty acids which are metabolized into phospholipids. A phospholipid-rich super-remnant is thus formed whose role is obscure, but which may represent chylomicron-derived LDL (Scheig 1979).

[80]Probably by either inhibiting adenylate cyclase which generates cAMP, or by promoting the production of the enzyme which breaks it down — *3', 5'-nucleotide phosphodiesterase,* or both (see Scheig 1979).

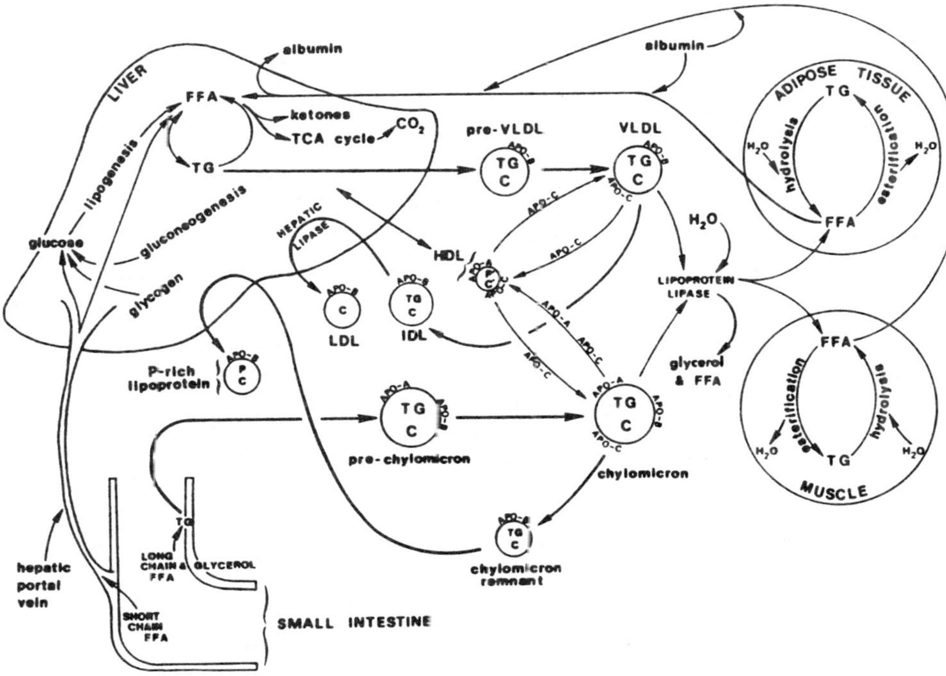

Figure 20. Lipid metabolism. C = cholesterol; C′= cholesterol ester; FFA = free fatty acids; P = phospholipid; P′= lysolecithin; TCA cycle = Krebs cyle; TG = triglyceride.

HDL are synthesized both in the liver and the intestine, and they are the major vehicle by which cholesterol is transported from extrahepatic tissues to the liver for breakdown and elimination. They carry the enzyme LCAT (lecithin-cholesterol acyl transferase) which transforms cholesterol into its ester and phospholipid into lysolecithin. LDL are further broken down in the liver and eliminated in the bile. The fate of the P-rich lipoprotein remnant of the chylomicron remnant is unknown. Adapted and modified from Mayes 1981 *in* Harper's Review of Biochemistry.

in a reaction requiring ATP. Long-chain fatty acids are converted into acyl co-A in the microsomes and on the outer membrane of the mitochondria; the acyl co-A thus formed is transported across the membranes to the inside of the mitochondria by a carrier molecule called *carnitine*. Short-chain fatty acids can be activated to acyl co-A inside the mitochondria without requiring carnitine. Inside the mitochondria, the acyl co-A is oxidized to acetyl co-A ($CH_3-\overset{\overset{O}{\|}}{C}\bullet S-\text{co-A}$) by a group of enzymes collectively called *fatty acid oxidase*. This is a highly complex series of reactions in which the fatty acid is shortened at each step by two carbon atoms with the splitting off of an acetyl co-A molecule. This process is repeated until the remaining acyl co-A radical is only four carbon atoms long. Each time the cycle is repeated flavoprotein (see footnote 19) is reduced and NAD^+ is reduced to $NADH + H^+$, and both reductions generate ATP in the electron transport chain. The 4-carbon fatty acid residue is completely oxidized in a final step with the generation of two acetyl co-A molecules. The acetyl co-A formed by beta-oxidation enters the TCA cycle and is metabolized to CO_2 and water with the production of ATP. In the case of acyl radicals with an odd number of carbon atoms, beta-oxidation proceeds until a 3-carbon residue is left, which is then converted into *succinyl co-A,* a constituent of the Krebs cycle which enters the cycle at the appropriate point. Two minor pathways for fatty acids also exist. α-oxidation occurs in brain tissue — it involves the removal of one carbon atom at a time; it does not necessitate co-A intermediates and it generates no ATP. Omega-oxidation involves the cytochrome P_{450} system in the microsomes in which the terminal methyl group ($-CH_3$) of a fatty acid is hydroxylated to $-CH_2OH$ and subsequently oxidized to $-COOH$.[81] The fatty acid is thus transformed into a *dicarboxylic acid:*

$$HO-\overset{\overset{\displaystyle O}{\|}}{C}-R-\overset{\overset{\displaystyle O}{\|}}{C}-OH.$$[82]

Although many anabolic and catabolic and oxidation and reduction processes are mere reversals of the same biochemical pathway, the synthesis of long-chain fatty acids from acetyl co-A involves quite a different set of enzymes than does the oxidation of fatty acids to acetyl co-A. Fatty acid oxidation occurs in the mitochondria, whereas most of the synthesis of fatty acids is extramitochondrial, occurring in the cytosol of the liver, kidneys, brain, lungs, mammary glands, and adipose tissue. The liver is quantitatively the most important site of endogenous lipogenesis in man; the adipose tissue performs that role in the rat. It requires energy as ATP and converts reduced NADPH into its oxidized form, $NADP^+$. Bicarbonate ion, $-HCO_3^-$, is a necessary cofactor as a source of CO_2 for the initial conversion of acetyl co-A into *malonyl co-A* ($HO-\overset{\overset{\displaystyle O}{\|}}{C}-CH_2-\overset{\overset{\displaystyle O}{\|}}{C}\cdot S-\text{co-A}$). Initially, glucose from a variety of sources[83] is converted into pyruvate in the cytosol. In this reaction, NAD^+ is reduced to $NADH + H^+$. This pyruvate then enters the mitochondria for conversion into acetyl co-A (Fig. 21) by the mitochondrial-bound enzyme *pyruvate dehydrogenase.* In order to move the acetyl co-A out of the mitochondria into the cytosol for action by the extramitochondrial enzymes involved in fatty acid synthesis, it is first converted into *citrate* by moving a short distance through the Krebs cycle (see Fig. 7). The citrate is then moved out of the mitochondria and reconverted

---

[81] $-COOH$ has the structural formula, $-\overset{\overset{\displaystyle O}{\|}}{C}-OH$.

[82] Recall that fatty acids have the general formula, $CH_3-R-\overset{\overset{\displaystyle O}{\|}}{C}-OH$.

[83] Including dietary glucose brought to the liver via the hepatic portal vein, glucose from glycogenolysis, and glucose synthesized *de novo* from amino acids (gluconeogenesis). (See also Fig. 20.)

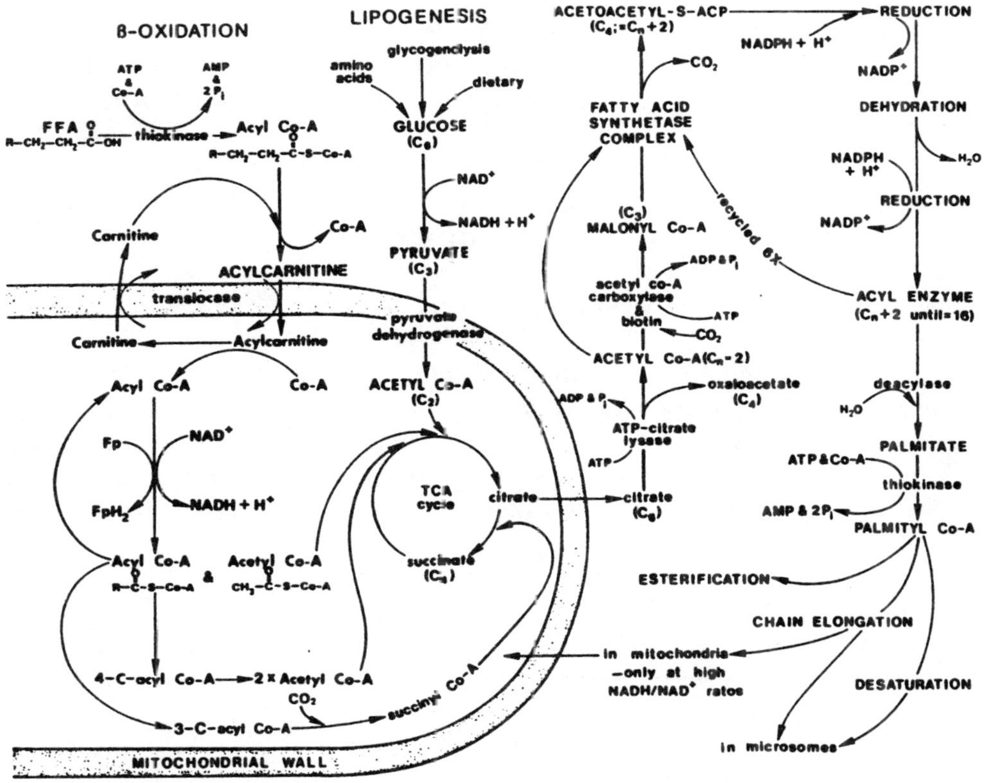

Figure 21. Fatty acid oxidation and lipogenesis. ADP = adenosine diphosphate; AMP = adenosine monophosphate; ATP = adenosine triphosphate; FFA = free fatty acids; Fp= flavoprotein (see footnote 19); FpH_2 = reduced flavoprotein; Pi = inorganic phosphate.

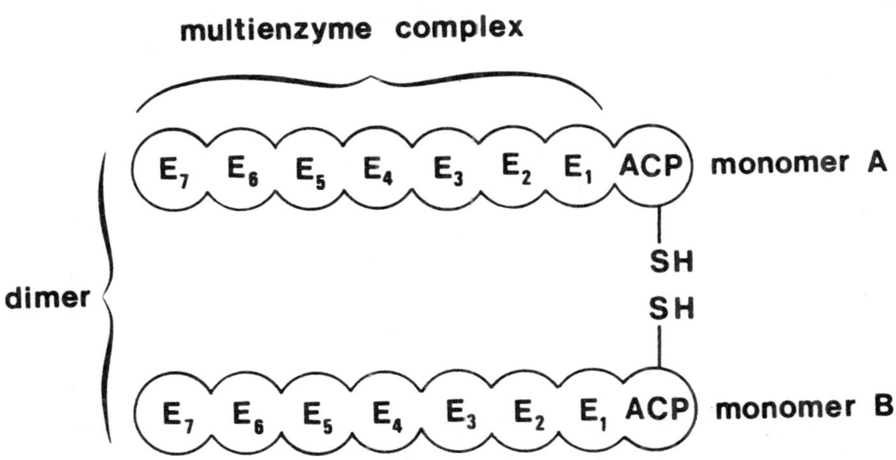

Figure 22. Fatty acid synthetase complex. E_1 through E_7 are the individual enzymes of the complex; E_7 = deacylase. Adapted and modified from Mayes 1981 *in* Harper's Review of Biochemistry.

back into acetyl co-A by a cytosolic enzyme, *ATP-citrate lysase.* The acetyl co-A is converted into malonyl co-A in a reaction requiring ATP and the enzyme *acetyl-co-A carboxylase.*[84] This step is the rate-limiting one for the synthesis of fatty acids.

The synthesis of fatty acids is catalyzed by a complex of seven enzymes collectively called the *fatty acid synthetase complex.* This complex is a *dimer* — that is, a super-molecule composed of two identical smaller molecules called *monomers.* Each monomer contains all seven of the enzymes of fatty acid synthetase complex plus a terminal *acyl carrier protein (ACP)* bearing a *sulfhydryl group* (—SH) as shown in Figure 22.

An initial priming molecule of acetyl co-A combines with an —SH group of one monomer of the complex, releasing co-A in a reaction catalyzed by *acetyl transferase.* Simultaneously, a malonyl co-A molecule formed from acetyl co-A (Fig. 21) combines with the —SH group on the other monomer, and is converted into *acyl malonyl enzyme* by another enzyme, *malonyl transferase:*

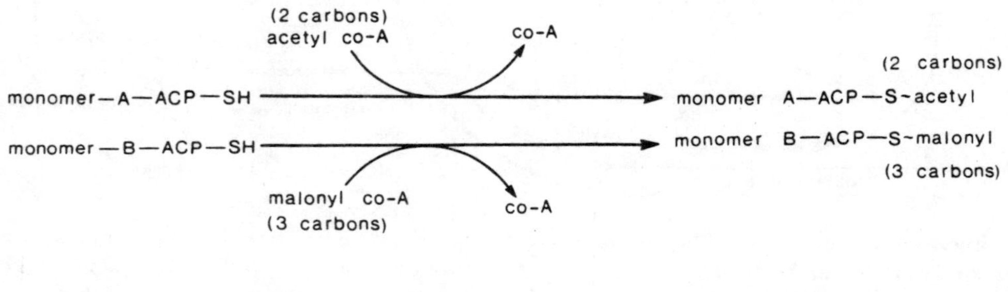

The acetyl now replaces the free carboxyl group from the malonyl—S—ACP, producing CO_2 as a by-product which contains the same carbon introduced by the CO_2 carried by biotin in the acetyl—co-A carboxylase reaction just described. Thus,

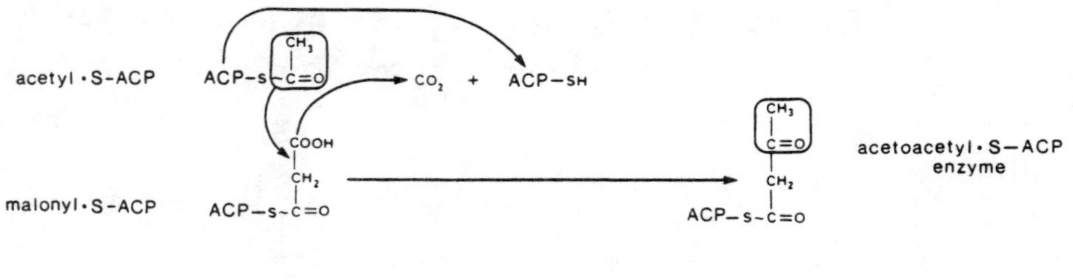

The resulting *acetoacetyl—S—ACP enzyme* (also called *beta-ketoacyl enzyme*) is then reduced in a reaction requiring the oxidation of NADPH + H^+ to

[84]This enzyme requires *biotin* (one of the vitamins B-complex) as the intermediate carrier of the CO_2 required in this process.

$NADP^+$, the product of that reduction is dehydrated, and the product of the dehydration is reduced once more in a reaction in which NADPH is again oxidized. The final product is *acyl enzyme* or *butyryl—S—ACP* (ACP—S•C(=O)—$CH_2-CH_2-CH_3$). Notice that acyl enzyme contains two more carbon atoms than did the acetyl co-A molecule which initiated the process. Acyl enzyme thus contains $C_n + 2$ carbon atoms. The sequence of reactions leading to acyl enzyme is repeated six more times (Fig. 21), yielding a final 16-carbon acyl radical known as *palmityl—S—ACP.* The palmityl—S—ACP is released by a hydrolysis reaction catalyzed by the seventh enzyme in the multienzyme complex, *deacylase* (Figs. 21-22). The complete set of cycles requires 14 NADPH molecules for the necessary reductions. The freed palmitate is activated to its acyl co-A form, *palmityl co-A,* in a reaction driven by ATP and catalyzed by the enzyme *thiokinase.* The palmityl co-A thus formed represents the activated fatty acid which can be esterified and transformed into triglyceride or cholesterol ester, or it can undergo desaturation and chain elongation.

Fatty acid chain elongation occurs primarily in the microsomes. Malonyl co-A serves as the donor of acetyl groups which convert both saturated and unsaturated fatty acyl co-A molecules into longer homologues by adding two carbon atoms each time in a reduction reaction driven by NADPH. ACP is not utilized in this process. The mitochondrial pathway for chain elongation operates only when the mitochondrial $[NADH]/[NAD^+]$[85] ratio is high — such as occurs in the liver with excessive ethanol oxidation. The process involves essentially a reversal of the same enzymatic pathway employed in the beta-oxidation of fatty acids (see Fig. 21), with one minor exception, and NADPH serves as the reductant.[86] Fatty acid *desaturation* (elimination of hydrogens attached to the carbon atoms with the formation of double bonds between adjacent carbons) occurs in the microsomes (endoplasmic reticulum) of the liver and to a lesser extent, in the adipose tissue. The double bonds are introduced into the fatty acids by specific *monooxygenases* located in the microsomes in NADPH- or NADH-requiring reactions.[87]

---

[85]Brackets around a compound indicate the *molar concentration* (moles of compound or substance per liter of solvent or medium) of that compound.

[86]The exception involves one of the steps in beta-oxidation not shown in Figure 21: a saturated acyl co-A substrate is converted into its corresponding unsaturated acyl co-A with the reduction of Fp to FpH_2 (the cofactor exchange is figured). The unsaturated acyl co-A is then hydrated into *hydroxy acyl co-A,* which undergoes two additional steps in its conversion into the 4-carbon acyl co-A plus two acetyl molecules. In mitochondrial fatty acid elongation, the reverse process of converting the unsaturated acyl co-A into the saturated form is accomplished by a separate enzyme (a reductase, rather than a dehydrogenase), and the reaction is driven by the oxidation of NADPH into $NADP^+$ instead of FpH_2 (Fp_{red}) into Fp (Fp_{ox}).

[87]This is a mixed-function monooxygenase involving *cytochrome b_5,* which is similar in function to cytochrome P_{450} (see Fig. 13). As in all cytochromes, electrons are carried from reduced flavoprotein and the iron atom of the heme moiety is reversibly interconverted between Fe^{3+} and Fe^{2+}.

Lipid can accumulate in the liver, mainly as triglyceride, and produce fatty liver in two major ways: (1) from an excess of free fatty acids supplied to the liver, and (2) by interference with the metabolism and transport of the lipids either reaching or synthesized within the liver. Excessive production of FFA can result from: (1) increased mobilization of FFA from the adipose tissue, (2) increased supply of dietary triglyceride in chylomicrons and/or increased hydrolysis of dietary triglyceride by extrahepatic lipoprotein lipase, and (3) increased synthesis of lipids within the liver itself. The FFA thus produced can accumulate in the liver because of interference with the triglyceride cycle, or from a metabolic block in plasma lipoprotein synthesis and/or release. This can include blockage or interference in the synthesis of apoprotein, of lipoprotein from the apoprotein and lipid moieties of phospholipids, of cholesterol and cholesterol esters, of the carbohydrate fraction of VLDL, or the failure of the secretory process. In addition, there may be decreased oxidation of lipid in the liver. Even in the absence of impaired hepatic beta-oxidation of lipid, the oxidative pathway can become saturated as FFA build up in the liver from other sources, thus causing further lipid accumulation. The overall rate-limiting step for hepatic lipid accumulation appears to be the production of VLDL for triglyceride export from the liver.

Considerable contradiction exists in the literature concerning the causes of altered lipid metabolism and the development of mild (usually) *hyperlipemia* (elevated levels of plasma lipid) and fatty liver injury associated with alcohol abuse. This confusion even includes conflicting reports on whether or not ethanol challenge produces an increase, decrease, or no change in certain measurable physiological parameters, such as levels of circulating lipoproteins, *ketone bodies* (a toxic product of lipid metabolism which will be discussed in more detail below), FFA mobilization from adipose tissue reserves, or the activity of enzymes such as *glucose-6-phosphatase.*[88] Many of these conflicting data appear to be due to differences by the various investigators in the handling of *in vitro* tissue cultures, routes of administration of ethanol as well as various agents which block the pathways being tested, and the types of diets provided test and control animals. Additional confusion results from attempts to compare the results obtained from laboratory rats with those occurring in human subjects. The presence of other, often unrelated, medical factors in human subjects (such as diabetes, essential hyperlipemia, or pancreatitis) introduces still further complications when comparing different studies. Nevertheless, certain clear patterns have begun to emerge concerning the toxicological effects of ethanol in humans, both in acute and chronic challenges to alcoholic and nonalcoholic subjects. Without attempting to treat the now quite considerable research

[88]An enzyme important in glucose metabolism. It catalyzes the *dephosphorylation* (removal of a phosphate group) of glucose-6-phosphate into glucose (see Fig. 26). This enzyme thus catalyzes the last step in gluconeogenesis (the synthesis of glucose from noncarbohydrate precursors).

literature in an exhaustive or systematic way, the major findings and implications can be summarized in a fairly straightforward manner. More detailed discussions can be found in Lieber & DeCarli 1978, Barboriak & Menahan 1979, Israel et al. 1979, and Scheig 1979.

As has been previously emphasized several times, the dramatic shift in hepatic redox state towards enhanced [NADH]/[NAD⁺] ratios resulting from the oxidation of large amounts of ethanol plays a major role in the development of metabolic abnormalities and the ensuing liver pathologies associated with chronic alcohol abuse. The excess of reducing equivalents inhibits the Krebs cycle by slowing down or even reversing the reactions of the cycle which require the reduction of NAD^+. The redox shift in favor of increased NADH can even cause the TCA cycle to run backwards under certain circumstances, with drastic consequences for carbohydrate metabolism, particularly gluconeogenesis. The increase in $[NADH]/[NAD^+]$ ratio also inhibits beta-oxidation of fatty acids, and may also cause an increase in the rate of endogenous lipogenesis as a means of disposing of the excess hydrogen equivalents (see footnote 59). The increased production of acetyl co-A resulting from the oxidation of ethanol can further enhance lipogenesis by serving as the direct source of the substrate for fatty acid synthesis, thus eliminating the need for converting glucose into pyruvate. Although acetyl co-A is normally converted into citrate in the TCA cycle for movement out of the mitochondria and secondarily converted back into acetyl co-A in the cytosol before entering the lipogenic cycle, at least some can pass directly out of the mitochondria into the cytosol via the "carnitine shuttle" involving enzyme *acetyl co-A carnitine acetyl transferase:*

$$\text{acetyl co-A} + \text{carnitine} \rightleftharpoons \text{acetyl carnitine} + \text{co-A.}$$

The increase in citrate produced by acetyl co-A buildup also stimulates the conversion of cytosolic acetyl co-A into malonyl co-A by acetyl co-A decarboxylase.[89]

A review of Figure 16 will show that both cytosolic and mitochondrial levels of NADH are increased by ethanol oxidation. Elevated levels inside the mitochondria favor the reversal of the malate-oxaloacetate step in the TCA cycle (see Figs. 7 and 26). This decreases the availability of oxaloacetate, a necessary constituent substrate and the major regulator of the TCA cycle. Excess reducing equivalents generated by ethanol oxidation also interfere with the oxidation of alpha-ketoglutarate by depressing the activity of the catalyzing *alpha-ketoglutarate dehydrogenase,* which requires unreduced NAD^+. Normally, this reaction proceeds as follows (see also Fig. 7):

[89] Some investigators (Barboriak & Menahan 1979, Reitz 1979, and Scheig 1979) insist that ethanol not only does not increase lipogenesis, but actually *decreases* it. However, this effect appears to be due to acute ethanol challenges, and to the dietary status of the test animals. Both chronic ethanol administration and fasting increase the biosynthesis of fatty acids as well as the activity of the enzymes involved in that process (Lieber & DeCarli 1978).

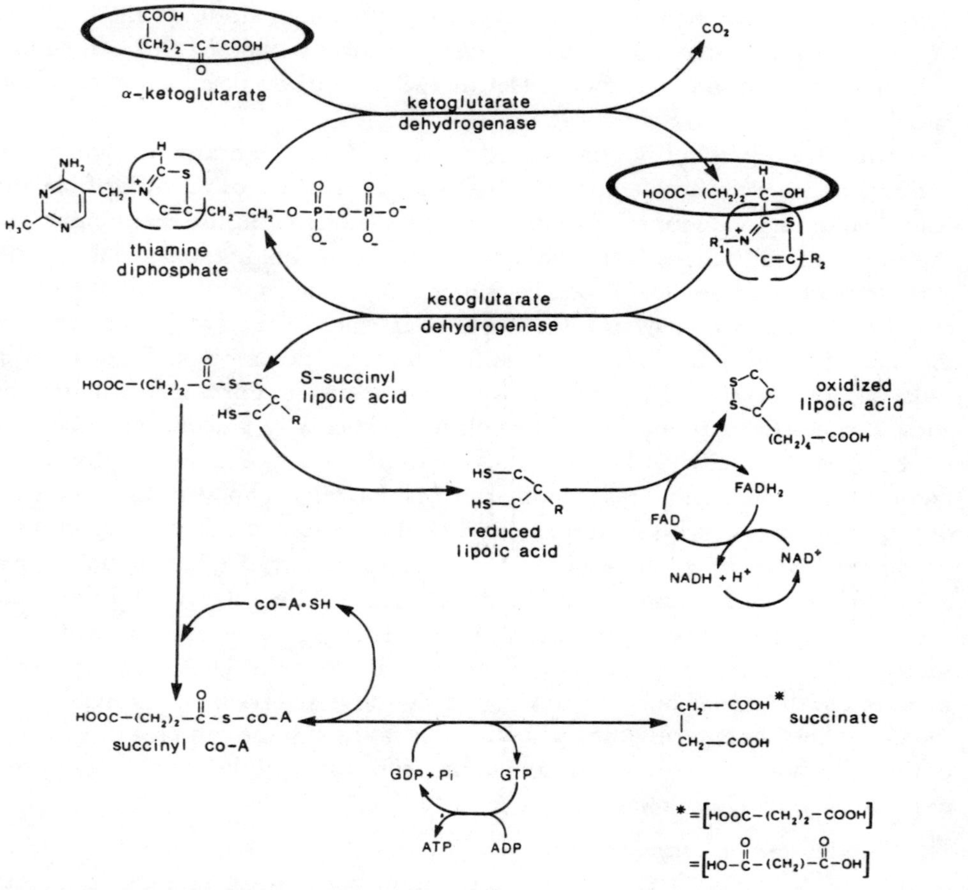

Figure 23. Oxidation of alpha-ketoglutarate. FAD = oxidized flavoprotein; $FADH_2$ = reduced flavoprotein. See text for details.

The redox shift accompanying ethanol oxidation also inhibits the generation of pyruvate from glucose and certain amino acids, thus decreasing the availability of this intermediary to the TCA cycle as well. Furthermore, the conversion of pyruvate into acetyl co-A follows exactly the same biochemical pathway as does the oxidation of ketoglutarate just described, except that the substrate is pyruvate instead of ketoglutarate, and the catalyzing enzyme is pyruvate dehydrogenase instead of ketoglutarate dehydrogenase. Lipoic acid is oxidized in the same manner, with the accompanying reduction of FAD to $FADH_2$ (which in turn reduces NAD^+ to $NADH + H^+$), and the oxidized lipoate is similarly involved in the conversion of pyruvate to S-acetyl lipoic acid. S-acetyl lipoic acid is converted into acetyl co-A by likewise absorbing a co-A group and releasing reduced lipoic acid. As a result of the depression of this pathway by excess reducing equivalents, whatever pyruvate that is produced in the reducing environment resulting from the oxidation of large amounts of ethanol is shunted into the formation of lactate (see footnote 21):[90]

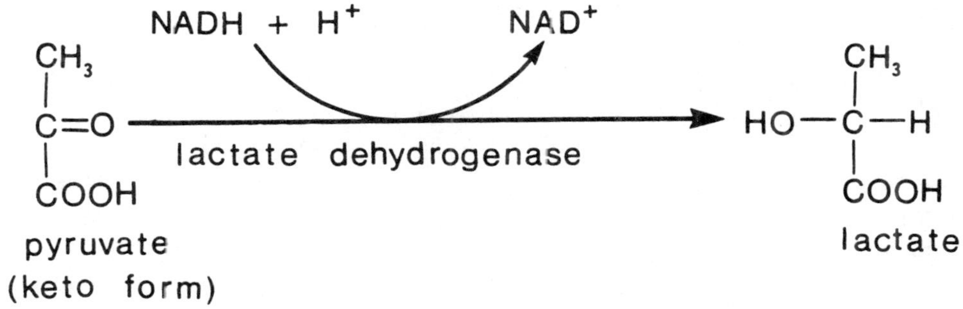

An additional factor inhibiting the conversion of pyruvate into acetyl co-A is the mass effect because of the excess of the latter substance resulting from ethanol oxidation. The increased generation and decreased utilization of pyruvate further augments the production of lactate, often resulting in *hyperlactidemia* or *lactic acidosis.*[91] Notice that thiamine (vitamin B_1) is required as a co-factor (Fig. 23) in the conversion of pyruvate to acetyl co-A (just as it is in the oxidation of ketoglutarate). Alcoholics are often thiamine deficient because of malabsorption secondary to intestinal injury from alcohol, as well as due to malnourishment resulting from poor dietary intake associated with an alcoholic lifestyle. The ensuing accumulation of pyruvate and hyperlactidemia which can develop from these complicating factors can be life-threatening (Mayes 1981b).

The reducing equivalents produced by ethanol oxidation are utilized by the electron transport chain to generate ATP. Since the TCA cycle is not only depressed but also saturated with the products of ethanol oxidation (acetyl co-A), acetyl co-A from the beta-oxidation of fatty acids is not needed, and this pathway is secondarily suppressed. This is in addition to the direct suppression caused by the excess of hydrogen equivalents which prevent beta-oxidation

[90]The full sequence in the oxidation of glucose to pyruvate involves 9 steps, each requiring its own enzyme (see Fig. 26). In the final step, a precursor molecule, *phosphoenol-pyruvate* (PEP), gives up its phosphate group to transform ADP into ATP, and in so doing is converted into *enol pyruvate* by the enzyme *pyruvate kinase* in a reaction which generates considerable energy loss as heat, and which is therefore irreversible. The enol pyruvate thus formed, $HOOC-\underset{OH}{\underset{|}{C}}=CH_2$, is spontaneously converted into the keto form of pyruvate, $HOOC-\underset{O}{\underset{\|}{C}}-CH_3$.

[91]Metabolic acidosis occurs whenever there is an acid buildup in the body, whether by a real net gain of acid or reducing equivalents, a relative increase due to loss of buffering base or alkalai, or a renal failure preventing normal acid excretion. Whatever the cause, there is a loss of bicarbonate and a corresponding decrease in *p*H, that is, a rise in $[H^+]$ (see footnote 42, page 61). Acidosis will be treated in more detail later in this chapter.

from going forward (see Fig. 21). Fatty acids that would normally be channeled into beta-oxidation thus accumulate in the liver together with lipid generated by enhanced lipogenesis, resulting in fatty liver disease.

Ethanol in stressful doses increases the mobilization of fatty acids from the adipose tissues by initiating the release of adipokinetic (lipolysis-enhancing) catecholamines (see above; also Lieber & DeCarli 1978). In fact, even low ethanol doses in man produce an increase in the urinary excretion of these catecholamines, reflecting an increased production (Scheig 1979). On the other hand, increased acetate levels resulting from ethanol metabolism are correlated with marked decreases in circulating FFA (Lieber & DeCarli 1978). This is due partly to an increased *de novo* synthesis of fatty acids because of the acetyl co-A resulting from the higher acetate levels (as well as from the enhanced [NADH/NAD^+] ratio). Since the rate of peripheral FFA mobilization is inversely related to the amount of circulating FFA because of negative feedback mechanisms (Scheig 1979), lipolysis in the adipose reserves would be depressed. Elevated acetate levels also directly inhibits peripheral FFA mobilization because the *ketone bodies* produced from it (via acetyl co-A) are oxidized by the extrahepatic tissues in preference to free fatty acids, which in turn are burned in preference to glucose. This preferential oxidation of ketone bodies (and probably also of acetate itself) causes a reduction of FFA mobilization (1) via the negative feedback mechanisms just described, and (2) via the stimulation of insulin output because of the spared glucose utilization.[92] The net result of an ethanol challenge will reflect the given circumstances in any particular case, and may thus account for many of the apparent contradictions in the literature (Lieber & DeCarli 1978). Moreover, extraneous variables such as nicotine intake, common among drinkers of beverage alcohol, can influence the mobilization of FFA by the excitement of sympathetic innervation of the adipose tissues (Bowman & Rand 1980).

Ethanol markedly increases the levels of circulating chylomicrons and VLDL in particular, and of the other plasma lipoproteins to a minor extent. When alcohol is consumed along with a diet rich in fat content, hepatic lipid accumulation comes mainly from dietary fat via the adipose tissues. When ethanol is taken with a low-fat diet, fatty liver is derived mainly from endogenously synthesized fatty acids (Lieber & DeCarli 1978). The hyperlipemia following both acute and chronic ethanol challenges in man is almost always due to the increase in VLDL (Scheig 1979). The VLDL in such cases resemble dietary fat in their makeup, rather than the lipid composition of the adipose reserves. Larger particles are broken down by the extrahepatic tissues more rapidly than smaller ones and chylomicrons are therefore catabolized more

[92] Glucose is the fuel which is burned last. The mobilization of adipose FFA is thus dependent upon a combination of interdependent effects whereby FFA spares glucose utilization in tissues such as heart and muscle, and glucose depresses lipolysis in the adipose tissues. This interaction is known as the *glucose-fatty acid cycle* (Mayes 1981).

quickly than are VLDL. It has also been suggested that chylomicron clearance from the blood is enhanced by ethanol, since there appears to be increased inclusion of fatty acids from chylomicrons into VLDL (Scheig 1979). The fatty acids deposited from the chylomicrons into the adipose tissues are quickly mobilized and transported to the liver where they are incorporated into VLDL. Increased fatty acid influx to the liver from all sources results in enhanced VLDL production, which, however, does not keep pace with the lipid buildup in the liver so that fatty liver develops. The increase in plasma VLDL and their slow clearance from the blood relative to chylomicrons causes the observed hyperlipemia involving dietary fat-containing VLDL.

There are at least two separate free fatty acid pools in the adipose tissues (Scheig 1979; Mayes 1981). Pool 1 contains FFA formed by lipolysis of triglyceride from the chylomicrons and VLDL, as well as from triglyceride already present within the adipose reserves (Fig. 20). It is from this small, rapidly turning over pool that FFA are re-esterfied and released back into the plasma without passing through a second, larger pool with a much slower turnover rate. Those FFA most recently taken up into pool 1 from the chylomicrons are the first to be released back into circulation. Once FFA are deposited into pool 2, they must be activated into acyl co-A by thiokinase in an ATP-requiring process (see Fig. 21) before they can undergo re-esterification into triglyceride and subsequent lipolysis and deposition back into pool 1, whence they can be mobilized into circulating FFA or recycled back through pool 2. Because the excess VLDL produced by the liver in response to ethanol exceeds the capacity of the adipose tissues to clear them from the blood, despite the probable increase in lipoprotein lipase activity also generated by an ethanol challenge, the hyperlipemia associated with alcohol intake is predominantly due to VLDL buildup in the blood. This appears to be true for both acute and chronic alcohol ingestion (Scheig 1979).

Actually, the individual response to ethanol is highly variable. Both normal and alcoholic subjects exhibit raised levels of plasma lipids, especially of the triglyceride fraction, via the mechanisms just described in response to an ethanol challenge. However, the response of alcoholics and individuals with abnormal carbohydrate and/or lipid metabolism is typically much exaggerated. For example, individuals with familial type IV hypertriglyceridemia[93] which is not associated with excessive carbohydrate intake will respond with seriously exacerbated hypertriglyceridemia at relatively low blood alcohol levels (< 50 mg-percent), whereas much higher levels of blood alcohol (>250 mg-percent) are needed to significantly enhance the hypertriglyceridemia in persons with a

[93]Type IV hypertriglyceridemia is characterized by elevated serum levels of VLDL, either in response to excessive caloric intake of carbohydrates (induced), or due to endogenous, inherited abnormalities of carbohydrate metabolism (familial). Type IV hypertriglyceridemia is associated with increased risk for coronary heart disease.

type IV disorder induced by excessive caloric intake (Scheig 1979). The normal postprandial rise in chylomicrons in healthy individuals is enhanced by ingesting small to moderate amounts of alcohol during or before a meal, and the resulting hyperlipidemia, either with or without alcohol, is increased by a high-fat dietary intake. In humans an initial hyperlipidemia associated with chronic alcohol intake declines after two or three weeks with continued drinking, due perhaps in part to progressive liver injury resulting in decreased lipoprotein production (Lieber & DeCarli 1978). Low to moderate doses of ethanol produce an adaptive increase in lipoprotein production by the liver in response to lipid accumulation in that organ. Very high doses, however, depress lipoprotein output because of direct hepatotoxic effects of the alcohol (about which more shortly).

It has been suggested that reduced peripheral uptake of circulating triglycerides may account for some of the hyperlipidemia associated with ethanol intake (Barboriak & Menahan 1979). However, it appears that only prolonged and chronic alcohol abuse, and not acute ethanol intoxication, can result in impaired ability to clear plasma triglycerides (Scheig 1979). Ethanol also stimulates the synthesis of triglycerides from fatty acids within the intestine, and some of the VLDL increase following ethanol ingestion is probably generated there as well. The effect of dietary fat upon ethanol-induced hyperlipidemia has already been discussed. The presence of carbohydrate in the diet appears to reduce the hyperlipidemic effect of alcohol because of the inhibitory effect of the associated elevated insulin levels on lipolysis (see footnote 77).

There is an inverse relationship between plasma levels of HDL-bound cholesterol and the occurrence of coronary heart disease. For some time evidence has been accumulating that ethanol ingestion increases plasma HDL levels. This, in turn, has been correlated with reduced coronary arterial occulsion and lowered rates of fatal myocardial infarction among *moderate* drinkers (2-3 drinks per day; Lieber 1984) relative to teetotalers (Barboriak & Menahan 1979; Haskell et al. 1984). Ethanol was thus thought to have a "protective" effect against myocardial infarction when taken moderately. Indeed, one report even suggested that "nonexercisers can maintain levels of HDL similar to those of individuals who jog regularly by ingesting three beers a day" (Hartung et al. 1983).

HDL is now known to be a group of heterogenous lipoproteins, however, with two major subclasses: HDL cholesterol is carried in approximately similar amounts on a less dense fraction called HDL_2 and a denser fraction known as HDL_3 (Haskell et al. 1984). Elevated plasma levels of HDL_2 are associated with a decreased risk for coronary heart disease, whereas plasma levels of HDL_3 have no relationship one way or the other with CHD. Women have higher HDL_2 levels than men, and running and the taking of high estrogen content oral contraceptives also enhance plasma levels of this fraction. Alcohol ingestion raises the levels of circulating HDL_3, but not of HDL_2, and abstention decreases levels of HDL_3, but not HDL_2.

The protective effect of moderate ethanol consumption against coronary heart disease thus does not appear to be related to its augmenting effect upon plasma HDL. HDL_3 is thought to be derived primarily from "nascent" HDL produced by the liver (Lieber 1984). Enhanced HDL production by the liver may be related to the inducing effect alcohol has upon the microsomal cytochrome P_{450} enzyme system within the liver; other drugs that induce liver microsomal activity also increase HDL levels in proportion to the changes they exert upon the microsomes. Moderate alcohol intake elevates HDL_3, but not HDL_2. By contrast, the chronic ingestion of ethanol by alcoholics significantly elevates HDL_2, but only moderately raises HDL_3 levels (Haskell et al. 1984). This increase in HDL_2 resulting from the consumption of large amounts of alcohol may be due to the enhanced breakdown of VLDL, whose production is enhanced following large doses of ethanol (Lieber 1984). This VLDL increase does not occur subsequent to prolonged alcohol abuse and probably reflects progressive liver disease.

Lieber (1984) has distinguished three different responses with regard to ethanol, HDL, and coronary heart disease: (1) moderate alcohol consumption produces an increase in plasma HDL_3, and perhaps irrelevantly, is also associated with a decrease in the incidence of coronary heart disease — the mechanism by which the protection against CHD occurs is unknown; (2) heavy alcohol consumption produces elevated levels of both fractions of HDL, but the increase in HDL_2 is more dramatic — at these high levels of alcohol consumption, however, no protective effect against CHD appears to occur; and (3) HDL levels are unaffected by alcohol intake as ethanol-induced liver injury progresses beyond a critical point.

Because of the hyperlactidemia which commonly occurs with chronic excessive alcohol intake (see footnote 76), blood levels of *uric acid*[94] may also become secondarily elevated. Uric acid exists in two *tautomeric* (chemically identical but structurally different) forms under physiological *p*H conditions: the protonated, *lactam* form, uric acid, and its *lactim* configuration which forms the monosodium salt, *sodium urate.*

[94]Uric acid is the relatively insoluble, completely oxidized metabolite of the *purine ribonucleotides* in certain mammals (the primates, including man, and the Dalmatian dog) and other vertebrates (the birds and certain reptiles). The purines are nitrogen-containing, double-ring, organic bases which, together with *pyrimidines* (single-ring organic bases), form DNA and RNA, the nucleic acids which make up the genetic code, and some of which (RNA) function in the transmission and translation of the code and the manufacture of the proteins stipulated by the code. Purines are also the basic building blocks for very important high-energy sources and regulatory messengers such as ATP and cAMP, respectively. Because these organisms can synthesize their own purines and pyrimidines *de novo,* the excess and exogenous supplies in the diet must be broken down and eliminated. In man the purines are excreted in the urine and to a lesser extent in the feces as uric acid. Pyrimidines are mostly broken down in the liver into highly soluble end products. The bulk of the nitrogen excreted in the urine of man consists of *urea,* a highly soluble end product of amino acid degradation.

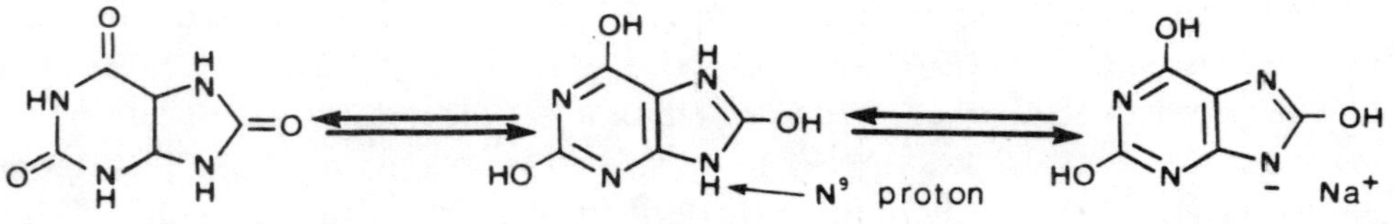

Figure 24. Uric acid-urate equilibrium and gout.

The *p*K (the negative log of the dissociation constant, which is equal to the *p*H at which the protonated and unprotonated forms of an acid are present in equal concentrations) of the N^9 proton is 5.75. Thus, at that *p*H value (see footnote 40) the concentration of sodium urate exactly equals that of uric acid. At *p*H values less than 5.75, uric acid will predominate, whereas at higher than *p*H = 5.75, sodium urate will be the most abundant species. Sodium urate is a polar, ionic compound which is 17 times more soluble in water than is uric acid. At normal physiological temperature of 37° C. (98.6° F.) and normal plasma *p*H of 7.4 the solubility of sodium urate is 7 mg/100 ml of plasma (7 mg-percent). When the serum sodium urate concentration exceeds its serum solubility, the serum becomes supersaturated, a condition known as *hyperuricemia,* and crystals of the urate may be precipitated out of solution. These crystals can be deposited in the joints where they are attacked by leukocytes, resulting in the inflammatory reaction known as *acute gouty arthritis*.

Two-thirds or so of the uric acid formed from enogenously synthesized and dietary purine bases is excreted in the urine; the remaining one-third is eliminated in the bile and further broken down by the intestinal bacteria. Both the sodium urate and uric acid fractions are completely filtered by the *glomerulus* into the *proximal convoluted tubule* in the kidney.[95] This filtrate is 90-95 percent or more resorbed back into the cells of the tubule; subsequently, most of it is secreted back into the lumen of the tubule. In the distal tubule and collecting ducts the urine becomes highly acidic and the *p*H drops to 5.0 or even less — far below the *p*K for uric acid of 5.75. As a result, uric acid becomes the predominant urate species in the urine. This highly insoluble substance is only maintained in solution because of the relatively large volume of water in the urine. When the blood and body fluids become acidotic due to lactic acid or

[95]The functional unit of the kidney is the *nephron,* consisting of a highly vascular glomerulus through which filtered plasma passes into the proximal convoluted tubule. Much of the filtrate is resorbed by the cells of the proximal tubule and then secreted back into the lumen as water moves passively back and forth between compartments due to both passive diffusion and along concentration gradients set up by active transport pumps. The urine carries polar metabolites into the *distal convoluted tubule* where a complex system of current and counter-current mechanisms concentrates it still further. It finally passes out of the nephron into the *collecting tubules* (see also footnote 26) and into the bladder via the *ureter.*

ketone body (see below) buildup from excess pyruvate, the fall in *p*H shifts the urate equilibrium towards uric acid. The sodium urate then becomes supersaturated and may precipitate out as crystals, causing gout attacks. The *renal threshold* of uric acid (the serum concentration necessary for it to spill into the urine) is also raised in response to the higher concentrations of the protonated form (uric acid) due to lowered *p*H. This elevated real threshold is at least partly accounted for by the higher partition coefficient of uric acid relative to sodium urate.[96] The raised renal threshold further elevates the concentration of uric acid in the serum along with the sodium urate still present at the new equilibrium concentrations at the reduced plasma *p*H prevailing under acidosis. For the foregoing reasons alcoholics are often prone to gouty episodes and alcohol is best avoided by persons with susceptibility to gout attacks. Alcoholic hyperuricemia is reversible with abstinence from alcohol (Korsten & Lieber 1976).

With an adequate dietary intake the acetyl co-A generated from carbohydrate metabolism is converted into malonyl co-A by acetyl co-A carboxylase, which is the rate-limiting step in the generation of palmitate (see Fig. 21). This results in enhanced lipogenesis. High concentrations of malonyl co-A inhibit acylcarnitine translocase activity, depressing the transportation of long-chain acyl groups across the mitochondrial membrane and thus suppressing beta-oxidation (Mayes 1981). The small amounts of FFA entering the liver are easily esterified into triglycerides and incorporated into VLDL. Under conditions of fasting or starvation, however, plasma insulin levels are decreased and glucagon output is enhanced, both of which stimulate peripheral lipolysis and raise plasma FFA. The long-chain acyl co-A molecules derived from the mobilized FFA competitively inhibit the synthesis of citrate, a necessary activator for aetyl co-A carboxylase, thus suppressing the activity of the latter enzyme. Lipogenesis is thus depressed via a negative feedback process and the inhibition on acylcarnitine translocase is released, permitting an increase in the beta-oxidation of FFA. The acetyl co-A produced can be either oxidized via the TCA cycle or converted into ketone bodies in the liver (see Fig. 20).

The three ketones or acetone bodies are: (1) *acetoacetate,* which spontaneously converts to (2) *acetone,* and which is also converted into (3) *beta-hydroxylbutyrate* by the enzyme *beta-hydroxybutyrase dehydrogenase* in a reaction requiring the oxidation of NADH. The redox state thus controls the equilibrium between acetoacetate and beta-hydroxybutyrate, and under acidosis, the

[96]The partition coefficient of a substance is the ratio of its solubility in a nonpolar solvent, usually *n*-octanol, relative to water. The greater the partition coefficient the more lipid soluble is the substance. The higher partition coefficient of uric acid is due to its covalent, nonpolar nature as contrasted with the charge-carrying sodium urate. It is thus more soluble in the lipid fraction of the cell membranes than in the aqueous medium of the urine. It is therefore retained to a greater extent within the cells than the urate, and higher serum levels of uric acid are required to achieve spillage into the urine for excretion.

latter ketone predominates in the blood. Ketogenesis is initiated when two molecules of acetyl co-A are condensed to form a molecule of acetoacetyl co-A which then combines a third acetyl co-A to form acetoacetate in a series of complex steps.

Ketones are continually released into the blood by the liver under normal circumstances. They are metabolized by the peripheral tissues, particularly by skeletal and cardiac muscle, where they are burned in preference to free fatty acids and glucose. The apportionment of acetyl co-A between the ketogenic and TCA pathways is regulated by a mechanism which ensures that the total energy bound up in ATP remains relatively constant. Since 1 mole of palmitate yields 129 moles of ATP when oxidized via the TCA cycle, and only 33 moles of ATP when converted into ketone bodies (Mayes 1981f), as plasma levels of FFA rise more of the acetyl co-A produced is converted into ketone formation and less is oxidized in the TCA cycle.

Acetoacetate and beta-hydroxybutyrate are both moderately strong acids which are buffered in the blood and other body fluids by cations such as Na^+, Mg^{2+} and K^+. When blood levels of ketones exceed the renal threshold, spillage into the urine occurs resulting in *ketonuria.* The continued excretion of ketones in the urine causes a general depletion in cations, particularly Na^+, lowering the alkalai reserve and resulting in a large *anion gap* (difference in concentration of positive and negative ions) in the plasma. The resulting acidosis is called *ketoacidosis,* and the excessive loss of buffering cations and fluid in the urine can cause profound depression of the central nervous system and severe dehydration, resulting in coma and even death. Whenever large amounts of ketone bodies are present in the blood and urine, a strong odor of acetone can usually be detected on the breath — the so-called "fruity" odor of diabetic ketoacidosis. Ketoacidosis is a common complication in uncontrolled diabetes. Although diabetics exhibit elevated blood glucose levels, the very metabolic defect that causes the hyperglycemia, insulin insufficiency, prevents the normal uptake and utilization of glucose by the cells of muscles and liver. This results in an effective carbohydrate "starvation," leading to the sequence of events which precipitate a ketoacidosis very similar to that seen in frank starvation. The only major difference is that in diabetes blood glucose levels are elevated far above the renal threshold, resulting in massive spillage into the urine and glycosuria.

Ketoacidosis is well known in chronic alcoholics, although the precise mechanisms underlying its pathogenesis remain to be clarified. Alcohol consumption potentiates the ketogenesis due to a low carbohydrate diet and ketone body production is also directly related to the amount of fat in the diet (Sargent et al. 1979; Reitz 1979); dietary fat has been suggested to play a "permissive" role in the development of alcoholic ketoacidosis. However, the ketonemia and ketonuria associated with excessive alcohol intake is typically a delayed effect, which follows several days of heavy drinking combined with significant decrease or cessation of food intake. Patients are typically female (Korsten & Lieber 1976) and present with severe vomiting during the previous 24 hours, confusion, dehydration (due to the protracted vomiting and excess urine loss associated with cation excretion), *tachycardia* (rapid pulse), *Kussmaul respiration,*[97] and metabolic acidosis characterized by elevated serum FFA and a marked increase in beta-hydroxybutyrate relative to acetoacetate (contrasting with diabetic ketoacidosis) accompanied by decreased plasma bicarbonate and a large anion gap. In many patients plasma *p*H may be at near normal levels despite the elevated ketones and depressed bicarbonate, suggesting an almost complete respiratory compensation (Sargent et al. 1979).[97]

Alcoholic ketoacidosis appears to be due to the combined effects of serum glucose depletion followed by glycogen exhaustion within 8-12 hours, and the associated suppression of gluconeogenesis and resulting mobilization of free fatty acids from the adipose tissues. Although beta-oxidation is initially depressed by heavy alcohol intake, it is subsequently enhanced in response to free fatty acid mobilization. Since the TCA cycle is depressed by the combination of excess hydrogen equivalents and the mass effect of acetyl co-A from the oxidation of ethanol, the acetyl co-A resulting from both beta-oxidation and ethanol metabolism are routed through the ketogenic pathway. The resulting ketoacidosis tends to exacerbate the hyperlactidemia due to alcohol consumption. Ketoacidosis secondary to pancreatic damage may also occur in chronic alcoholics because of insulin failure which can result in an induced diabetes mellitus. The effects of ethanol upon lipid metabolism are summarized in Figure 25.

ALCOHOL AND CARBOHYDRATE METABOLISM

I have previously mentioned several different effects that ethanol can have on carbohydrate metabolism. This is an appropriate juncture at which to integrate these various processes into a more coherent system of interrelated events and to discuss the interaction between ethanol and carbohydrate biochemistry in somewhat more detail.

Because glucose is essential to the metabolism of nervous tissue and erythrocytes, provides a source of glyceride-glycerol for the adipose tissues, helps to maintain the level of intermediate compounds in the TCA cycle, and functions as a fuel source for skeletal muscles under anaerobic conditions, the body has devised a method of providing a constant source of glucose from noncarbohydrate derivatives in the event of starvation and glycogen depletion. This

---

[97] Labored, paroxysmal gasping due to the body's attempts to compensate for the acidosis. The hyperventilation increases the exchange of CO_2 (an acid) in the lungs, thus reducing the PCO_2 (partial pressure of CO_2) in the blood and at least partially compensating for the metabolic acidosis.

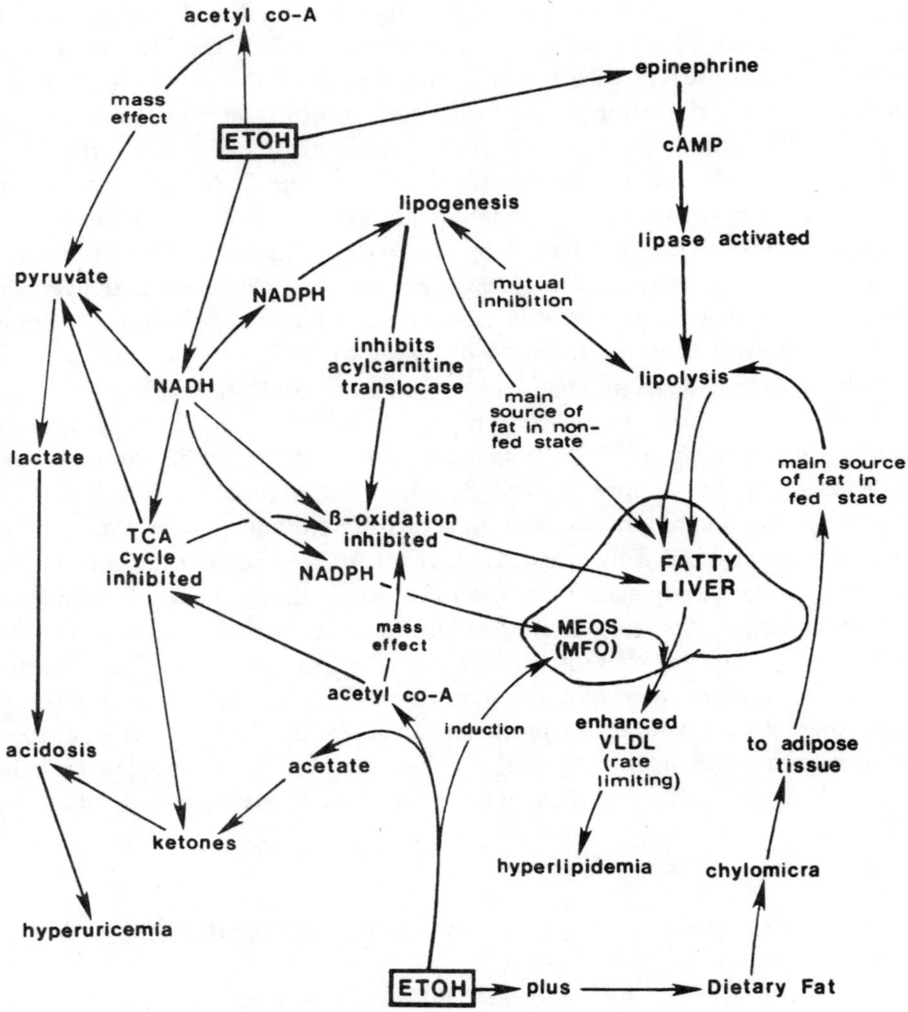

Figure 25. Effects of ethanol on lipid metabolism. ETOH = ethanol.

pathway is essentially a reversal of the glycolytic[98] pathway and the TCA cycle (respiration), but with some minor modifications. Let us first consider the Embden-Meyerhof glycolytic pathway (Fig. 26).

The Embden-Meyerhof pathway by which glucose is converted into pyruvate occurs entirely in the extramitochondrial cytosol in nearly all tissues. Glucose, a 6-carbon sugar is first converted into *glucose 6-phosphate* in a phosphorylation process in which ATP is converted into ADP along with the release of considerable energy. The reaction is catalyzed by the enzyme *hexokinase,* and

[98] Glycolysis refers to the oxidation of glucose or glycogen to pyruvate.

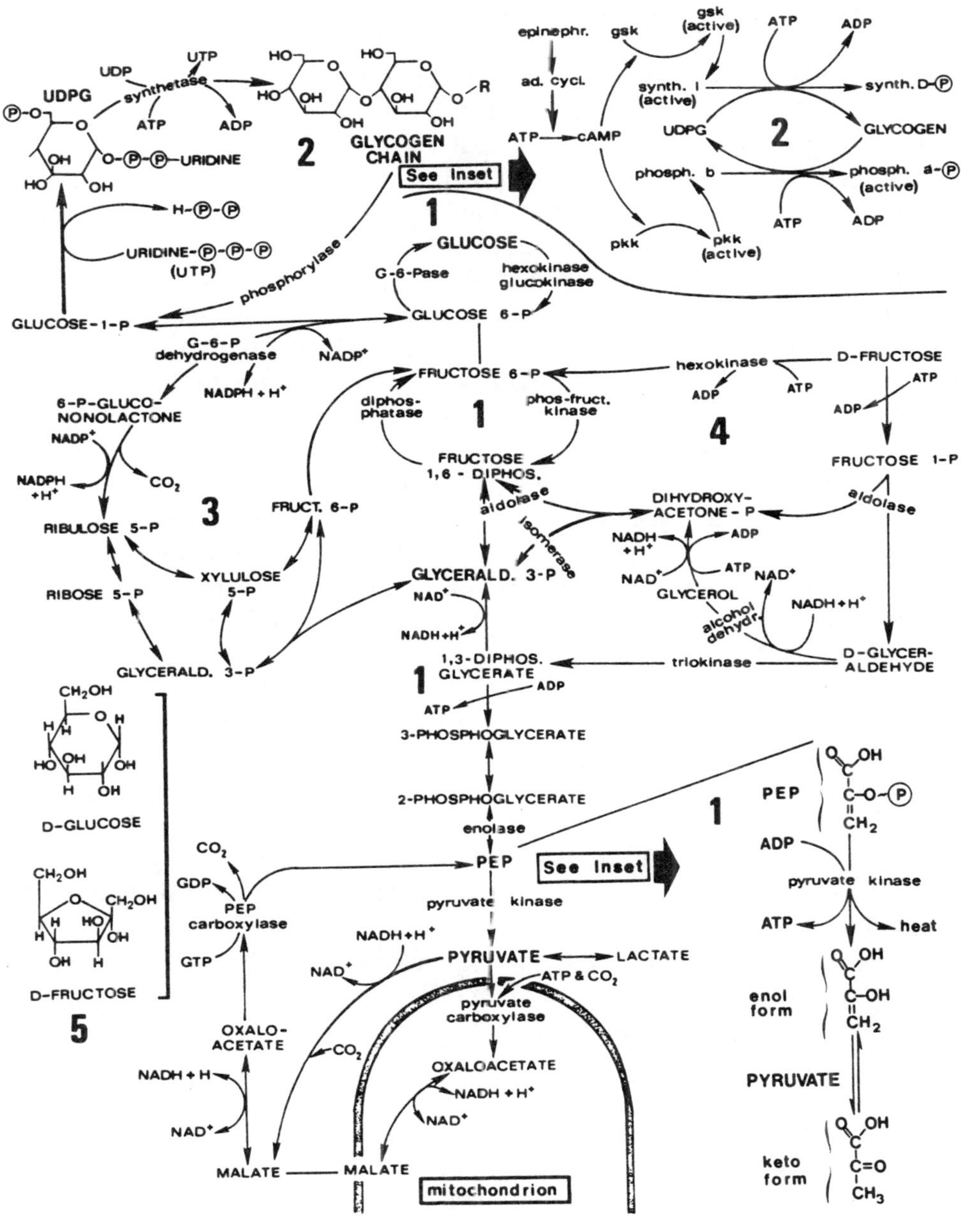

Figure 26. Carbohydrate metabolism. 1 = Embden-Meyerhof pathway; 2 = glycogenesis and glycogenolysis; 3 = hexose monophosphate shunt; 4 = fructose metabolism; 5 = structural configurations of glucose and fructose. UDPG = uridine diphosphate glucose; PEP = phosphoenolpyruvate; ad. cycl. = adenylate cyclase; gsk = glycogen synthetase kinase; pkk = phosphorylase kinase kinase; UDP = uridine diphosphate; UTP = uridine triphosphate. Adapted and modified from Mayes 1981c and Bowman & Rand 1980.

in the liver, also by a second, inducible enzyme (depending upon the nutritional state), *glucokinase.* Because of the significant energy loss during this step, the reaction is for all practical purposes an irreversible one (compare with footnote 90). Hexokinase has a low *Km* for glucose and thus guarantees that a steady supply of this compound is metabolically available even when blood glucose levels are low. Glucokinase serves mainly to lower postprandial blood glucose concentrations; its *Km* for glucose is high and it is most active at plasma glucose levels above 100 mg-percent (Mayes 1981).

Glucose 6-phosphate can be routed either into the formation of glycogen by being first converted into *glucose 1-phosphate* and stored in the liver, or converted into *fructose 6-phosphate*[99] along with the main glycolytic pathway.[100] The next step in the glycolytic pathway is another phosphorylation which requires the conversion of another ATP molecule into ADP, and again the loss in energy results in the process being irreversible. The *fructose 1,6-diphosphate* thus formed is split into two 3-carbon molecules by the enzyme *aldolase: dihydroxyacetone phosphate* and *glyceraldehyde 3-phosphate.* Because the glyceraldehyde phosphate thus formed is metabolized in the subsequent steps of the Embden-Meyerhof pathway, and the dihydroxyacetone phosphate is converted into glyceraldehyde phosphate by an isomerase in a reversible reaction, all subsequent reactions in glycolysis are processed twice to account for the complete glycolysis of one glucose molecule.

The two glyceraldehyde molecules resulting from the splitting of fructose 1,6-diphosphate are oxidized by a dehydrogenase known variously as *glyceraldehyde 3-phosphate dehydrogenase* or *triose phosphate dehydrogenase* (because glyceraldehyde phosphate is a 3-carbon-containing triose) into *1,3-diphosphoglycerate.* In this reaction NAD^+ is reduced to NADH plus H^+, and the energy gained from this reduction is used to attach an inorganic phosphate to the number 1 carbon (the carbonyl carbon) in a high-energy bond.[101] This high-energy phosphate bond just formed is removed from the 1,3-diphosphoglycerate by diphosphoglycerate kinase and used to convert ADP into ATP. The resulting molecule is known as *3-phosphoglycerate,* and it is converted into *2-phosphoglycerate* by the enzyme *phosphoglycerate mutase* which transfers the remaining phosphate group from the number 3 carbon to the number 2 carbon. The 2-phosphoglycerate is next dehydrated by *enolase* to form a high-energy phosphate bond by redistributing the energy within the molecule, and converting 2-phosphoglycerate into *phosphoenolpyruvate.* The enzyme *pyruvate kinase* then

[99]Glucose and fructose are both hexoses (sugars containing 6 carbons) and they have the same chemical formula ($C_6H_{12}O_6$); they differ only in their structural arrangements. Glucose has a 6-sided ring whereas fructose has a 5-sided ring structure (see Fig. 26).

[100]Glucose 6-phosphate can be also converted back into glucose in a dephosphorylation process catalyzed by glucose 6-phosphatase (see also footnote 88).

[101]Notice that the first two phosphate groups to be attached during glycolysis (in forming glucose 6-phosphate and, later, fructose 1,6-diphosphate) do *not* form high-energy bonds.

transfers the high-energy bond from phosphoenolpyruvate (PEP) to ADP, converting it into ATP, and converting PEP into *enolpyruvate* (the enol form of pyruvate; see also footnote 90). The enolpyruvate spontaneously converts to the keto form, *ketopyruvate,* which is a more stable form at metabolic pH conditions [standardly defined as $p\text{H} = 7.0$]. The pyruvate thus formed is available for conversion into acetyl co-A for processing through the TCA cycle when the [NADH]/[NAD^+] ratio is not excessively high. When the redox milieu is a reducing one, pyruvate is shunted off to form lactate and/or oxaloacetate (see below).

The famous Second Law of Thermodynamics has many expressions, one of which is: *any system will undergo spontaneous changes towards a state of statistical randomness or increased* entropy *until an equilibrium state is reached.* Solutes in a concentrated solvent in immediate contact with a dilute solution will therefore diffuse into the latter until they are uniformly distributed throughout the entire system and equilibrium is attained, that is, no further change is possible without the addition of energy from an outside source. The change in total energy that occurs when a system goes to equilibrium is called the *enthalpy;* this enthalpy is lost irretrievably to the system as heat unless new energy is supplied from outside the system. The *free energy G* of such a system can be defined as

$$G = H - TS$$

where H = the enthalpy, S = the entropy, and T = the absolute temperature (in degrees Kelvin). The *change in free energy* is

$$\triangle G = \triangle H - T\triangle S,$$

and for a system not at equilibrium,

$$\triangle G = -W,$$ [102]

where W is the total work done by the change in total energy.

Therefore, nonequilibrial systems can proceed spontaneously only in the direction of negative free energy change, and when a system has reached equilibrium, the available free energy is zero. The free energy varies with the logarithm of the concentration:

$$G = G^\circ + RT\ ln[concentration],$$

where ° is the *standard free energy* in mol/liter, R = the gas constant,[103] and T is the absolute temperature. For a reaction:

$$aA + bB \rightleftharpoons cC + dD$$

[102]For a system not in equilibrium, $\triangle H < T\triangle S - W$; therefore, $-W = \triangle H + (-T\triangle S)$, $-W = \triangle H - T\triangle S$, and by substitution, $\triangle G = -W$.

[103]R = pressure × volume ÷ mole × degrees Kelvin; depending upon the units employed, it is variously equal to: 0.083 liter × atmosphere × degree^{-1} × mole; 8.3×10^{-7} ergs × degrees^{-1} × mole^{-1} (cgs system); 8.3 joules × degree^{-1} × mole^{-1} (mks system); or 1.9 calories × degree^{-1} × mole^{-1}.

where A, B, C, and D are the reactants and their products, and a, b, c, and d are the exponents of their concentrations, the *equilibrium constant,* K'_{eq}, can be defined as:

$$K'_{eq} = \frac{[C]^c[D]^d}{[A]^a[B]^b}$$

(recall that brackets around a substance indicate molar concentration). The free energy change is:

$$\triangle G = \triangle G^{\circ} + RT \times \ln K'_{eq}$$

where $\triangle G^{\circ}$ is the *standard free energy change,* and $\ln K'_{eq}$ is the natural logarithm of the equilibrium constant. When the reaction is at equilibrium, $\triangle G$ equals zero no matter what the starting concentrations may be. Thus,

$$\triangle G^{\circ} = -RT \times \ln K'_{eq}$$

and

$$\triangle G^{\circ} = -1,420 \times \log_{10} K'_{eq}.$$

Therefore a tenfold change in the value of K'_{eq} means a change in $\triangle G^{\circ}$ of 1,420 calories per mole. The higher the value of K'_{eq} is in a positive direction, the greater is the negative value of $\triangle G^{\circ}$.[104] And the greater the negative value of $\triangle G^{\circ}$, the stronger is the tendency for the reaction to proceed towards equilibrium.

The reaction catalyzed by pyruvate kinase (or more correctly, pyruvate phosphokinase) in which PEP gives up its high-energy phosphate to ADP, and which forms the products ATP and pyruvate, has a very high positive equilibrium constant, and thus a correspondingly large *negative* value for the standard free energy change of the reaction:

$$(1)\ K'_{eq}\ \frac{[pyruvate][Mg^{++} - ATP^{4-}]}{[PEP][Mg^{++} - ADP^{3-}]} = 2 \times 10^5$$

(2) $\triangle G^{\circ} = -7,500$ cal/mole (White et al. 1978).

The reaction, therefore, proceeds very strongly towards the right side of the equation, the PEP is essentially totally converted into pyruvate, and the reverse reaction is energetically impossible under metabolic conditions. Phosphoenolpyruvate is simultaneously an *anhydride* (an acid derivative from which a water molecule has been abstracted) of two strong acids: phosphoric acid (H_3PO_4) and pyruvic acid, both of which have a very strong tendency to dissociate.

As PEP is hydrolyzed into pyruvate, the enol form of the latter compound is formed first, which spontaneously converts to the more stable keto tautomer (see inset, Fig. 26 and footnote 105). This enol to keto shift provides an extra

[104] $\triangle G^{\circ}$ is also equal to the difference between the standard free energy of the reactants and that of the products formed:

$\triangle G^{\circ} = \triangle G^{\circ}$ products $- \triangle G^{\circ}$ reactants. That is, $\triangle G^{\circ} = (cG^{\circ}_C + dG^{\circ}_D) - (aG^{\circ}_A + bG^{\circ}_B)$.

"tug" to the overall equilibrium, rendering the likelihood of a reversal even more remote. Once pyruvate is formed, it cannot be run backwards through the Embden-Meyerhof glycolytic pathway without first bypassing the step catalyzed by pyruvate kinase.[105]

There is a collateral glycolytic pathway known variously as the *hexose monophosphate shunt, pentose phosphate pathway,* or the *pentose shunt* (see Fig. 26). This shunt consists of a multicyclic process which converts 3 molecules of glucose 6-phosphate into 3 molecules of CO_2 plus three 5-carbon residues. Two of the 5-carbon residues are converted into fructose 6-phosphate and the third into glyceraldehyde 3-phosphate; all three products reenter the Embden-Meyerhof pathway at the appropriate places. The major function of the hexose monophosphate shunt appears to be the generation of reduced NADPH required by a variety of extramitochondrial anabolic pathways such as lipogenesis and the mixed-function monooxygenases (see also above, Fig. 13 and footnote 59; the NADH and NADPH systems are also linked together, and $NADP^+$ can be reduced by transhydrogenation from NADH). The hexose monophosphate shunt does not appear to be of major significance to ethanol metabolism.

Fructose of "fruit sugar" (see footnote 99) can be phosphorylated into fructose 6-phosphate by hexokinase and thus enter the Embden-Meyerhof pathway directly (see Fig. 26). However, by far the most important route quantitatively for fructose metabolism is its phosphorylation into *fructose 1-phosphate* by the hepatic enzyme *fructokinase.* Fructose 1-phosphate is in turn converted into *dihydroxyacetone phosphate* and *D-glyceraldehyde* by an *aldolase.* D-glyceraldehyde is readily reduced to glycerol by alcohol dehydrogenase (the very same) involving the oxidation of NADH to NAD^+; this results in an oxidized alcohol dehydrogenase-NAD^+ complex. The glycerol is then converted into dihydroxyacetone phosphate in a two-step sequence involving phosphorylation and reoxidation (it can also be esterified into triglyceride and incorporated into VLDL). Dihydroxyacetone phosphate then enters the Embden-Meyerhof pathway by being converted into either glyceraldehyde 3-phosphate or fructose 1, 6-diphosphate. Still another liver enzyme, *triokinase,* converts D-glyceraldehyde into 2-

---

[105]The enol form of a tautomer has the structure $-\overset{|}{C}=C-OH$; the word derives from *-ene* for the carbon-carbon double bond, and *-ol* for the alcohol or $-OH$ group. Keto structures contain a $C=O$ bond and the hydrogen of the $-OH$ group on the enol form is transferred to one of the carbon atoms, breaking the $C=C$ bond: $-\underset{H}{\overset{|}{\underset{|}{C}}}-C=O$. Because of the high degree of polarity of the $-O-H$ bond, the hydrogen is readily separated. This, or another hydrogen may then reattach to the oxygen atom or to one of the carbon atoms. Once it bonds to the carbon, however, it tends to remain there because carbon-hydrogen bonds are much stronger than oxygen-hydrogen bonds, and they are not easily broken. This causes the tautomeric equilibrium to shift very strongly in the direction of the keto tautomer, and the enol configuration is present in such small quantities that it is essentially absent (see also inset on Fig. 26).

phosphoglycerate, and this may be the most important pathway in D-glyceraldehyde metabolism (Mayes 1981). [Notice that all of the steps in fructose metabolism prior to entering the Embden-Meyerhof pathway are *one way,* except for the interconversion of D-glyceraldehyde and glycerol.] [106]

A ready supply of carbohydrate reserves is stored in the liver and muscles, and to a much lesser extent in other tissues in the form of glycogen. Muscle glycogen is primarily stored as an instantaneous glucose reserve for use by the muscle tissues themselves. Hepatic glycogen stores are much larger and serve mainly to maintain blood glucose levels during periods of fasting (e.g., between meals and overnight). Both *glycogenesis,* or the synthesis of glycogen from glucose, and *glycogenolysis,* its degradation into glucose (in the liver), or pyruvate and lactate (in muscle), leave or enter the Embden-Meyerhof pathway via the conversion of glucose 6-phosphate into or from *glucose 1-phosphate,* respectively. This conversion requires a magnesium-dependent enzyme, *phosphoglucomutase.* All glucose taken in or synthesized in excess of that required for the immediate energy needs of the body is converted into glycogen up to a maximum limit.[107]

Glycogen is a many-branched *polysaccharide* consisting of a series of linked *glucosyl* units held together by oxygen-carbon bonds (Fig. 26). Glycogen stores are augmented by merely adding additional glucosyl units to existing glycogen chains. Glucose 1-phosphate is phosphorylated to form an active nucleotide, *uridine diphosphate glucose (UDPG);* this conversion requires the dephosphorylation of *uridine triphosphate (UTP)* into *uridine diphosphate (UDP)* plus inorganic pyrophosphate.[108] The inorganic pyrophosphate is subsequently hydrolyzed by *inorganic pyrophosphatase* in a reaction whose $\triangle G^\circ = -7.0$ kcal/mole, thus rendering the formation of UDPG from glucose 1-phosphate irreversible. The UDPG is then attached to the growing glycogen chain by *glycogen synthetase* in a dephosphorylation process converting UDP back into UTP. Glycogen synthetase exists in an active, or dephosphorylated form *(synthetase I)* as well as in an inactive, or phosphorylated form *(synthetase D).* Synthetase I is converted into synthetase D by another enzyme, *glycogen synthetase kinase,* which in turn is activated by cyclic AMP. Catecholamines, and in particular epinephrine, stimulate adeylate cyclase activity, which in turn converts ATP into cAMP (see footnote 80); epinephrine thus has a major inhibitory effect upon glycogenesis,

[106]The NADH/NAD$^+$-dependent step occurring between the conversion of glycerol to dihydroxyacetone phosphate is also reversible, but the overall conversion is not.

[107]As much as 6 percent of the wet weight of the liver and about 1 percent of that of muscle tissue may consist of glycogen; there is an additional 0.1 percent of glucose in the extracellular fraction (Mayes 1981c). Carbohydrate in excess of these levels is converted into fatty acids via the lipogenic pathway.

[108]High energy phosphate complexes can be formed with several nucleosides: adenosine, guanine, uridine, and cytidine. Both ATP and GTP (see Fig. 23) transfer phosphate groups to drive energy-requiring reactions. UDP is the carrier molecule by which activated glucosyl groups are joined to form a variety of polysaccharides.

as does its precursor, norepinephrine, and the pancreatic hormone, glucagon.

Glycogen is broken down into glucose 1-phosphate by another pathway involving the enzyme, *glycogen phosphorylase.* This enzyme also exists in an active, and in this case phosphorylated, form *(phosphorylase a)* and an inactivated, dephosphorylated form *(phosphorylase b).* Activated glycogen phosphorylase *a* converts glycogen back into glucose 1-phosphate. Cyclic AMP also serves in this case to activate an enzyme two steps removed from the generation of glucose 6-phosphate, *viz. phosphorylase kinase kinase,* which in turn activates *phosphorylase kinase* which converts glycogen phosphorylase from the inactive to the active state. Epinephrine thus has a dual effect upon glycogen reserves because of its stimulation of adenyl cyclase: (1) it restricts the synthesis of glycogen from glucose 1-phosphate, and (2) enhances its breakdown into glucose 6-phosphate.

Gluconeogenesis occurs primarily in the mammalian liver and kidney. It is essentially a reversal of the Embden-Meyerhof glycolytic pathway, except that several energy barriers must be bypassed by alternate routes: (1) the step between pyruvate and PEP, (2) between fructose 1, 6-diphosphate and fructose 6-phosphate, and (3) between glucose 6-phosphate and glucose.[109] By far the most important of these energy barriers with respect to ethanol metabolism is the block between the conversion of pyruvate to phosphoenolpyruvate. This obstacle is neatly circumvented by the mitochondrial enzyme *pyruvate carboxylase,* a biotin-dependent enzyme which converts pyruvate and CO_2 into oxaloacetate in an ATP-requiring reaction. This process is very similar to the one in which acetyl co-A is converted into malonyl co-A by acetyl co-A carboxylase (see footnote 84). Pyruvate carboxylase is activated by acetyl co-A partly via an *allosteric*[110] mechanism, but also due to the mass effect of large amounts of that substance which prevents the conversion of pyruvate into additional acetyl co-A for oxidation via the TCA cycle, ketone body formation, or lipogenesis. The oxaloacetate thus formed from pyruvate cannot reenter the cytosol from the mitochondria. However, it can be converted into malate by running backwards a short distance through the TCA cycle, a process which tends to occur under

[109]There is also an energy barrier between glucose 1-phosphate and glycogen, which has just been discussed in some detail. Glycerol from fructose or lipid metabolism is also converted into glucose via dihydroxyacetone phosphate as described above, and is an important source of carbohydrate in starvation.

[110]Allosteric modification of the activity of an enzyme involves a highly specific attachment site on that enzyme for either the modifying agent itself (in the case of allosteric inhibition) or for a second, inhibiting molecule (in allosteric activation). When the allosteric site is occupied the active site on the enzyme to which the reacting substrate attaches is stereochemically altered so that the substrate molecule no longer fits. In allosteric activation, the activating molecule removes the blocking agent from the allosteric site, thus permitting the reacting substrate to bind with the enzyme. Acetyl co-A changes the tertiary conformation of pyruvate carboxylase and thus lowers the *Km* value for bicarbonate ion (which is the source of the CO_2 required in the reaction). Allosteric modification is a highly sensitive feedback regulator because the enzyme's activity is modified in direct proportion to the amount of modifier present.

enhanced mitochondrial [NADH]/[NAD^+] ratios. Malate can leave the mitochondria and once in the cytosolic portion, it is readily reoxidized into oxaloacetate by the reduction of NAD^+. The oxaloacetate can be then converted into phosphoenolpyruvate by ***phosphoenolpyruvate carboxylase,*** and thus reenter the Embden-Meyerhof pathway. This complicated series of steps constitutes an essential detour around the energetically disallowed conversion of pyruvate directly into PEP as the first step.

Pyruvate can also be converted directly into malate in the cytosol via an energy-consuming reaction incorporating CO_2 and requiring the oxidation of NADH plus H^+ to NAD^+. This malate can either be converted directly into oxaloacetate or routed through the TCA cycle (either forwards or backwards, depending upon the intramitochondrial redox state).

Now that we have negotiated to some extent the tortuous and complex biochemical pathways involved in basic carbohydrate metabolism, we are in a good position to understand the many diverse, and often apparently contradictory, effects that ethanol oxidation and its sequalae exert upon these systems.

Under conditions of adequate nutrition and with adequate glycogen stores, alcohol enhances the rate of glycogenolysis and elevates plasma glucose concentrations (by up to 10% according to Becker et al. 1974). This appears to be largely due to the release of catecholamines from the adrenal glands in response to the physiological stress that a significant ethanol challenge has upon an organism. As we have seen epinephrine enhances the activity of adenylate cyclase which stimulates a variety of phosphorylases, resulting in enhanced glycogenolysis and suppressed glycogenesis. Catecholamine release due to physiological (or psychological) stress also stimulates the pancreatic alpha cells to release glucagon, whereas insulin release from the beta cells is correspondingly suppressed. Glucagon augments glycogenolysis by stimulating the activity of adenylate cyclase in a manner similar to epinephrine. Norepinephrine and epinephrine also directly inhibit insulin release, thus decreasing the peripheral utilization of glucose.

On the other hand, ethanol in the fasted state results in a severe hypoglycemia because of exhaustion of the glycogen reserves and the direct inhibition of gluconeogenesis. Because the oxidation of ethanol and acetaldehyde generates a large excess of both reducing equivalents and acetyl co-A, the normal operation of the TCA cycle is severely impaired or even reversed; the conversion of glucose and amino acids into pyruvate, and of pyruvate into acetyl co-A is likewise similarly restricted. The altered redox state favors the conversion of pyruvate into malate, both in the cytosol and the mitochondria. However, the conversion of malate to oxaloacetate requires the reduction of NAD^+, and in a highly reducing environment this step is not possible. Glucogenesis is therefore restricted or halted completely and the buildup of malate prevents further channeling along that pathway. The only route still open for pyruvate is its reduction to lactate, a process that is augmented by a reducing environment (see footnote 21). An additional factor inhibiting the conversion of pyruvate into acetyl co-A in chronic alcoholics is the associated deficiency in vitamins B-complex commonly seen in this group — especially of thiamine.

The liver normally contains enough glycogen in well-nourished individuals to supply the body with adequate glucose for about 8 to 12 hours with fasting. The enhanced mobilization of glycogen reserves and the suppression gluconeogenesis frequently causes a profound hypoglycemia in alcoholics and patients often present in emergency rooms with blood glucose levels as low as 5 mg-percent (Becker et al. 1974). Such patients are in coma or near coma and may have a number of neurological signs such as seizures and muscular weakness on one side of the body. Most medical authorities are in agreement that prompt treatment with intravenous glucose is an essential life-saving measure in such patients (for example, Becker et al. 1974; Korsten and Lieber 1976). However, it has also been suggested that thiamine-deficient alcoholics and those with an already severe lactic acidosis may be precipitated into a life-threatening pyruvate accumulation and exacerbated hyperlactidemia if glucose is administered (Mayes 1981).

Alcohol-induced hypoglycemia may occur up to 30 hours following the last drink and the mortality rate for such patients is about 10 percent (Becker et al. 1974). Insulin does not appear to be involved in alcoholic hypoglycemia. On the contrary, the normal stimulatory effect of glucagon on insulin is inhibited by ethanol, insulin levels can be normal in patients with alcoholic hypoglycemia, and blood glucose levels can be depressed in decompensated, insulin-dependent and alcoholic diabetics. But besides inhibiting gluconeogenesis and depleting glycogen stores, ethanol does potentiate the hypoglycemic effect of insulin and other similar agents. The issue is complicated by the fact that a high proportion of alcoholics with alcoholic liver disease exhibit marked glucose intolerance even in the absence of ethanol. The evidence, however, strongly suggests that this does not result from the liver injury itself. On the contrary, a peripheral resistance to glucose utilization (Reitz 1979) is probably correlated with *decreased* insulin output due to stress-related catecholamine release. Individuals with severe alcoholic pancreatic damage, however, often exhibit a chronic, reactive hypoglycemia due to insult to the beta cells (see footnote 43); frank diabetes mellitus often also results from such permanent pancreatic injury.

The administration of fructose enhances the clearance of alcohol from the blood in intoxicated persons by as much as 80 percent. Even severely intoxicated patients have been sobered up to an alert and functional state within 2½ hours after receiving fructose (Becker et al. 1974). However, there is much variation in this response (Erickson 1979) and the acceleration of ethanol oxidation produced by fructose may range from 15 percent to more than 100 percent (Alkana and Noble 1979). This enhanced clearance of ethanol from the blood is due to the conversion of fructose into D-glyceraldehyde, and the subsequent reduction of D-glyceraldehyde to glycerol by alcohol dehydrogenase (see Fig. 26). The accompanying generation of oxidized ADH-NAD^+ complexes counters the increased [NADH]/[NAD^+] due to ethanol and acetaldehyde oxidation, thus allowing an accelerated rate of ethanol metabolism.[111] The effect of fructose is most evident at higher blood concentrations of ethanol.

Gluconeogenesis is also stimulated by fructose via the hexokinase to fructose 6-phosphate and thence via the phosphohexose isomerase to glucose 6-phosphate route, and fructose is sometimes given to patients with ethanol-induced hypoglycemia. Fructose is also rapidly metabolized to pyruvate, dihydroxyacetone phosphate, and D-glyceraldehyde (see Fig. 26). These three substances are each in turn reduced to lactate, glycerol 3-phosphate,[112] and glycerol, respectively; all of these reduction steps are accompanied by the oxidation of NADH and H^+ to NAD^+, a process enhanced by the excess hydrogen equivalents due to ethanol metabolism. In a reducing milieu glycerol would tend not to oxidize into dihyroxyacetone phosphate, but would become esterified into triglyceride, incorporated into VLDL, and enter the various lipid metabolic pathways. Similarly, the glyceraldehyde 3-phosphate deriving from dihydroxyacetone phosphate and fructose 1,6-diphosphate (from glycogenolysis) would be blocked from its NAD^+-dependent oxidation into 1,3-diphosphoglycerate under a high [NADH]/[NAD^+] ratio. Most of the fructose converted into pyruvate would follow the pathway from D-glyceraldehyde to 1,3-diphosphoglycerate in an ATP-requiring step catalyzed by triokinase.

As has been noted, this pyruvate is shunted into the formation of lactate by high concentrations of reducing equivalents. This can precipitate or exacerbate a previously existing hyperlactidemia and may have life-threatening metabolic consequences. Because the increase in ethanol clearance from fructose administration is small (never more than two-fold under the highest doses) and the danger of serious metabolic consequences high, the use of fructose in detoxifying acutely intoxicated patients is not recommended by most medical authorities. Particular care must also be taken to ensure that the patient has not consumed methanol if fructose is to be employed, since it will also enhance the rate of production of formaldehyde.

---

[111]Glycerol can be metabolized only by those tissues which possess the activating enzyme glycerokinase: the liver, kidney, intestine, brown adipose tissue, and the lactating mammary gland. Glycerol derived from D-glyceraldehyde (as well as from other sources) is converted into dihydroxyacetone phosphate, accompanied by the reduction of NAD^+ to NADH and H^+. However, in the highly reducing environment produced by ethanol oxidation this step would be severely curtailed; the glycerol from D-glyceraldehyde reduction could then be esterified into triglyceride, transported by VLDL, and utilized in the various lipid pathways and cycles.

[112]Glycerol is converted first into glycerol 3-phosphate with the dephophorylation of ATP into ADP, and then oxidized into dihydroxyacetone phosphate by the conversion of NAD^+ to NADH and H^+ in a step not shown in Figure 26.

Several authors have suggested (for example, Higgins 1979; Bowman and Rand 1980) that the rate limitations for ethanol oxidation by ADh may also be energy-linked and thus dependent upon the [ATP]/[ADP] ratio. Therefore, agents which uncouple oxidative phosphorylation, such as *dinitrophenol* and *carbonylcyanide*-m-*chloropheylhydrazone* (variously abbreviated as CCCP or FCCP) which cause a marked increase in the metabolic rate and thus of oxygen utilization, should increase the rate of alcohol clearance.[113] This has repeatedly been shown to be the case, although the results are quite variable (Rognstad & Grunnet 1979) and the acceleration in alcohol clearance too small (50% at near toxic doses) to justify using such highly dangerous uncoupling agents. It has also been suggested that the enhanced ethanol metabolism due to fructose is at least partly caused by the increased utilization of ATP during its metabolism into glucose or pyruvate (Higgins 1979). However, the mechanism is not at all understood and there are several apparently contradictory facts that require clarification. For example, the rate of ethanol metabolism is inversely correlated with the relative tissue concentrations of ATP, ADP, and AMP, in that order, which seems to exhibit a clear link between energy and alcohol oxidation. However, the inhibitor constants for these phosphate carriers are: $K_i^{ATP} = 700$ μM, $K_i^{ADP} = 180$ μM, and $K_i^{AMP} = 32$ μM, respectively (Higgins 1979).[114]

It is obvious, then, that the adenosine phosphate complexes are increasingly potent inhibitory agents of aldehyde dehydrogenase progressing from ATP to ADP to AMP. As ATP concentrations decrease and ADP and AMP levels increase, therefore, the release of inhibition by ATP as it disappears should more than be offset by the increasing inhibitory effect from the more potent inhibitors, ADP and AMP. Precisely the reverse appears to be the case! There does appear to be a strong relationship between energy-state and ethanol oxidation, but it is an inverse one and the mechanism are completely obscure thus far.

---

[113]These agents completely eliminate the oxidative phosphorylation of ADP to ATP, but they do not inhibit the oxidative processes of the respiratory chain itself. Continuing redox reactions in the respiratory chain therefore yield energy in the form of heat which is lost to the system, rather than as chemical energy used to form ATP. The increased loss of energy causes a compensatory increase in metabolic rate and a corresponding increase in oxygen consumption. The effect of this metabolic acceleration is to enhance the rate of ethanol and acetaldehyde oxidation.

[114]ATP, ADP, and AMP are competitive inhibitors for the NAD-binding site on the enzyme alcohol dehydrogenase. Consider the equation $E + S \rightleftharpoons ES$, on page 75. In the analyogous case of competitive inhibition, the competitive inhibitor I reacts with the binding site on enzyme *E* to reversibly form the complex *EI*. Since the *EI* complex cannot form further reaction products (as can the ES complex on page 75), the inhibitor constant K^N_i can be defined: $K^N_i = [E][I] : [EI]$. The greater the binding affinity of I for E (that is, the lower the value of K^N_i), the more completely bound will be the inhibitor when its molar concentration exceeds that of the enzyme. But when the concentration of the enzyme increases, the inhibitor becomes rapidly saturated and the proportion of unbound enzyme also

→

The effects of ethanol upon carbohydrate metabolism are summarized in Figure 27.

We left our discussion of alcoholic fatty liver disease on page 86 to undertake the long and involved detour through the biochemical and metabolic processes by which this is precipitated by ethanol ingestion. This is an appropriate point to resume that discussion and to lead into the factors that result in the far more dangerous progression into hepatitis and cirrhosis.

As we have seen, fatty liver disease due to alcohol intake arises from a great many different processes. It is also amply clear that this is not due to the malnutrition commonly seen in alcoholics as was formerly thought, but rather to the direct toxic effects of alcohol and its metabolites. Fatty liver can develop remarkably quickly in response to ethanol. Nonalcoholic human subjects showed significant fatty liver changes within a few days when given 10 ounces of 86-proof whiskey per day along with a nutritionally adequate diet. This fat content increased nearly eightfold in only 18 days (Lieber 1976). Larger doses (18-24 ounces per day) produced fatty liver change within *two days* (Rubin & Lieber 1968).

Hepatic protein accumulation occurs simultaneously with fat buildup and it is as important quantitatively as fat deposition in the early development of alcoholic hepatomegaly (Lieber & DeCarli 1978). Minor increases in mitochondrial and microsomal proteins are seen, but the major protein accumulation occurs in the cytosol, especially of transport proteins like albumin and transferrin. The increase of the hepatic Golgi apparatus which occurs with a similar increase in both rough and smooth endoplasmic reticulum due to ethanol may be partly responsible for this, since the Golgi apparatus is the site of production

---

increases rapidly in proportion. The higher the affinity of I for E, the steeper is the rate of increase of unbound enzyme as its total concentration increases, according to the equation:

$$R = \text{slope of inhibited reaction} = \frac{K_m}{V_{max}} \times \left[1 + \frac{[I]}{K_i}\right],$$

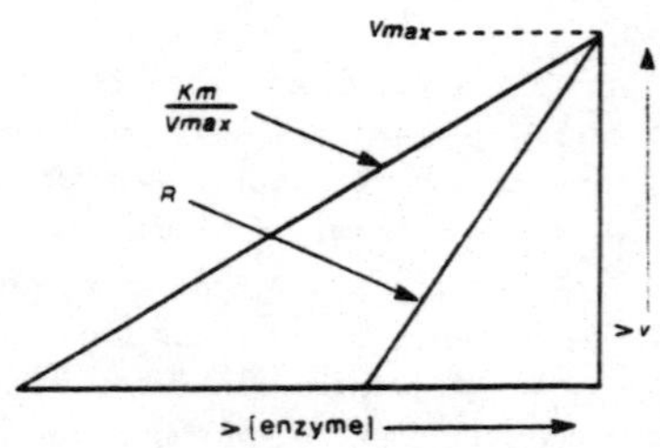

where $K_m + V_{max}$ = slope of the uninhibited reaction (see also pages 71 and 72 and Figs. 14-15 for explanation of symbols). The increase in slope in the presence of the inhibitor is therefore $1 + [I]/K^{N}_{i}$. At any concentration of I there is a concentration of enzyme (although it may be very high) which will give full enzyme activity. Unlike the case in noncompetitive inhibition, V_{max} is not changed in any way by the inhibition.

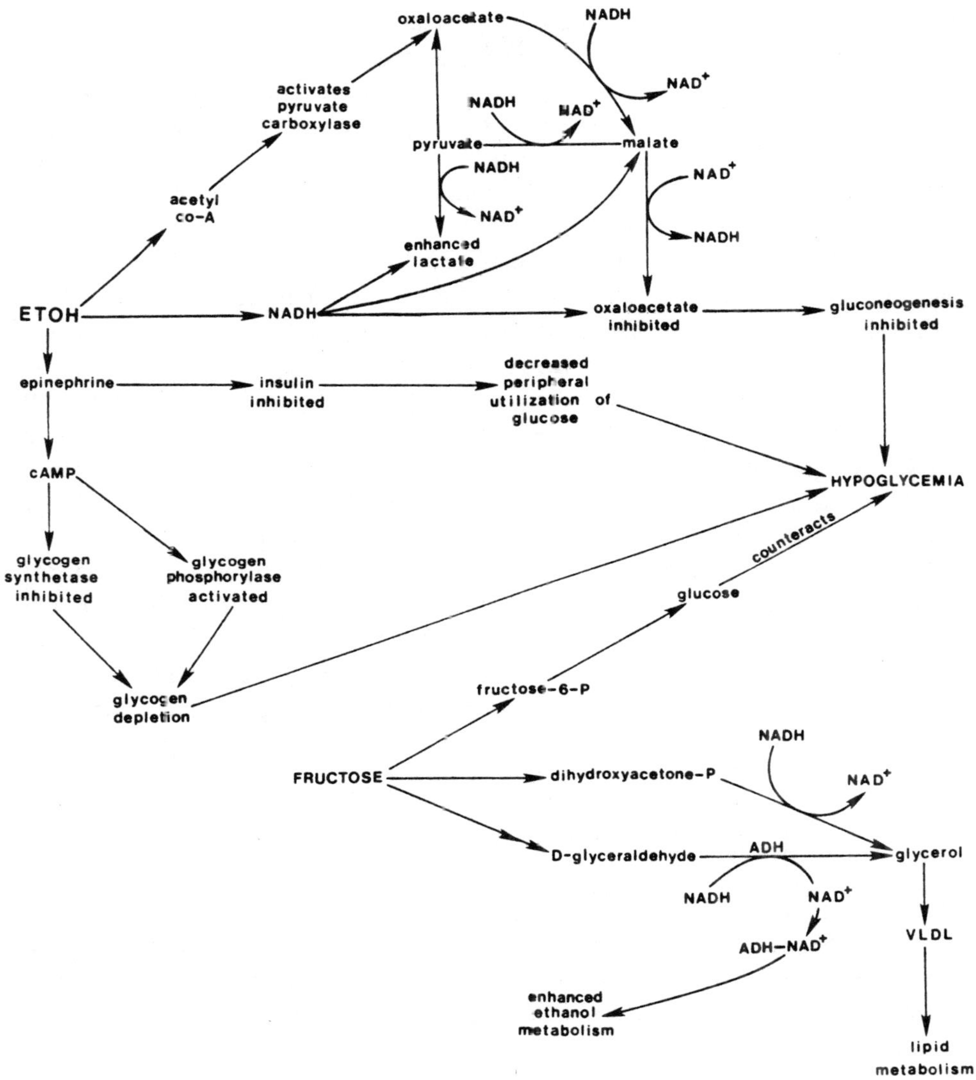

Figure 27. Effects of ethanol on carbohydrate metabolism.

of the protein moiety of lipoproteins. The Golgi apparatis is also closely associated with the endoplasmic reticulum. Proteins manufactured in the ribosomes associated with the rough ER are moved either directly into condensing vacuoles pinched off the endoplasmic reticulum, or into the Golgi apparatus and subsequently into vacuoles derived therefrom. These vacuoles then fuse with the plasma membrane of the cell in a Ca^{2+}-dependent process, and the contents are released to the exterior. It appears that the export of proteins from the hepatocytes is impaired by ethanol, perhaps because of the general disruptive effects of ethanol upon membrane systems, particularly with regard to Ca^{2+}-binding. The decreased protein export acting in concert with increased protein production contributes to hepatycytic protein accumulation.

Chronic ethanol insult causes a *decrease* in rough ER membrane surface area, quite in contrast to the effects of acute ethanol challenges (Lieber & DeCarli 1978). The correlation between this and alterations in protein synthesis are not clear, and decreased protein manufacture may depend upon the nutritional state of the organism. Lipoprotein output does decrease with chronic ethanol intake, resulting in decreasing plasma lipids (in contrast to the initial hyperlipemia) possibly associated with progressive liver injury.

The mitochondria are also grossly disturbed by chronic alcohol intake. They typically become swollen and engorged with massive distortion of the membrane architecture. This appears to be due to the direct toxic effects of both ethanol and its immediate metabolite, acetaldehyde, as well as possibly to some of the congeners in certain alcoholic beverages. In this regard, pure grain alcohol was found to be less destructive to mitochondria than bourbon (Lieber & DeCarli 1978). As the mitochondria suffer increasingly greater injury, their ability to metabolize acetaldehyde becomes increasingly impaired. Since most of the acetaldehyde is oxidized in the mitochondria (see Fig. 16), this may account for the increasd serum levels of acetaldehyde seen in alcoholics relative to normal controls. Mitochondrial disruption probably also exacerbates the inhibition of beta-oxidation of fatty acids resulting from increased [NADH]/[NAD^+] ratios.

HEPATITIS, CIRRHOSIS, AND PORTAL HYPERTENSION

It is still unclear whether reversible alcoholic fatty liver disease represents the initial lesions that progress into hepatocellular inflammation and necrosis. Most investigators, however, believe that this is probably the case. Both fatty change (Fig. 28) and necrosis usually begin in the peripheral regions of the liver acinus in alcoholics, that is, the centrilobular area. This region lies in acinar zone 3 (see Figs. 18 & 28) which lies most distally to the point of entry of the blood from the portal vein. It therefore has the lowest oxygen tensions. When oxygen consumption is accelerated by ethanol oxidation, the PO_2 is further reduced.[115] Alcohol dehydrogenase activity is reported to be greater in the centrilobular than in the periportal region (Mezey 1979). Furthermore, the microsomal enzymes are also concentrated in the centrilobular zone, and this system comes into play at high concentrations of ethanol. All of this depletes the already low oxygen tension in the centrilobular area still further. The resulting hypoxia is the probable cause of cell death and necrosis in acinar zone

[115]The *partial pressure* of oxygen (see also footnote 96). The pressure of a gas mixture is equal to the sum of the partial pressures of its constituent gases.

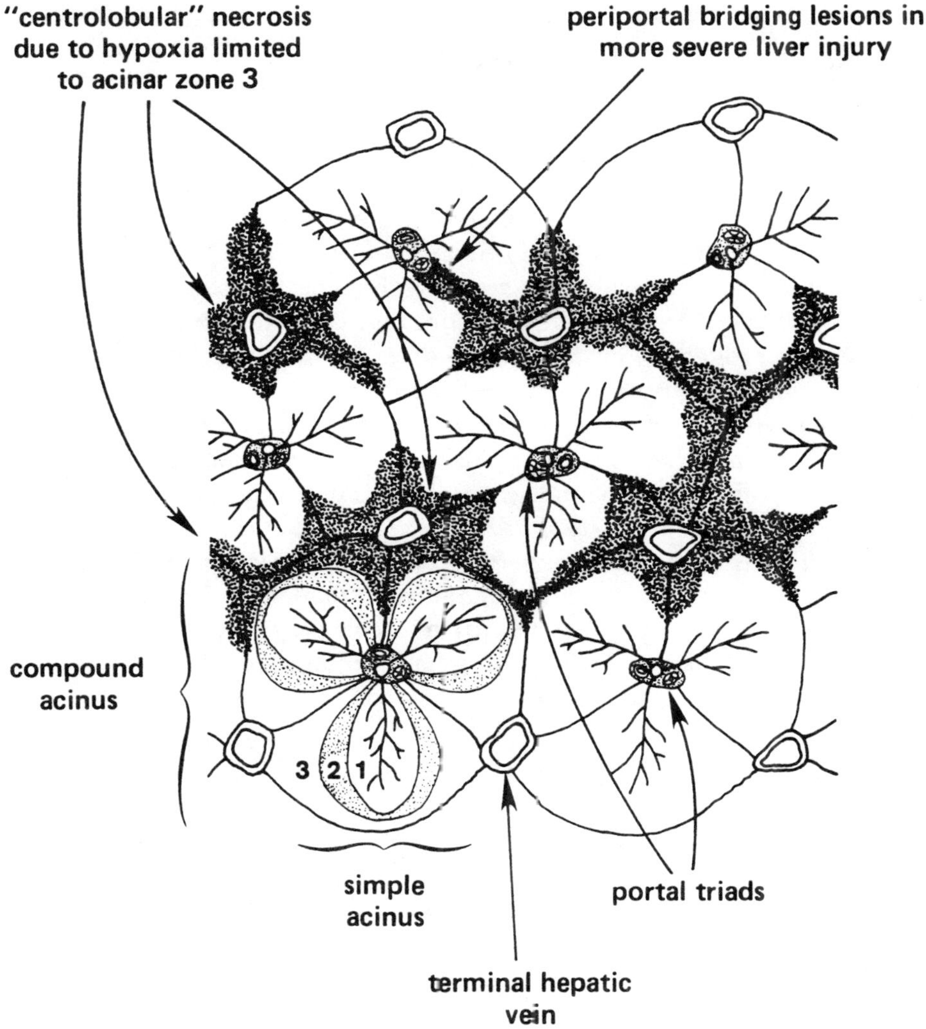

Figure 28. Alcoholic liver injury. Adapted and modified after Rappaport 1975. Numbers refer to acinar circulatory zones.

3, producing the typical centrilobular necrotic lesions of alcoholic hepatitis (Israel et al. 1979). Such advanced liver injury usually only occurs after years of excessive alcohol intake and it is likely that other factors also play an important role. This model also implies that enhanced ethanol clearance rates associated with increased microsomal activity induced by chronic ethanol intake would augment the formation of centrilobular necrosis. This is supported by the fact that alcoholics with liver necrosis do appear to metabolize ethanol 60 percent faster than alcoholics without such lesions (Israel et al. 1979).

Centrilobular collagen deposition and ensuing fibrosis is the hallmark of advanced alcoholic liver disease (Figs. 28 & 29). Collagen is the most abundant protein in vertebrates and it is unique in containing the amino acids *hydroxyproline* and *hydroxylysine*. Proline and hydroxyproline constitute about 21 percent of the entire collagen chain. Collagen is produced by *fibroblasts*[116] or their derivatives. It is first secreted by groups of ribosomes known as *polysomes* as a very high molecular weight protein called *procollagen*. While these procollagen chains are still attached to the polysomes, the proline and lysine residues are hydroxylated by the enzymes *proline* (or *prolyl*) *hydroxylase* and *lysine (lysyl) hydroxylase* into hydroxyproline and hydroxylysine, respectively. The procollagen chains are extruded from the cell and three of the chains intertwine to give a triple helical, ropelike strand through the formation of hydrogen bonds by the hydroxyamino acids. Once this configuration is formed, hydroxylation of proline and lysine ceases. The assembled procollagen then forms *tropocollagen* by splitting off excess peptide sequences (amino acid chains). The tropocollagen then forms a series of cross-linkages between the strands, becoming converted into parallel strands of collagen.

The enzymes necessary for converting proline into hydroxyproline and its lysine hydroxylating counterpart are both mixed-function oxygenases bound to the microsomal membranes. They require molecular oxygen, ascorbic acid (vitamin C), and the TCA cycle substrate alpha-ketoglutarate, plus Fe^{2+}, in addition to the specific amino acid to be hydroxylated. The reaction is:

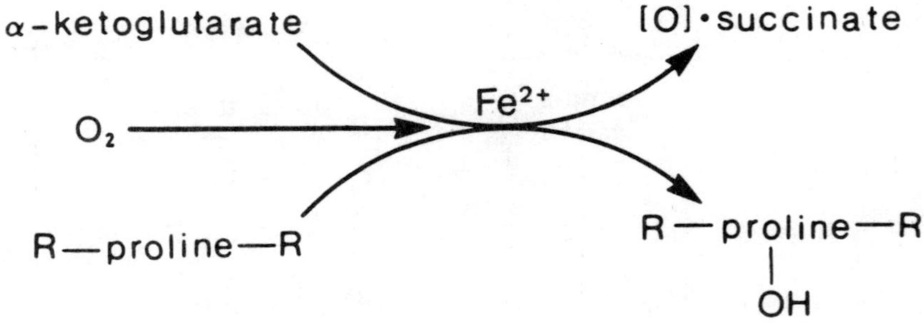

The reaction involving lysine hydroxylase is exactly analogous. Ascorbic acid is required as a necessary cofactor to convert the precursor molecules of proline and lysine hydroxylase into their active forms. This appears to involve the aggregation of shorter protein chains with a molecular weight only one-third that of the active enzyme (Stassen et al. 1973).

Hypoxia and lactate, in addition to ascorbate, also are capable of activating proline and lysine hydroxylase (Comstock and Udenfriend 1970; Levene &

[116] Generalized, undifferentiated, embryonic or *mesenchymal* cells capable of differentiating into a variety of cell types. They secrete many different kinds of connective tissue material, including collagen, clotting fibers, cartilage, and bone.

Bates 1976; Mezey 1979). Although molecular oxygen is required for the hydroxylation of proline, low oxygen tensions appear to paradoxically stimulate the active production of collagen. This is done indirectly by shifting the cellular machinery from aerobic to anaerobic glycolysis with the resulting buildup of lactate. Lactate apparently can function in the place of ascorbate as the necessary cofactor catalyzing the aggregation of precursors into active proline hydroxylase. It is, however, much less effective than ascorbic acid in this capacity. Although very little oxygen is available under such anoxic conditions, there is enough present in trace quantities to support the reaction but not enough to support normal cell growth and aerobic glycolysis (Levene & Bates 1976).

In summary, centrilobular hypoxia resulting from the metabolism of ethanol can produce lactate buildup by promoting anaerobic glycolysis, as well as shunting pyruvate over into lactate production because of the excess reducing equivalents generated by ethanol and acetaldehyde oxidation. This lactate activates proline and lysine hydroxylase from precursor proteins and paradoxically causes the formation of collagen resulting in fibrosis in the region of the central hepatic vein. This process is very likely augmented by the proliferation of the microsomal membranes induced by chronic alcohol intake, since both hydroxylases are mixed-function oxidases bound to this fraction. The resulting lesions are shown in Figure 28.

In early alcoholic hepatitis the lesions are confined largely to the centrilobular areas. The majority of acini are usually affected and the central hepatic veins may become completely occluded. As alcoholic hepatitis progresses, fibrosis may expand to form bridges linking the hepatic venules (veins) to the portal tracts, commonly associated with bile duct proliferation (Fig. 28). The attendant swelling and lateral compression of the cytoplasm has already been mentioned. *Mallory bodies* are commonly present in the cytoplasm surrounding the nucleus. These are small, discrete, brightly staining, hyalin particles which appear to represent destroyed remnants of the endoplasmic reticulum or possibly also of the mitochondria. Mallory bodies have been considered by many authors to be almost diagnostic of alcoholism. However, they can and do occur in many other disorders, and their presence is not required for a diagnosis of alcoholic hepatitis. They are typical nonetheless, and together with fibrosis around the central hepatic venule (*centrilobular sclerosis* of some authors) present a characteristic portrait of alcoholic hepatitis and associated fibrosis. For patients who stop drinking at an early stage of the disease, hepatocytic inflammation may reverse with only remnant fibrosis persisting in acinar zone 3; in other cases the fibrosis may progress despite abstinence from alcohol.

As the fibrosis progresses to form bridges between hepatic venules and the portal tracts, fibrous septa develop along these routes. As these septa contract the normal architecture of the liver becomes grossly distorted (Fig. 29). The remaining liver parenchyma in acinar zones 1 & 2 often partially regenerates and forms a variable pattern of small micronodules of the same size as or somewhat

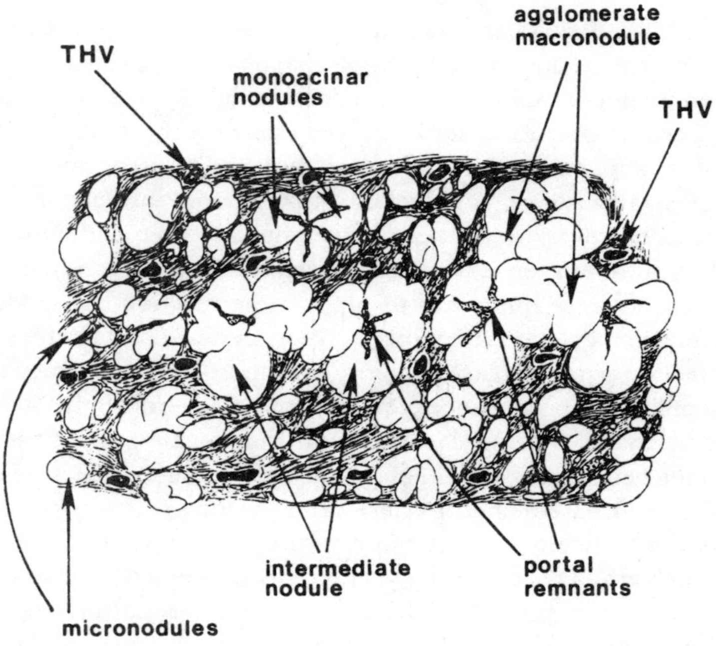

As fibrosis progresses and becomes general in acinar zone 3, the surviving liver parenchyma in zone 1 (zone 2 is really a transition between zones 1 and 3 and as zone 3 is destroyed, zone 2 becomes incorporated into zone 1) undergoes partial regeneration and hyperplasia. As the "centrolobular" fibrous zones contract, the entire liver architecture is destroyed. Surviving remnants of simple acini are partially regenerated into small monoacinar nodules. Much smaller micronodules are formed out of small acinar remnants. Intermediate nodules are generated out of surviving remnants of complex acini, and the much larger agglomerate macronodules are formed out of the extreme hyperplasia of intact complex acinar agglomerates. It should be emphasized that the peripheral boundaries of the acini are not visible under normal circumstances. However, as necrosis and fibrosis progress in zone 3, the acini become delineated by bands of pathological tissue. THV = terminal hepatic vein.

Adapted and modified after Rappaport 1975.

Figure 29. Severe micronodular cirrhosis. THV = terminal hepatic vein.

smaller than the normal hepatic lobule. At some point in this progression the patient has passed from alcoholic hepatitis into liver cirrhosis, commonly called *Laennec's cirrhosis* or *micronodular cirrhosis.* This is the most advanced and dangerous form of alcoholic liver injury, and it is irreversible. As the cirrhosis progresses, nodules of different sizes may appear *(macronodular cirrhosis).* The transition from micronodular to macronodular cirrhosis appears to be due to the differential growth of regenerative nodules from the parenchyma (Korsten & Lieber 1976). Late in the course of cirrhosis the liver shrinks into a small, hard, nodular or "hobnail," brown-colored structure often weighing less than 1,000 grams (Robbins 1974). This disease has a slow and insidiously progressive course over a span of from 5 to 20 years or more. It results from the direct hepatotoxic effects of ethanol itself and is not due to nutritional deficiencies, either from inadequate dietary intake or malabsorption, as been claimed previously. Poor nutrition can, of course, play an auxiliary role and exacerbate the course of the cirrhosis, but it cannot by itself produce the signs of alcoholic hepatitis and cirrhosis. Baboons given a nutritionally adequate diet along with ethanol equal to 50 percent of the total caloric intake developed the entire range of alcoholic liver disease (Korstein & Lieber 1976), including fatty liver (100% of the test animals), alcoholic hepatitis (31%), and about 38 percent developed liver cirrhosis in two to four years (Lieber & DeCarli 1978).

The development of fibrosis in the region around the terminal hepatic venules results in occlusion of the venules and associated sinusoids (Fig. 30). This causes an increase in the portal blood pressure. The blockage is partially compensated for by the development of collateral shunts between the terminal portal and terminal hepatic venules. However, the flow of blood to the sinusoids is markedly reduced, exacerbating an already severe hypoxia in the distal portions of the sinusoids. As the liver shrinks in size and becomes massively fibrous and indurated, the *portal hypertension* already initiated by sclerotic occlusion of the hepatic venules becomes even more severe. Both the hepatic venules and the sinusoids are compressed by the regenerating parenchyma of the nodules resulting in a primarily sinusoidal and postsinusoidal portal hypertension. Although the development of pariacinar fibrosis initiates this process, nodule regeneration appears to be the most important factor in the genesis of portal hypertension associated with alcoholic liver cirrhosis (Huet et al. 1975). The increased portal back-pressure causes the anastomoses between the portal venules and hepatic arterioles (Fig. 30) to become enlarged and engenders the development of abnormal shunts between the two systems. The consequent shunting of arteriolar blood under arteriolar pressures directly into the portal venules causes the portal flow to be reversed.[117]

Portal hypertension has many serious medical consequences, including (1) *ascites* or leakage of serous fluid into the body cavity, (2) the development of collateral venous channels wherever the *systemic* (main body) and portal circulations share a common capillary network, and (3) *splenomegaly* or gross spleen enlargement (also termed *congestive splenomegaly*).

Ascites occurs in about 46 percent of patients with liver cirrhosis (Robbins 1974), and its appearance represents a poor prognosis with significant mortality. Ascites may present with many liters of fluid accumulating in the body cavity with massive abdominal swelling. Portal hypertension and *hypoalbuminemia*

---

[117]The valves formed by flaps of tissue present in most veins to prevent backward flow of the blood are lacking in the hepatic portal system.

[118]In two fluids separated by a semipermeable membrane in which the relative concentrations of solute (e.g., salt) and solute (e.g., water) differ, *osmosis* is the tendency for each of the fractions to migrate from regions of higher to regions of lower concentrations of itself. Thus, water will flow from more dilute solutions (greater concentrations of water relative to the solute) to more concentrated solutions (greater concentrations of solute relative to water) and vice versa. An equilibrium between the two systems is eventually reached in which the concentrations of solvent and solute are approximately identical (ignoring Donnan equilibrium factors). Proteins act to increase the osmotic pressure along with such electrolytes as N^+ and K^+; as they are removed from the blood, the osmotic pressure of the blood drops and fluid is lost to the "exterior" (peritoneal or body cavity).

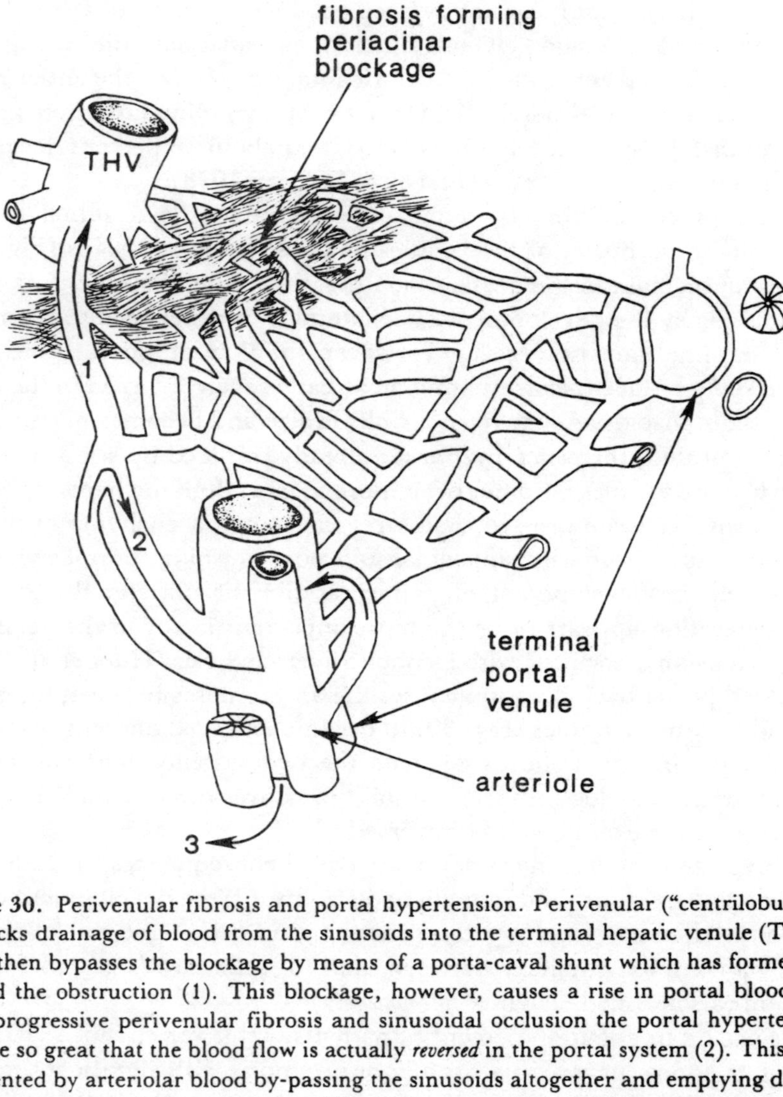

Figure 30. Perivenular fibrosis and portal hypertension. Perivenular ("centrilobular") fibrosis blocks drainage of blood from the sinusoids into the terminal hepatic venule (THV). This blood then bypasses the blockage by means of a porta-caval shunt which has formed a detour around the obstruction (1). This blockage, however, causes a rise in portal blood pressure. With progressive perivenular fibrosis and sinusoidal occlusion the portal hypertension may become so great that the blood flow is actually *reversed* in the portal system (2). This reversal is augmented by arteriolar blood by-passing the sinusoids altogether and emptying directly into the portal venules. With general liver fibrosis the reversal of portal flow may be such that massive leakage of serum into the body cavity occurs causing ascites and *caput Medusae,* as well as jaundice, and/or lethal hemorrhage from esophageal and/or gastric varices (3). Based on a Drawing by Rappaport 1975.

enhance the filtration of serous fluid into the body cavity because of the resulting imbalance between hydrostatic and osmotic forces.[118] The fluid is protein-rich (primarily albumin) and it contains water soluble substances such as sugar, Na^+, and K^+ in similar concentrations to those in the blood. The rate of exchange between the ascitic fluid and the blood is as much as 80 percent per hour (Robbins 1974). Thus, attempts to relieve the pressure by tapping off the intraperitoneal fluid are rarely successful and the fluid rapidly reaccumulates.

The *left gastric vein* or *coronary vein* runs along the length of the lesser curvature of the stomach and intermingles with the capillary bed it forms jointly with the *esophageal veins* (Fig. 31). It then turns and runs downward to join the hepatic portal vein just above the junction between the latter and the *splenic vein* (from which arises the inferior mesenteric vein — see also Figs. 11 & 31). The back pressure resulting from portal hypertension often causes the esophageal-gastric capillaries to become dilated and the capillary walls to be distended and weakened. Such esophageal and gastric *varices* occur in about two-thirds of all patients with advanced liver cirrhosis (Robbins 1974). Ruptures and massive hemorrhage occur in these varices in about a quarter of these patients, nearly always with fatal consequences.

Similarly, the systemic and portal circulations anastomose in the *rectal venous plexus*. The *middle rectal vein* drains the rectal plexus into the *internal iliac vein* and thence into the inferior vena cava, and thus belongs to the systemic circulation. However, it also drains into the *superior rectal vein* which empties into the *inferior mesenteric vein* and which thus belongs to the portal circulation. The vessels of the rectal plexus are located within very loose connective tissue and they receive very little support. They are thus very susceptible to increased blood pressure. Portal hypertension very readily causes these vessels to become distended and outpouched resulting in the rectal varices known as hemorrhoids. Unlike the life-threatening esophageal and gastric varices associated with alcoholic portal hypertension, hemorrhoids are not a serious medical problem. But they certainly add to the overall pain and discomfort of the sufferer. Between 30 and 50 percent of all patients with liver cirrhosis develop hemorrhoids (Robbins 1974).

The persistent remnants of the *left umbilical vein*[119] runs from the left branch of the hepatic portal vein to anastomose with the *epigastric veins* of the systemic circulation. Portal hypertension frequently causes the epigastric complex to become distended, producing a characteristic pattern of varicose veins radiating from the umbilicus. This condition is known as the *caput Medusae* or Medusa's head because of the resemblance of the tangle of snakes on the head of that mythical figure (Fig. 31).

Congestive splenomegaly results from portal backflow through the *splenic vein* into the spleen (Fig. 31).

---

[119]The fetus receives its entire oxygen supply from the placenta via the embryonic umbilical veins, of which only the left one persists throughout later fetal existence. These veins carry oxygenated blood into the inferior vena cava, both directly and via a temporary embryonic shunt, the *ductus venosus*. The oxygenated blood from the placenta is mixed with returning deoxygenated blood in the vena cava before it enters the right atrium of the heart. Most of this blood passes directly into the left atrium through a temporary fetal opening called the *foramen ovale* and is sent directly to the oxygen-dependent and vulnerable brain through a pulmonary bypass, the *ductus arteriosus*. All of these temporary structures disappear within a very few minutes after birth and the blood is routed to the lungs for oxygenation. A small portion of the left umbilical vein persists throughout life, however, which connects the portal and systemic circulations.

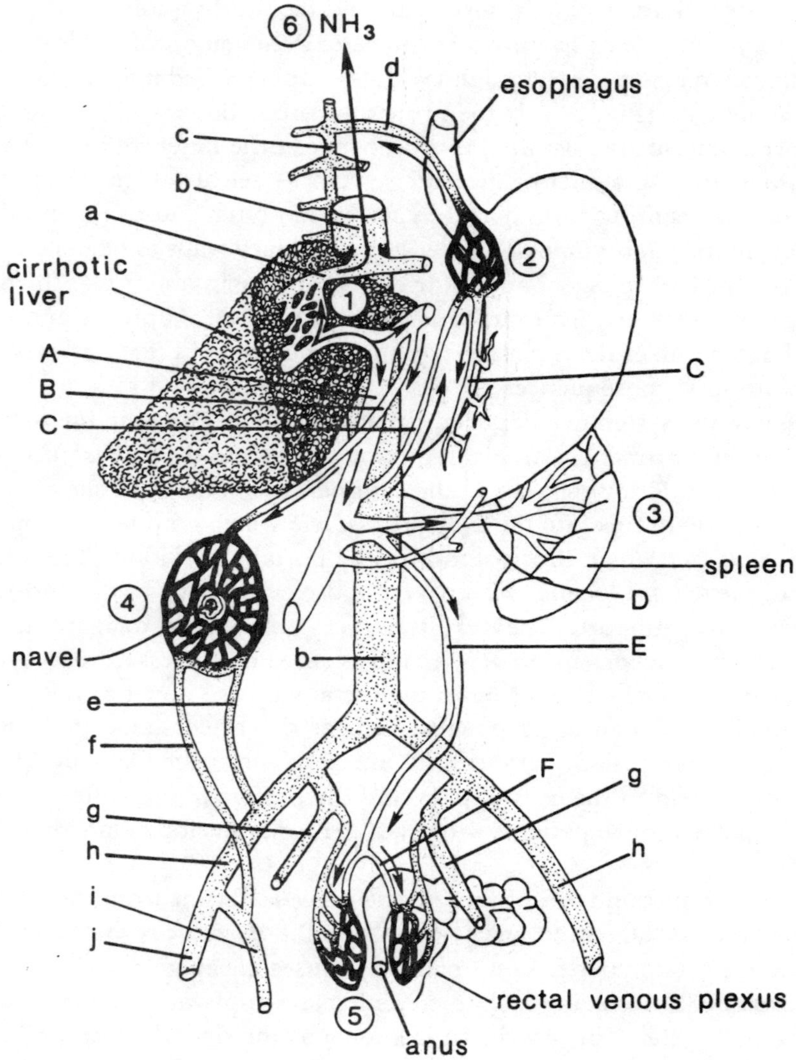

Figure 31. Consequences of liver failure and portal hypertension. **Hepatic portal venous circulation** [upper-case letters and no stippling]: A = hepatic portal vein; B = remnant of left umbilical vein; C = left gastric (coronary) vein; D = splenic vein; E = inferior mesenteric vein; F = superior rectal vein. **Systemic venous circulation** [lower-case letters and light stippling]: a = hepatic vein; b = inferior vena cava; c = azygous vein; d = esophageal vein; e = inferior epigastric vein; f = superficial epigastraic vein; g = internal iliac vein; h = external iliac vein; i = great saphenous vein; j = femoral vein. **Anastomosing plexi between portal and systemic circulations** shown by heavy stippling: 1 = porta-caval shunt; 2 = esophageal-gastric varcies; 3 = splenomegaly; 4 = *caput Medusae* formed in epigastric plexus; 5 = hemorrhoids; 6 = liver failure and transport of non-detoxified NH_3 to the brain where it interferes with the TCA cycle, causing hepatic encephalopathy. Arrows indicate direction of circulatory flow.

Alcoholic liver cirrhosis is sometimes accompanied by *hepatorenal syndrome,* a grave kidney disorder characterized by *oliguria* (frequent urination) and *azotemia* (increased blood urea concentration). There is a decline in the rate of glomerular filtration and renal blood flow and the blood is shunted intrarenally from the cortex (outer kidney region) to the medulla (inner zone) by mechanisms that are not clear. An increased sodium retention is characteristic of this syndrome which may be partly due to the fact that medullary nephrons have longer loops of Henle than do cortical ones. However, increased sodium retention is seen in cirrhotics prior to the onset of hepatorenal syndrome (Korsten & Lieber 1976).

Patients with liver failure involving cirrhosis and portal shunting may develop a severe, chronic or recurrent, but largely reversible neuropsychiatric disorder known as *hepatic* or *metabolic encephalopathy.* It is characterized by personality changes, confusion, agitation, clouded consciousness which may progress to deep coma, and a flapping tremor of the outstretched hands known as *asterixis* or *liver flap.* A characteristic pungent, sweet-sour breath odor, *fetor hepaticus,* is commonly produced presumably by the exhalation of *mercaptans* (R—C—SH) generated by the bacterial breakdown of the sulphur-containing amino acid *methionine.* The disease may develop in the absence of frank liver failure in patients with surgical postcaval shunts. The most likely cause of this disorder is an increase in the blood levels of ammonia (Robbins 1974; Korsten & Lieber 1976; Bowman & Rand 1980).

Dietary amino acids are transaminated and deaminated (see pp. 64 & 65) primarily in the liver into their corresponding α-keto acids and ammonia. The highly toxic ammonia thus formed is normally detoxified and cleared from the portal venous blood in the liver via the urea or *ornithine cycle* which converts ammonia into a harmless and water-soluble metabolite, urea, which is then excreted via the kidneys. Ammonia is also produced by the normal intestinal bacteria from urea by bacterial *urease,* and it is normally excreted in the feces as ammonium ion. Gastrointestinal bleeding such as caused by alcoholic gastritis and/or esophageal-gastric varcies and azotemia such as occurs in hepatorenal syndrome along with dietary protein can increase the production of ammonia by augmenting the amount of urea in the gut. In severe liver failure, the detoxification of ammonia is compromised and the peripheral blood, which normally has no trace of ammonia, may contain as much as 3 ug/ml (Bowman & Rand 1980). Amino acid metabolism is also impaired causing an accumulation of those substances in the plasma and urine — particularly of methionine, cystine, and tyrosine.

Excess ammonia combine with *glutamate (glutamic acid)* to form the amino acid *glutamine.* By so doing it shifts the mass effect to favor the conversion of *alpha-ketoglutarate,*[120] an essential substrate in the TCA cycle, into

[120]The formation of alpha-ketoglutarate is a necessary step in the complex sequence of reactions by which citrate is converted into succinate (see Figs. 7 & 23).

glutamate.[121] The brain is thus deprived of alpha-ketoglutarate, which interferes with the TCA cycle in this organ, impairing the operation of the electron transport mechanism and interfering with the generation of new ATP. The detoxification of ammonia also requires the consumption of ATP, further depleting that energy-rich compound. This interferes with the active sodium-potassium-dependent transport pump and inhibits the repolarization of discharged neurons, further impairing CNS function. The important inhibitory neurotransmitter *gamma-aminobutyric acid* or *GABA* requires glutamate as an essential precursor for its synthesis (see also footnote 105). The enhanced conversion of glutamate into glutamine in the detoxification of excess ammonia reduces its availability for the generation of GABA. The role played by the resulting inhibitory release due to decreased GABA production is unclear, although it probably functions in the agitation and asterixis seen in hepatic coma. Glutamate itself has a potent excitatory effect upon most neurons and its reduced availability as a neurotransmitter potentiates the increased inhibitory consequences and CNS depression due to excess ammonia. The major conversion route in ammonia detoxification within the CNS is:

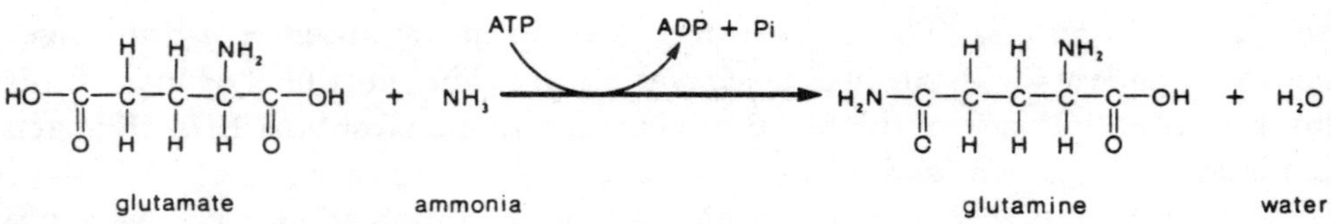

SUMMARY

Alcohols are carbon-containing organic compounds bearing one or more hydroxyl groups. Because they are both water and fat soluble they are quickly dispersed throughout the body water as well as dissolved into the lipid or fatty portions of cell membranes. By packing into the phospholipid bilayers of biological membranes, they cause them to expand or fluidize, thus distorting their normal architecture so that ionic gates and other membrane proteins are unable to function normally. This causes active transport systems to become impaired so that electrolytes cannot be properly exchanged across cell membranes. This inhibits the flux of sodium and potassium ions from one side of neural membranes to the other, so that nervous transmission is compromised. This is the major mechanism by which ethanol causes central nervous system depression, although it also alters the activity of certain specific receptors in the brain.

---

[121]Glutamate interacts with the TCA cycle in a number of ways and it plays a central role in brain metabolism. It also serves as a substrate from which oxaloacetate, the major regulator of the TCA cycle, is generated via alpha-ketoglutarate (see page 98). It is the precursor for *gamma-aminobutyric acid (GABA)*

→

Alcohol is oxidized to acetaldehyde primarily in the liver by the enzyme alcohol dehydrogenase. This oxidation reaction requires the reduction of the cofactor nicotinamide adenine dinucleotide, or NAD^+, into NADH plus a free hydrogen ion (H^+). Alcohol dehydrogenase (ADH) catalyzes this reaction by bringing the alcohol and NAD^+ into close proximity so that the cofactor removes a specific methylene hydrogen atom from the alcohol molecule. In exactly the same manner, the enzyme aldehyde dehydrogenase catalyzes the removal of hydrogen from the toxic intermediate, acetaldehyde, also by using NAD^+, converting the aldehyde into acetic acid or acetate. When large amounts of alcohol are oxidized in the liver, the conversion of nearly all the NAD^+ into NADH plus free H^+ or reducing equivalents causes a shift in the redox state of the body. That is to say, the resulting accumulation of hydrogen ions is synonymous with an increase of acidity in the body (hydrogen ion concentration is the chemical definition of acidity).

Because a great many biochemical reactions are dependent upon the reduction of NAD^+, such a shift to greater acidity and corresponding depletion of oxidized NAD^+ generally causes drastic alterations in the directions and rates of reaction, or both, in many of these pathways. Food is normally broken down into acetyl co-A, either directly as in the case of fats or indirectly via pyruvate or specific amino acids. This acetyl co-A then enters the Krebs cycle — the body's furnace by which food is converted into energy — where it is used to

---

and both are important neurotransmitters in the central nervous system (this is discussed in detail in volume 2 of this series). The role played by glutamate can be summarized:

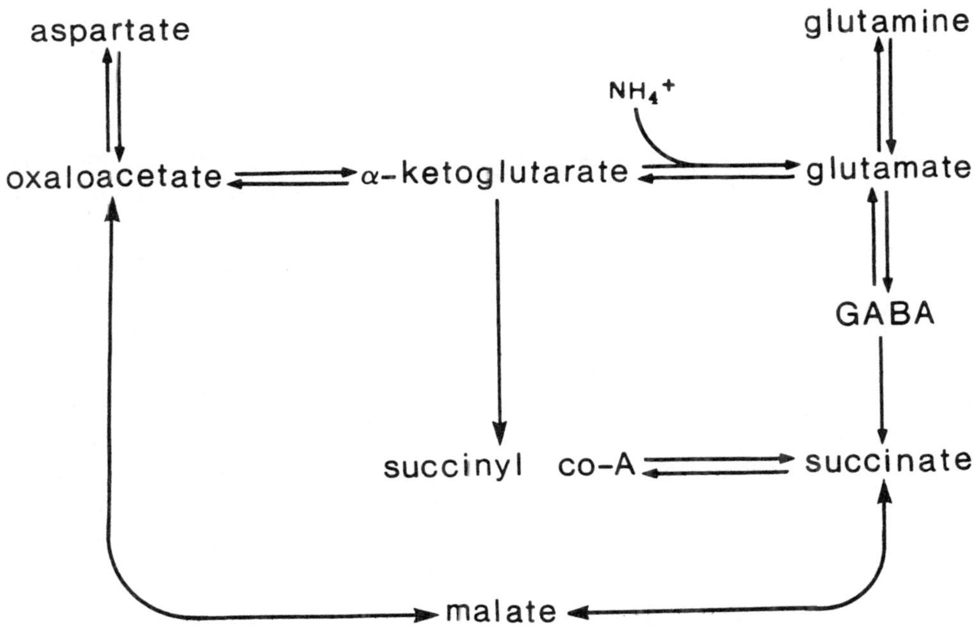

generate energy-rich ATP and to produce the body's waste by-products, carbon dioxide and water. Ethanol itself is oxidized as described into acetate which is then converted into acetyl co-A and routed through the Krebs cycle.

Because it is a simple molecule, alcohol is more readily burned as fuel by the body than other substrates. This is because it requires less energy to break the bonds holding the alcohol molecule together. Thus massive amounts of acetyl co-A are produced when large amounts of alcohol are consumed. This acetyl co-A saturates the Krebs cycle and the mass effect of so much of this substance prevents the conversion of pyruvate into acetyl co-A. Pyruvate consequently accumulates and is shunted off into other biochemical pathways, primarily the production of lactic acid. Because the conversion of pyruvate into lactate requires the oxidation of NADH into NAD^+, the excess of hydrogen ions actually favor this latter pathway. When carried far enough, lactic acidosis can result which only exacerbates the acidosis produced by the oxidation of alcohol itself. Hyperlactidemia associated with chronic excessive alcohol intake upsets the balance between uric acid and sodium urate. At *p*H values less than 5.75 uric acid becomes the predominant species, and since it is less soluble in water than sodium urate, it precipitates out as crystals in joints causing gouty arthritis.

Like other sedative-hypnotic drugs, ethanol depresses the higher portions of the brain first. Complex, reverberating neural networks such as those found in the higher cerebral cortex are the first to be affected. As these higher centers become relaxed, lower portions of the brain become disinhibited. This permits unbridled emotional responses generated by the limbic system to surge up and become expressed without regard for the circumstances in which the individual finds himself. This is why people become more talkative and uninhibited at cocktail parties. This apparent excitation due to CNS depression is termed "paradoxical excitement." It has also been shown that small amounts of alcohol inhibit the sodium-potassium pump. This would tend to reduce the resting potential, thus facilitating the propagation of nervous impulses and augmenting the excitatory responses early in the course of intoxication. With moderate amounts of alcohol, however, CNS function is only depressed.

As intoxication progresses, the limbic system itself becomes depressed, and hypothalamic functions become disinhibited. The limbic system is the site where emotions are experienced; the hypothalamus is the site where emotions are expressed. Hypothalamic disinhibition can thus give rise to uncontrollable rage, weeping or joy, depending upon personality factors and circumstances. The complex reverberating system of the cerebellum also becomes depressed about this time, giving rise to ataxia and loss of motor coordination. As intoxication proceeds still further, the reticular activating system in the brainstem becomes involved and loss of consciousness occurs. Such an alcoholic coma is indistinguishable from a surgical one, and the comatose drinker is very close to the threshold between life and death. Further alcoholic depression involves the respiratory and heart rate centers of the lower brain, and death may rapidly ensue.

Women contain more body fat than men, and their total body water amounts to 50 percent and 60 percent respectively. Because of this, women become drunker faster than do men of equivalent weight on similar amounts of alcohol — their blood alcohol concentrations are somewhat higher at first. However, because alcohol is soon sequestered from the blood into the fat reserves, women become sober more quickly than men.

Tolerance to the effects of alcohol are due to both metabolic and pharmacodynamic adaptation. High concentrations of alcohol induce the activity of a collateral system by which alcohol is oxidized in the liver — the mixed-function monoxygenase system, also referred to as the microsomal enzyme oxidizing system (MEOS). Chronic heavy drinkers can thus induce an enhanced clearance of ethanol from the body by as much as 30 percent. But by far the most important mechanism underlying tolerance to alcohol is pharmacodynamic adaptation. The neural membranes become resistant to the fluidizing effects of alcohol, so that it takes more of the drug to achieve the same state of intoxication. As alcohol abuse continues, these membranes can become so rigid that they can only function properly in the presence of alcohol or similarly acting agents such as barbiturates. The CNS is now not only tolerant to the effects of alcohol but physically dependent upon the drug in order to function at all.

Alcohol is rapidly absorbed from the gastrointestinal tract. It exerts a corrosive effect upon the gastric and intestinal mucosa and it removes the protective mucin, thus exposing the mucosal tissues to direct cytotoxic injury. It promotes the secretion of hydrochloric acid by the stomach which causes yet further damage to that organ, and because it causes constriction of the pyloric sphincter, prolongs the damage due to alcohol and HCl. Although at first absorbed almost immediately from the stomach, continued alcohol insult causes the gastric capillaries to shut down, so that alcohol tends to remain in that organ. Once it enters the small intestine, alcohol is continuously absorbed very rapidly by the intestinal lining, which it also damages as in the case of the stomach.

Because of the high caloric content of alcohol (one pint of whiskey contains half the daily caloric requirement for an average adult), chronic heavy drinkers do not tend to eat adequate or balanced meals. As a result they often suffer from a variety of vitamin and mineral deficiencies. Even with an adequate dietary intake, however, alcoholics still suffer from vitamin lack because of malabsorption from the damaged mucosa of the stomach and small intestine. Avitaminosis B is the most common deficit seen in alcoholics and it results in a variety of severe neurological, cardiac, and other damage, including polyneuropathy, alcoholic beriberi, reduced red blood cell count and resulting anemia, further gastrointestinal damage because of failure for the mucosa to adequately replace itself, and in severe cases, pellagra and Wernicke-Korsakoff syndrome. Life-threatening hemorrhages of the upper gastrointestinal tract due to the combined effects of alcohol upon the mucosa and the failure of those tissues to replace themselves are common among chronic alcoholics. And the anemia due to vitamin B deficiency is only made worse.

Prolonged alcohol abuse is associated with greatly increased rates of cancer of the mouth and esophagus, both of which are greatly exacerbated by the concomitant abuse of tobacco so common among alcoholics. Severe relapsing pancreatitis is also common among these people. Alcohol increases the release of gastric HCl which in turn promotes the release of secretin by the duodenum, which then causes the pancreas to release pancreatic juice which contains a complete complement of digestive enzymes. Because alcohol causes the partial or complete constriction of the pancreatic sphincter (as in the case of the pyloric sphincter), these enzymes remain trapped within the pancreas and they begin to digest the very organ that produced them. Damage to the pancreatic islet cells often underlies a chronic, reactive hyglocemic syndrome in abstinent, recovering alcoholic patients.

Lipid metabolism is grossly disrupted by chronic alcohol insult. The mass effect of acetyl co-A and the buildup of reducing equivalents (hydrogen ions) resulting from the oxidation of large quantities of ethanol inhibit the oxidation of fatty acids by the liver. These two factors also depress the Krebs cycle which further inhibits fatty acid oxidation. Because of suppression of the Krebs cycle, alcohol-derived acetate forms ketone bodies (such as occur in diabetes) which contribute to the acidosis resulting from lactate buildup and the excess of hydrogen ions. This can ultimately result in electrolyte depletion causing severe neurological damage. The buildup of hydrogen equivalents also promotes the synthesis of new lipids from acetyl co-A. And the physiological stress induced by alcohol consumption results in the release of epinephrine (adrenalin) via the sympathetic nervous system pathway, which causes the release of free fatty acids from the fat depots. All of these factors contribute to the buildup of fat in the liver cells.

Fat globules accumulate in the hepatocytes which crowd the cell substance or cytoplasm to one side. Such fatty liver disease becomes apparent upon liver biopsy in persons who have drunk moderate amounts of alcohol for as little as a week or two. This condition is readily reversible upon cessation of alcohol intake. When alcohol abuse is prolonged and extreme, however, the accumulation of fat in the liver can result in cell inflammation (hepatitis) and death (necrosis). Dead liver cells are replaced by fibrous scar tissue — this constitutes liver cirrhosis, an irreversible condition. This process is enhanced by increased microsomal activity induced by alcohol metabolism.

Recent evidence suggests that moderate alcohol consumption is associated with both decreased risk of myocardial infarction and elevated levels of plasma high-density lipoproteins (HDL). Because plasma HDL levels are directly related to a reduced risk of coronary heart disease (CHD), it has been assumed that this is the mechanism underlying the association between moderate drinking and reduced CHD. Exercise is also known to increase plasma HDL and is also correlated with reduced risk for CHD. HDL are now known to comprise a heterogeneous group of lipoproteins, however, some of which do and some of which do not give protection against myocardial infarction. HDL_2 are believed to be causally associated with reduced CHD risk and they are produced by exercise. Alcohol ingestion, however, produces elevated levels of HDL_3, which does not reduce the risk for cardiac disease. The mechanism underlying the association between alcohol intake and reduced incidence of CHD is not known, therefore — the relationship between HDL_3 and lowered rates for CHD do not appear to be relevant. Chronic consumption of alcohol by advanced alcoholics does raise circulating HDL_2 levels, but this does not produce any protection against CHD. This is probably associated with advanced liver disease in this population.

Alcohol has an equally disruptive effect upon carbohydrate metabolism. It stimulates catecholamine release (epinephrine) from the adrenal glands and when adequate glycogen stores are present, elevates plasma glucose levels. However, epinephrine also inhibits insulin production from the pancreatic islet cells. Without circulating insulin peripheral cells cannot take up and utilize plasma glucose when it is present. The result is effective glucose starvation such as occurs in diabetes. Because elevated levels of epinephrine produced by alcohol stimulate glucagon release and thus enhance the rate at which glycogen is converted into glucose, the glycogen reserves become depleted more rapidly than otherwise. When sustained alcohol consumption takes place in the absence of adequate dietary intake, as is common in alcoholic binges, severe hypoglycemia ensues which occasionally leads to death. This problem is exacerbated by the fact that gluconeogenesis or the synthesis of glucose from amino acids derived from endogenous sources is impeded because of the altered redox state associated with excess hydrogen equivalents. Alcohol-induced hypoglycemia may occur up to 30 hours following the last drink and it has a mortality rate of about 10 percent.

Hepatic oxygen concentrations are most severely restricted in the perivenular regions of the liver, even under normal physiological conditions. This oxygen depletion is severely aggravated by the oxidation of large amounts of alcohol, particularly when the microsomal enzymes become activated. This oxygen depletion not only can result in perivenular necrosis; perivenular hypoxia also activates enzymes which convert procollagen into fibrotic strands of collagen. These fibrotic strands block the normal circulation of blood from the hepatic portal venules through the liver sinusoids to the central veins.

These obstructions result in a backpressure within the hepatic portal system leading to dangerous varices wherever this system anastomoses with the systemic venous system. Esophageal and gastric varices, spleen enlargement, *caput Medusae,* and even hemorrhoids are the result. Severe portal backpressure also causes leakage of the serum from the walls of the blood vessels into the body cavity, causing a grossly distended abdomen known as ascites. About 45 percent of patients with liver cirrhosis develop ascites, most of whom soon die.

Consequent to the development of perivenular blockage portacaval shunts are spontaneously formed which route the blood and its products of digestion around the obstruction and into the systemic venous circulation. Under normal circumstances dietary amino acids from protein breakdown are deaminated and transaminated in the liver sinusoids. The ammonia thus formed is detoxified and cleared by the liver cells before it reaches the hepatic vein where it would be circulated to the rest of the body. In severe liver failure the detoxification of ammonia is compromised and significant amounts reach the brain where it results in profound hepatic or metabolic encephalopathy or coma. In the CNS it combines with glutamate to form glutamine. The resulting unavailability of glutamate depresses the TCA or Krebs cycle in central neurons, which reduces ATP levels so that the sodium-potassium pump is depressed. This reduces the resting potential across neural membrane systems and impairs nervous transmissions. Glutamate is also an excitatory neurotransmitter as well as a precursor for the inhibitory transmitter GABA. The release of inhibition on those portions of the brain utilizing those substances may be responsible for the agitation and asterixis seen in hepatic coma.

BIBLIOGRAPHY

Alkana, R. L., and Noble, E. P.: Amethystic agents: reversal of acute ethanol intoxication in humans. In Machrowicz, E., and Noble, E. P. (Eds.): *Biochemistry and Pharmacology of Ethanol.* New York: Plenum Press, 1979, vol. 2, pp. 349-374.

Anonymous: *Alcoholics Anonymous* (revised edition). New York: Alcoholics Anonymous World Services, 1955.

Anonymous: Alcoholism: new victims, new treatments. *Time:* 75-81, April 22, 1974.

Baraona, E., and Lindenbaum, J.: Metabolic effects of alcohol on the intestine. In Lieber, C. S. (Ed.): *Metabolic Aspects of Alcoholism.* Baltimore: University Park Press, 1978, pp. 81-116.

Barboriak, J. J., and Menahan, L. A.: Hyperlipemic effects of ethanol. In Machrowicz, E., and Noble, E. P. (Eds.): *Biochemistry and Pharmacology of Ethanol.* New York: Plenum Press, 1979, vol. 2, pp. 349-374.

Becker, C. E., Roe, R. L., and Scott, R. A.: *Alcohol as a Drug: A Curriculum on Pharmacology, Neurology and Toxicology.* Baltimore: The Williams and Wilkins Co., 1974.

Beeson, P. B., and McDermott, W.: *Textbook of Medicine.* Philadelphia: W. B. Saunders Company, 1975.

Berry, M. S., and Pentreath, V. W.: The neurophysiology of alcohol. In Sandler, M. (Ed.): *Psychopharmacology of Alcohol.* New York: Raven Press, 1980, pp. 43-72.

Bowman, W. C., and Rand, M. J.: *Textbook of Pharmacology* (second edition). Oxford: Blackwell Scientific Publications, 1980.

Burns, M.: Women and alcohol: an overview. In Burtle, V. (Ed.): *Women Who Drink: Alcoholic Experience and Psychotherapy.* Springfield: Charles C Thomas, 1979, pp. 5-11.

Butters, N., and Cermak, L. S.: *Alcoholic Korsakoff's Syndrome: An Information-Processing Approach to Amnesia.* New York: Academic Press, 1980.

Cahalan, D., Cisin, I. H., and Crossley, H. M.: *American Drinking Practices: A National Study of Drinking Behavior and Attitudes.* New Haven: College and University Press, 1969.

Calvin, W. H., and Ojemann, G. A.: *Inside the Brain.* New York: New American Library (Mentor), 1980.

Carlsson, A., and Lindquist, M.: Antidepressants and brain monoamine synthesis. *Journal of Neural Transmission, 43*:73, 1978.

Christensen, E. L., and Higgins, J. J.: Effect of acute and chronic administration of ethanol on the redox states of brain and liver. In Machrowicz, E., and Noble,

E. P. (Eds.): *Biochemistry and Pharmacology of Ethanol,* New York: Plenum Press, 1979, vol. 1, pp. 191-247.

Cohen, G.: Interaction of catecholamines with acetaldehyde to form tetrahydroisoquinoline neurotransmitters. In Sharp, C. W., and Abood, L. G. (Eds.): *Progress in Clinical and Biological Research.* New York: Alan R. Liss, Inc., 1979, pp. 73-90.

Collins, M. A.: Neuroamine condensations in human subjects. In Begleiter, H. (Ed.): *Biological Effects of Alcohol.* New York: Plenum Press, 1980, pp. 87-102.

Comstock, J. P., and Udenfriend, S.: Effect of lactate on procollagen proline hydroxylase activity in cultured L-929 fibroblasts. *Proceedings of the Nationals Academy of Science 66*:552-557, 1970.

Cornish, H. H.: Solvents and vapors. In Doull, J., Klassen, C. D., and Amdur, M. O. (Eds.): *Casarett and Doull's Toxicology: The Basic Science of Poisons* (second edition). New York: Macmillan Publishing Co., Inc., 1980, pp. 468-496.

Criteria Committee, National Council on Alcoholism: Criteria for the diagnosis of alcoholism. *Annals of Internal Medicine 77*:249-258, 1972.

Cytryn, L., and McKnew, D. H., Jr.: Affective disorders. In Kaplan, H. I., Freedman, A. M., and Sadock, B. J. (Eds.): *Comprehensive Textbook of Psychiatry/III* (third edition), Baltimore: Williams & Wilkins, 1980, vol. 3, pp. 2798-2809.

The Diagram Group: *The Brain: A User's Manual.* New York: G. P. Putnam's Sons, 1982.

Erickson, C. K.: Factors affecting the distribution and measurement of ethanol in the body. In Machrowicz, E., and Noble, E. P. (Eds.): *Biochemistry and Pharmacology of Ethanol,* New York: Plenum Press, 1979, vol. 1, pp. 9-26.

Faiman, M. D.: Biochemical pharmacology of disulfiram. In Machrowicz, E., and Noble, E. P. (Eds.): *Biochemistry and Pharmacology of Ethanol.* New York: Plenum Press, 1979, vol. 2, pp. 325-348.

Feuerlin, W.: Alcohol withdrawal syndromes. In Sandler, M. (Ed.): *Psychopharmacology of Alcohol.* New York: Raven Press, 1980, pp. 215-228.

Field, P. B.: A new cross-cultural study of drunkenness. In Pittman, D. J., and Snyder, C. R. (Eds.): *Society, Culture, and Drinking Patterns.* Carbondale and Edwardsville: Southern Illinois University Press, 1962, pp. 48-74.

Ganong, W. F.: *Review of Medical Physiology* (sixth edition). Los Altos: Lange Medical Publications, 1973.

Geller, I., and Purdy, R. H.: Interrelationship between ethanol consumption and circadian rhythm. In Machrowicz, E., and Noble, E. P. (Eds.): *Biochemistry and Pharmacology of Ethanol,* 1979, vol. 2, pp. 453-465.

Glatt, H. M.: Group therapy in alcoholism. *British Journal of Addiction 54,* 1957.

Glass, G. B. J., Slomiany, B. L., and Slomiany, A.: Biochemical and pathological derangements of the gastrointestinal tract following acute and chronic ingestion of ethanol. In Machrowicz, E., and Noble, E. P. (Eds.): *Biochemistry and Pharmacology of Ethanol,* New York: Plenum Press, 1979, vol. 1, pp. 551-586.

Golden, C. J., Graber, B., Blose, I., Berg, R., Coffman, J., and Bloch, S.: Difference in brain densities between chronic alcoholic and normal control patients. *Science 211*:508-510, 1981.

Gomberg, E. S.: Drinking patterns of women alcoholics. In Burtle, V. (Ed.): *Women Who Drink: Alcoholic Experience and Psychotherapy.* Springfield: Charles C Thomas, 1979, pp. 26-48.

Goodman, L. S., and Gilman, A. (Eds.): *The Pharmacological Basis of Therapeutics* (fifth edition). New York: Macmillan Publishing Co., Inc., 1975.

Goodwin, D. W.: *Is Alcoholism Hereditary?* Oxford: Oxford University Press, 1976.

Goodwin, D. W., and Guze, S. B.: *Psychiatric Diagnosis* (second edition). Oxford: Oxford University Press, 1979.

Hartung, G. B., Foreyt, J. P., Mitchell, R. E., Reeves, J. G., and Gotto, A. M., Jr.: Effect of alcohol intake on high-density lipiprotein cholesterol levels in runners and inactive men. *Journal of the American Medical Association 249*:747-750, 1983.

Haskell, W. L., Camargo, C., Jr., Williams, P. T., Vranizan, K. M., Krauss, R. M., Lindgren, F. T., and Wood, P. D.: The effect of cessation and resumption of moderate alcohol intake on serum high-density lipoprotein subfractions. *New England Journal of Medicine 310*:805-810, 1984.

Higgins, J. L.: Control of ethanol oxidation and its interaction with other metabolic systems. In Machrowicz, E., and Noble, E. P. (Eds.): *Biochemistry and Pharmacology of Ethanol,* 1979, vol. 1, pp. 249-351.

Hoff, E. C.: The alcoholisms. In Keller, M., and Coffey, T. G. (Eds.): *Proceedings of the 28th International Conference on Alcohol and Alcoholism,* Highland Park: Hillhouse Press, 1969, vol. 2, pp. 84-90.

Holden, C.: Identical twins raised apart. *Science 207*:1323-1328, 1980.

Horn, J. M.: Factors associated with criminality. *Science 200*:647-649, 1978.

Horton, D.: The functions of alcohol in primitive societies: a cross-cultural study. *Quarterly Journal of Studies on Alcoholism.*

Huet, P. M., Marleau, D., Légarté, A., Lavoie, P., and Viallet, A.: The hepatic circulation and portal hypertension in alcoholic cirrhosis. In Khanna, J. M., Israel, Y., and Kalant, H. (Eds.): *Alcoholic Liver Pathology.* Toronto: Alcoholism and Drug Addiction Research Foundation of Ontario, 1975, pp. 69-95.

Israel, Y., Kalant, H., Orrego, H., Khanna, J. M., Phillips, M. J., and Stewert, D. J.: Hypermetabolic state, oxygen availability, and alcohol-induced liver damage. In Machrowicz, E., and Noble, E. P.: *Biochemistry and Pharmacology of Ethanol,* 1979, vol. 1, pp. 433-444.

Iversen, L. L.: The chemistry of the brain. *Scientific American 241*:134-149, 1979.

Jellinek, E. M.: *The Disease Concept of Alcoholism.* New Haven: Hillhouse Press, 1960.

Jellinek, E. M.: Phases of alcohol addiction. In Pittman, D. J., and Snyder, C. R. (Eds.): *Society, Culture, and Drinking Patterns.* Carbondale and Edwardsville: Southern Illinois University Press, 1962, pp. 356-368.

Johnson, W. H., Delanney, L. E., Williams, E. C., and Cole, T. A.: *Principles of Zoology* (second edition). New York: Holt, Rinehart, and Winston, 1977.

Kaplan, H. I., and Sadock, B. J.: Neurophysiology of behavior. In Kaplan, H. I., Freedman, A. M., and Sadock, B. J. (Eds.): *Comprehensive Textbook of Psychiatry/III* (third edition), Baltimore: Williams & Wilkins, 1980, vol. 1, pp. 189-211.

Keller, M.: The definition of alcoholism and the estimation of its prevalence. In Pittman, D. J., and Snyder, C. R. (Eds.): *Society, Culture, and Drinking Patterns.* Carbondale and Edwardsville: Southern Illinois University Press, 1962, pp. 310-329.

Khanna, J. M., Chung, S., Ho, G., and Shah, G.: Acute metabolic interaction of ethanol and drugs. In Galanter, M. (Ed.): *Currents in Alcoholism, Volume VII, Recent Advances in Research and Treatment.* New York: Grune & Stratton, 1980, pp. 93-108.

Klein, D. F., Gittleman, R., Quitkin, F., and Rifkin, A.: *Diagnosis and Drug Treatment of Psychiatric Disorders: Adults and Children* (second edition). Baltimore: Williams & Wilkins, 1980.

Korsten, M. A., and Lieber, C. S.: Medical complications of alcoholism. In Tarterman, R. E., and Sugarman, A. S. (Eds.): *Alcoholism: Interdisciplinary Approaches to an Enduring Problem.* Reading: Addison-Wesley Publishing Company, Inc., 1976, pp. 107-169.

Kulkarni, A., and Hodgson, E.: Hepatotoxicity. In Hodgson, E., and Guthrie, F. E. (Eds.): *Introduction to Biochemical Toxicology.* New York: Elsevier, 1980, pp. 341-356.

Lehninger, A. L.: *Biochemistry.* New York: Worth Publishers, Inc., 1970.

Levene, C. I., and Bates, C. J.: The effect of hypoxia on collagen synthesis in cultured 3T6 fibroblasts and its relationship to the mode of action of ascorbate. *Biochimica et Biophysica Acta 444*:446-452, 1976.

Lieber, C. S.: The metabolism of alcohol. *Scientific American 243*:25-33, 1976.

Lieber, C. S.: Metabolism of alcohol. In Lieber, C. S. (Ed.): *Metabolic Aspects of Alcoholism.* Baltimore: MTP (University Park Press), 1978, pp. 1-29.

Lieber, C. S.: *Medical Disorders of Alcoholism: Pathogenesis and Treatment.* Major Problems in Internal Medicine. Philadelphia: W. B. Saunders Company, 1982, vol. XXII.

Lieber, C. S.: To drink (moderately) or not to drink? *New England Journal of Medicine 310*:846-848, 1984.

Lieber, C. S., and DeCarli, L. M.: Metabolic effects of alcohol on the liver. In Lieber, C. S. (Ed.): *Metabolic Aspects of Alcoholism.* Baltimore: MTP University Park Press, 1978, pp. 31-79.

Lindros, K. O., Pikkarainen, P., Pekkanen, L., Sipponen, P., Väänänen, H., and Salaspuro, M.: An improved animal model for production of alcoholic liver damage using a nutritionally adequate diet containing ethanol and 4-methylpyrazole, In Eriksson, K., Sinclair, J. D., and Kiianmaa (Eds.): *Animal Models in Alcohol Research.* London: Academic Press, 1980, pp. 445-452.

Lishman, W. A., Ron, M., and Acker, W.: Computed tomography of the brain and psychometric assessment of alcoholic patients — a British study. In Sandler, M. (Ed.): *Psychopharmacology of Alcohol.* New York: Raven Press, 1980, pp. 33-41.

Lumsden, C. J., and Wilson, E. O.: *Genes, Mind, and Culture.* Cambridge: Harvard University Press, 1981.

Madden, J. S.: *A Guide to Alcohol and Drug Dependence.* Bristol: John Wright & Sons Limited, 1979.

Martin, J.: *Chalk Talk on Alcohol.* Aberdeen: Kelly Productions, 1972.

Massarelli, R.: Effects of ethanol on the cholinergic system. In Machrowicz, E., and Noble, E. P. (Eds.): *Biochemistry and Pharmacology of Ethanol.* New York: Plenum Press, 1979, vol. 2, pp. 223-240.

Mayes, P. A.: Carbohydrates. In Martin, D. W., Mayes, P. A., and Rodwell, V. W.: *Harper's Review of Biochemistry* (eighteenth edition). Los Altos: Lange Medical Publications, 1981a, pp. 141-151.

Mayes, P. A.: The citric acid cycle — the catabolism of acetyl co-A. *Op. cit.,* 1981b, pp. 152-159.

Mayes, P. A.: Metabolism of carbohydrate. *Op. cit.,* 1981c, pp. 160-185.

Mayes, P. A.: Metabolism of lipids: I. Fatty acids. *Op. cit.,* 1981d, pp. 199-221.

Mayes, P. A.: Metabolism of lipids: II. Role of the tissues. *Op. cit.*, 1981e, pp. 222-243.

Mayes, P. A.: Regulation of carbohydrate and lipid metabolism. *Op. cit.*, 1981f, pp. 245-261.

Melchior, C. L.: Long-lasting effects of tetrahydroisoquinolines. In Sandler, M. (Ed.): *Psychopharmacology of Alcohol.* New York: Raven Press, 1980, pp. 149-153.

Mendelson, W. B.: Pharmacologic and electrophysiologic effects of ethanol in relation to sleep. In Machrowicz, E., and Noble, E. P. (Eds.): *Biochemistry and Pharmacology of Ethanol.* New York: Plenum Press, 1979, vol. 2, pp. 467-484.

Mezey, E.: Ethanol and hepatic fibrogenesis. *Op. cit.*, 1979, vol. 1, pp. 459-478.

National Council on Alcoholism: Definition of alcoholism. *Annals of Internal Medicine 85*:764, 1976.

Noble, E. P., and Tewari, S.: Metabolic aspects of alcoholism in the brain. In Lieber, C. S. (Ed.): *Metabolic Aspects of Alcoholism.* Baltimore: MTP (University Park Press), 1978, pp. 149-185.

O'Briant, R. G., and Lennard, H. L.: *Recovery From Alcoholism: A Social Treatment Model.* Springfield: Charles C Thomas, 1973.

Oswald, W., and Azevedo, I.: Chemical sympathectomy due to tetrahydroisoquinolines derived from adrenalin. In Begleiter, H. (Ed.): *Biological Effects of Alcoholism.* New York: Plenum Press, 1980, pp. 131-136.

Rappaport, M.: Liver architecture and microcirculation. In Khanna, J. M., Israel, Y., and Kalant, H. (Eds.): *Alcoholic Liver Pathology.* Toronto: Alcoholism and Drug Addiction Research Foundation of Ontario, 1975, pp. 43-67.

Reitz, R. C.: Effects of ethanol on the intermediary metabolism of liver and brain. In Machrowicz, E., and Noble, E. P. (Eds.): *Biochemistry and Pharmacology of Ethanol.* New York: Plenum Press, 1979, vol. 1, pp. 353-382.

Restak, R. M.: *The Brain.* Toronto: Bantam Books, 1984.

Roach, M. K.: Changes in the activity of Na^+, K^+-ATPase during acute and chronic administration of ethanol. In Machrowicz, E., and Noble, E. P. (Eds.): *Biochemistry and Pharmacology of Ethanol.* New York: Plenum Press, 1979, vol. 2, pp. 67-80.

Robbins, S. L.: *The Patholic Basis of Disease.* Philadelphia: W. B. Saunders Company, 1975.

Rognstad, R., and Grunnet, N.: Enzymatic pathways of ethanol metabolism. In Machrowicz, E., and Noble, E. P. (Eds.): *Biochemistry and Pharmacology of Ethanol.* New York: Plenum Press, 1979, vol. 1, pp. 65-85.

Rottenburg, H., Waring, A., and Rubin, E.: Tolerance and cross-tolerance in chronic alcoholics: reduced membrane binding of ethanol and other drugs. *Science 213*:583-584, 1981.

Rubin, E., and Lieber, C. S.: Hepatic microsomal enzymes in man and rat: induction and inhibition by ethanol. *Science 162*:690, 1968.

Sargent, W. Q., Beard, J. D., and Knott, D. H.: Acid-base balance following ethanol intake during acute withdrawal from ethanol. In Machrowicz, E., and Noble, E. P. (Eds.): *Biochemistry and Pharmacology of Ethanol.* New York: Plenum Press, 1979, vol. 2, pp. 17-25.

Scheig, R.: Ethanol, lipids, and adipose tissue metabolism. *Op. cit.,* vol. 1, pp. 603-622.

Scheuer, P. J.: *Liver Biopsy Interpretation.* (third edition). London: Bailliere Tindall, 1980.

Schuckit, M. A.: Alcoholism and sociopathy: diagnostic confusion. *Quarterly Journal of Studies on Alcoholism 34*:157-164, 1973.

Schuckit, M. A.: *Drug and Alcohol Abuse: A Clinical Guide to Diagnosis and Treatment.* New York: Plenum Medical Book Company, 1979.

Schuckit, M. A., Pitts, F. N., and Reich, T.: Alcoholism: I. Two types of alcoholism in women, *Archives of General Psychiatry 20*:301-306, 1969.

Segel, I. H. *Enzyme Kinetics.* New York: John Wiley & Sons, 1975.

Seiden, L. S., and Dykstra, L. A.: *Psychopharmacology: A Biochemical and Behavioral Approach.* New York: Van Nostrand Reinhold Company, 1977.

Shaw, S., and Lieber, C. S.: Amino acids and ethanol. In Machrowicz, E., and Noble, E. P. (Eds.): *Biochemistry and Pharmacology of Ethanol.* New York: Plenum Press, 1979, vol. 1, pp. 383-406.

Siegel, S., Hinson, R. E., Krank, M. D., and McCully, J.: Heroin "overdose" death: contribution of drug-associated environmental cues. *Science 216*:436-437.

Stassen, F. L. H., Cardinale, G. J., and Udenfriend, S.: Activation of prolyl hydroxylase in L-929 fibroblasts by ascorbic acid. *Proceedings of the National Academy of Science USA 70:* 1090-1093, 1973.

Stevens, C. F.: The neuron. *Scientific American 241*:54-65, 1979.

Vaillant, G. E.: Alcoholism and drug dependence. In Nicholi, A. M. (Ed.): *The Harvard Guide to Modern Psychiatry.* Cambridge: The Bellknap Press of Harvard University Press, 1982, pp. 567-577.

Wartburg, J. P. von: The metabolism of alcohol in normals and alcoholics: enzymes. In Kissn, B., and Begleiter, H. (Eds.): *The Biology of Alcoholism, vol. 1: Biochemistry.* New York: Plenum Press, 1971, pp. 63-102.

Warwick, R., and Williams, P. L.: *Gray's Anatomy* (thirty-fifth British edition). Philadelphia: W. B. Saunders Company, 1973.

Weiner, H.: Acetaldehyde metabolism. In Machrowicz, E., and Noble, E. P. (Eds.): *Biochemistry and Pharmacology of Ethanol.* New York: Plenum Press, 1979, pp. 121-144.

White, A. Handler, P., Smit, E. L., Hill, R. L., and Lehman, I. R.: *Principles of Biochemistry.* New York: McGraw-Hill Book Company, 1978.

Winokur, G., Reich, T., Rimmer, J., and Pitts, G.: Alcoholism: III. Diagnosis and familial psychiatric illness in 259 alcoholic probands. *Archives of General Psychiatry 23*:104-111, 1970.

World Health Organization Alcoholism Subcommittee: *Second Report. Technical Report Series No. 48,* 1952.

INDEX